SHABBOS TABLE IMPACT!

SHORT STORIES ON THE PARSHA
WITH AN IMMEDIATE MESSAGE

DOVID KAPLAN

SHABBOS TABLE IMPACT!

SHORT STORIES ON THE PARSHA
WITH AN IMMEDIATE MESSAGE

DOVID KAPLAN

Published and distributed by:
Shanky's Judaica, Jerusalem
Tel 02-538-6936
Fax: 02-538-6921
sales@shankysjudaica.com

Distributed in the United States by:
Israel Bookshop Publications
Tel. (732) 901-3009
www.israelbookshoppublications.com

Printed in Israel

THIS BOOK IS DEDICATED
IN MEMORY OF MY DEAR FRIEND

Harav Dovid Speyer zt"l.

HE WAS A TRUE *EVED HASHEM* AND A
SOURCE OF INSPIRATION TO HIS FAMILY,
FRIENDS AND *TALMIDIM.*

YEHI ZICHRO BARUCH

SPECIAL TRIBUTE
TO OUR PARENTS,

Rabbi and Mrs. Marshal Kaplan

AND

Mr. and Mrs. Eugene Cohen

MAY THIS BOOK BE A SOURCE OF
NACHAS FOR THEM, AND MAY
HAKADOSH BARUCH HU GRANT THEM
GOOD HEALTH AND NACHAS FROM ALL
OF THEIR OFFSPRING.

TABLE OF CONTENTS

FOREWORD

HAGAON HARAV MENDEL WEINBACH *ZT"L*
Rosh Yeshiva, Yeshivas Ohr Somayach
(Reprinted with permission from Rebbetzin Weinbach telit"a)

"**T**ELL me a story."
This is not merely the classical request of a child at bedtime; it is the unspoken request of every audience, whether it is in a classroom or a lecture hall. Even if the listener of a lesson or a speech soon forgets much of what he heard from the teacher or speaker, he will usually remember the story that was told.

While information feeds the intellect, the story stimulates the imagination and provides a listener and a reader with an opportunity to utilize both of these faculties in internalizing the message. This is why our Talmudic Sages and Torah giants throughout the generations have made so much use of the *mashal*, the parable, which is really nothing more than a story that never happened.

Rabbi Dovid Kaplan has done the same with stories that did happen. As a highly successful teacher of Torah in Yeshivas Ohr Somayach for so many years, he has learned to appreciate the "impact" his true stories have on his students. Following the success of his earlier works on Talmud study and parenting, the author is now sharing those stories with the broader public. Parents and teachers will find a short story on a wide variety of subjects to have an impact on their children and students – and everyone will find in this book enjoyable reading, which will have an inspiring impact on his life.

Rabbi Zev Leff

Razbbi of Moshav Matityahu
Rosh HaYeshiva—Yeshiva Gedola
Matityahu

הרב זאב לף

מרא דאתרא מושב מתתיהו
ראש הישיבה—ישיבה גדולה
מתתיהו

D.N. Modiin   Tel: 08–976–1138 טל'   Fax: 08–976– פקס'   ד.נ. מודיעין

THE Michtav M'Eliyahu relates that one of the pleasures of the World to Come will be when a person is able to recount the stories of his life's experience and relish in the successes he had in dealing with the challenges with which he was faced. He further explains that this is one of the reasons why each one's life's experiences are so different than another's, for, how boring it would be if everyone told the same story.

In this world, stories of an individual's life's experiences serve to acquaint us with the many and varied challenges and opportunities that perhaps we did not experience personally but through them we can gain vicarious benefit.

Since every person is unique and every situation is different and dependent on time, place and circumstances we cannot learn practical *halachos* from even the stories of how great Torah personalities functioned in specific situation. However, we can definitely derive inspiration, insights, aspirations, and general guidelines from the stories of others.

In addition, our awareness and recognition of Hashem comes predominately from our observation of Divine providence. Since G-d's orchestrations are not always visible or comprehensible, when someone experiences an obviously clear manifestation of G-d's kindness and mercy in his personal life, it is incumbent upon him not only to acknowledge it and express his gratitude, but also to share the story with others. As we say daily in our Shmone Esrei *"nodeh l'cha"*, "I will acknowledge my gratitude to You", *"unesapare t'helassecha"*," and recount to others Your praises".

An additional type of story that is effective can be illustrated as follows: Yaakov Aveinu informed his brother Eisav that he dwelt with Lavan and kept all six hundred and thirteen mitzvos but did not learn from Lavan's evil ways, the Chofetz Chaim explains that Yaakov was not boasting but rather deprecating himself. He bemoaned the fact that he did not learn from the zeal and ardor with which Lavan performed his evil chicanery to perform his own righteousness in a similar manner.

Additionally, we can explain that Yaakov also bemoaned that he didn't learn sufficiently from Lavan what not to do and how not to act. Sometimes stories about those less than desirable to emulate can at least give us a motivation to be inspired from their zeal and ardor for the negative and channel it into our lives for a positive purpose. Sometimes stories of such individuals also teach us what not to do or be.

Rabbi Dovid Kaplan, a fine *Talmid Chochom*, renowned educator, and a dear personal friend, presents in a masterful manner short poignant stories from which we can derive all these benefits.

Rabbi Kaplan is to be commended for this book and all his previous books.

May Hashem grant him the wherewithal to continue to benefit the community in many and varied ways. May his stories have the desired impact on all his readers which will in turn impact on the rich personal story he will be able to relate for all eternity.

Sincerely,

With Torah blessings

Rabbi Zev Leff

Rav, Moshav Matityahu

Rosh Yeshiva, Yeshiva Gedolah Matisyahu

Impact can mean force, collision or influence. Sometimes, though rarely, it can mean all three. When ideas and impressions are delivered with alacrity and professionalism, those ideas can come together into one.

Reb Dovid's scholarship and life experience are once again brought together into a blend of ideas and insights that will **impact** complacency and awaken inspiration and introspection.

May he and his ever-growing audience continue to be privileged to be **impact**ed.

Rabbi Nota Schiller
Rosh Yeshiva, Yeshivas Ohr Somayach
ירושלים
חשון, תשע"ד

ACKNOWLEDGMENTS

A NY form of thanks begins with an expression of gratitude to the *Ribbono shel Olam* for all His help and kindness, both in the publication of this book and in all areas of life.

Heartfelt thanks, of course, to my parents and parents-in-law for everything.

I would like to thank the *roshei yeshiva* of the two great palaces of Torah that I am so fortunate to be a part of: Harav Hagaon Rav Mendel Weinbach *zt"l*, and *yblch"t*, Harav Hagaon Rav Nota Schiller *shlit"a*, of Yeshivas Ohr Somayach, and Harav Hagaon Rav Doniel Lehrfield *shlit"a*, of Yeshivas Bais Yisroel.

Very special thanks to my brothers, Harav Hagaon Rav Yosef Kaplan *shlit"a*, and Harav Hagaon Rav Michel Kaplan *shlit"a*, who have served as role models for me in so many ways. Much of their wisdom and outlook is expressed throughout the **Impact** books.

I would like to thank all who have shared stories with

me, whether they were included in this collection or not.

Special thanks to Rabbi Jeremy Golker, whose encouragement was instrumental in moving this project along.

Special thanks to R' Meir and Devora Weiner for their competence and efficiency. It has been a pleasure working with them.

Of course, I must thank my children and son-in-law for impacting me in so many ways.

Finally, this book is a team effort, with me in the role of player and my wife as coach. So, as all players who wish to remain on the team say, I say, "Thanks, coach – couldn't have done it without you." Only, in this case it's true.

I would be delighted, dear reader, if you would share your comments and stories with me. I can be reached at (02) 583-4140 or at myimpactstory@gmail.com.

INTRODUCTION

T is with much gratitude to *Hashem Yisbarach* that we present this volume of the **Impact** series to the English speaking public.

The main purpose of this book is to provide Torah education for readers and Torah tools in the form of stories for parents, speakers and educators. A parent looking for a good bedtime story or two, or for a captivating story to tell at the Shabbos table, doesn't usually have the time to read a full-length story. The same is true for a *rebbe* who wants to spice up his *shiur* with a couple of inspirational stories or a speaker who wants to liven up his talk. This book serves as a resource to come up with one or more stories on short notice on a variety of subjects, along with a suggested message. For this reason, I've kept the stories short while trying to make them enjoyable reading, adding in far fewer descriptive details than found in standard full-length stories. Anyone using these stories for these or other beneficial purposes should definitely embellish them if they feel that's what the listeners need.

One of the questions people have continuously asked after reading the first books is, "Is that story true?" The stories are true in that I either heard them or read them. I definitely have added and changed details to make the stories more enjoyable, dramatic or shocking. Sometimes I've even taken one small incident that I've heard about and turned it into a story with all new details while retaining the essential lesson or message. What I have *not* done is researched the stories to check on their accuracy. In general, I think it is safe to assume that most stories people tell do have *some* basis in fact.

There are two categories of stories which appear in the book. The first is the standard type of "learning from what Jews have done" stories. These are incidents involving *tzaddikim, gedolim* or ordinary people and what we can learn from their behavior or words. The second category is stories from the world at large. This includes interesting news stories or strange events which have occurred in the contemporary world. I have found these to be particularly helpful in serving as the *mashal* for the Torah idea a parent wants to communicate to a child or that a speaker or teacher wants to get across to an audience. Sometimes you'll find the connection to the Torah idea quite distant. However, as any experienced speaker or educator will tell you, the trick is to get your audience's attention. A catchy story which you use as a lead-up to the idea you want to convey does just that. Of course, if you've thought of an idea that it connects to more directly, then by all means you should use it for that.

Most of the comments which follow the stories are meant to point out the lesson most obvious to me which is contained in the story. In a book of this nature it is inevitable that several stories will carry the same message. In such cases I've tried to make a comment that will make for more enjoyable reading. In other cases I've merely stated the message even though it appears by other stories too.

In this book, I have divided the stories according to the *parshas hashavua* to make it user-friendly for the Shabbos table. In some cases, the connection between the *parsha* and the story might be a bit tenuous. Please don't let that stop you from enjoying the story.

It is my hope that the book serves a beneficial purpose for anyone who picks it up, whether through education, inspiration or motivation. If you have benefited in any way and it's helped even slightly in your *avodas Hashem* and growth as a Jew, then all the time and energy invested will have been well worthwhile. I hope you enjoy the book.

Dovid Kaplan

BERAISHIS

BERAISHIS

"I WILL MAKE FOR HIM A HELPMATE
OPPOSITE HIM" (Beraishis 2:18)

WHEN Meir Shlomo Goodman's family got up from *shiva*, the children were understandably worried about his wife Zehava. The two had been married for over sixty years, and it had been a long and beautiful relationship. They became understandably worried when Zehava steadfastly refused to go to any of their homes for Shabbos. "But we don't want you to be alone," they protested.

"Don't worry about me. I won't be alone," she assured them. The kids knew she was quite social and had other friends who were widows, so they decided to let her be.

On the third or fourth Shabbos after she had again refused their offers, her daughter and son-in-law were uneasy. "Let's go over to Mama and see what's doing," her daughter suggested. Her husband agreed it was a good idea. So they walked over to pay Bubby a surprise visit with all eleven of their kids.

Not wanting to alarm her, they knocked on the door and waited instead of just walking in, as they normally did. "Mama, we were worried about you! We just wanted to make sure you weren't alone," her daughter said when her mother answered the door.

"Oh, that's so sweet," Zehava answered with a soft smile. "But, you know, I haven't been alone for a Shabbos yet." They followed her into the dining room, but didn't see any of her friends there. They then looked towards the table and saw it was set with two places. One was where Zehava had obviously been sitting, as the partially eaten food on her plate indicated. The other was by Meir Shlomo's seat at the head of the table, complete with sparking clean *kiddush* cup and *challa* cover. "I told you I wouldn't be alone," Zehava said through her tears. "I have Shabbos with Zaidy."

COMMENT: *Every husband reading this should ask himself if after* meah v'esrim *his wife will feel about him as Zehava did about Meir Shlomo. If he's not sure what the answer is, a review of his behavior to his wife, and perhaps his priorities in general, is in order.*

"I WILL MAKE FOR HIM A HELPMATE OPPOSITE HIM" (Beraishis 2:18)

Rashi says that if a man is deserving, his wife will help him. If not, she'll wage war against him.

H ARRY hated his wife Bertha with a passion. The marriage had never been great, and like most husbands, Harry blamed his wife. She didn't do this and she wasn't like that and she always did the other. And as is the case with most husbands, Harry was far more to blame for the problems than his wife. Be that as it may, they eventually decided to split up.

Harry was difficult about giving his wife a *get*. Matters dragged on, and eventually Bertha got a *dayan* from a local *beis din* involved. He invited Harry in for a meeting. "I'll give that miserable wretch a *get* when I'm good and ready," Harry growled. "She made my life miserable, so now it's my turn for payback. Let her sweat a little. Maybe in a year or two… I don't know." The *dayan* listened patiently to Harry's ranting.

When he finished, the *dayan* said, "You know, Harry, as long as you haven't given her a *get* you're one hundred percent married. That means that if you suddenly die – and, Harry, a person never knows when he's going to go – the two of you will be together for *all* eternity." Three days later Bertha had her *get*.

🗡 COMMENT: *Harry thought that giving the* get *would be the right solution because he just couldn't bear the thought of being together with Bertha for eternity. But he forgot one thing. He forgot that he must live with* himself *for eternity. In my* shalom bayis shiurim *for men, I always advise the husbands to ask themselves the following question: "How would I like to be married to* me*?" Some husbands might* *cringe with shame thinking of the answer. Others will be comfortable. Why not get comfortable?*

"FOR YOU ARE DIRT AND TO THE DIRT YOU SHALL RETURN" (Beraishis 3:19)

IRV was one of those guys you see in just about every *shul.* You know, the little bald guy who sits in the back with the young crowd and tells them jokes and stories. And between Shabbos *mincha* and *maariv* of *motzai Shabbos,* when he's really in his element, he puts on what could aptly be described as a performance. I'm sure you know exactly what I'm talking about.

Well, Irv had a bunch of nutty brothers, each of whom was the guy in the back in his respective shul. One day, the brothers and their families got together for some sort of celebration. Always the king at these family gatherings, Irv pulled one that had everyone on the floor. He lay down on the couch with a wreath of flowers in his hands and his arms folded across his chest and his eyes closed. "I don't want to wait until I actually die to be able to hear the wonderful things you're all gonna say about me," he announced. "I want to hear some eulogies now. And you better make 'em good."

One by one, the people got up and started talking about him. A good time was had by all.

 COMMENT: *Believe it or not, Irv was actually on the*

*right track. While his method was somewhat, uh, irregu-
lar, the concept in and of itself is correct.* Chazal *say that
the way a person is eulogized is an indication of his station
in* Olam Haba. *If people are effusive in their praise of the
deceased, he's going to do very well in the next world. If
they're groping for something positive to say, he's probably
going to be in for a bit of trouble up there. So it's a good
idea to think about what people will say in the end. If you
reach the unpleasant conclusion that there isn't a whole lot
of good to say, you should probably start making sure there
is. Just one thing, no matter what we can learn from the
Irvs of the world, behavior in* shul *is not one of them.*

"AND ADAM CALLED HIS WIFE CHAVA"
(Beraishis 3:20)

*It's a bit odd that after being told about his punishment, Adam
then gives his wife a nostalgic name. We would have expected to see
some sort of rebuke or verbal tongue-lashing for having gotten him
and all of future mankind into trouble. One of the commentaries
explains that we see from here that due to his appreciation for her
other qualities, he didn't bear a grudge against her for her mistake.*

A TALMID *chacham* in Bnei Brak once had to ask the
Chazon Ish *zt"l* an important question. When he
got to the house, he knocked on the door but there
was no response. He then went around the back and peeked
through a window. He saw the Chazon Ish lying in bed with
zero energy. When we say zero energy about the Chazon
Ish, who was known to push himself to the absolute limits of

what a human is capable of, we mean *zero* energy.

Desperate, the man opened the window and lowered himself into the room. He approached the bed and presented his question to the Chazon Ish, who was focused on him with his eyes open, but utterly motionless. The Chazon Ish didn't even have the energy to shake his head "no" or to nod his head "yes." Getting no response, the man climbed back out the window into the night.

The next day, after some introspection, the man realized he'd gone a bit too far. He went to the Chazon Ish and apologized for what he'd done. "I hope you don't have a *kepaida* against me," the man pleaded.

"I don't have the product called '*kepaida*' anywhere in my store," the Chazon Ish answered gently.

COMMENT: *We sometimes have* kepaidas *on people for things much less severe than intruding into our homes. Perhaps it's time to do an inventory check on what products we* have in *our stores.*

"SHE THEN BORE HIS BROTHER HEVEL"
(Beraishis 4:2)

IT was the early forties. The State of Israel had not yet been officially ratified by the United Nations. Yoseph Meirovich, who had come to Palestine with the secular liberal left-wing Habonim movement, was unhappy about the state of affairs in the land. He decided to take matters into his own hands and negotiate with his neighbors himself. He left his small town of Zichron Yaakov and entered an Arab village to begin making peace. Yoseph Meirovich… was never seen again. He left behind his wife Nurit, now an *agunah*, and two small sons, ages three and one.

On the advice of a religious relative, his wife moved near a *yeshiva* so that the *yeshiva* would fill in some of the emptiness of the father's absence. The three eventually became *shomer Shabbos*.

The boys, Ariel and Yoav, were as close as brothers could be, practically inseparable. They did just about everything together and went just about everywhere together. Eventually Ariel got married and moved away, working as an architect. Yoav became a criminologist. Though it took him a little longer to find a wife, six years after his brother's marriage he brought home the great news that he was engaged.

What should have been a source of joy and *nachas* gave Nurit more aggravation than she had ever experienced – even more than the disappearance of her husband. It turned out that Yoav's *kallah* was from a different ethnic background than Ariel's wife, and Ariel's wife was not willing to accept her into the family.

Each husband sided with his wife and the brothers really had it out. Matters turned ugly and the brothers stopped talking to each other. All efforts on the part of their relatives to bring about a reconciliation failed. They went their separate ways and had absolutely nothing to do with each other. They didn't even attend each other's *simchas* as their children grew up. Nurit, after over sixty years of suffering as an *agunah*, was *niftar*, never seeing her sons back on speaking terms.

COMMENT: *"Stop behaving like children" is a common expression used to chide adults engaged in unreasonable behavior. Frankly, it would be more accurate to tell unreasonable children to stop behaving like adults. Even if the time had come for the rebuilding of the* Bais Hamikdash, *this sort of behavior would probably prevent it. What a crying shame.*

"IS MY SIN TOO GREAT TO BEAR?"
(Beraishis 4:13)

ARTHUR and Dina had been married over forty years, and they hadn't been good ones. Arthur treated his wife miserably – insulting her in public, belittling her, constantly yelling and, in spite of being a man of means, rarely providing her with spending money. Dina stuck it out for the sake of the kids, but many nights she wept silently into her pillow. Afraid of her husband, she just rolled with whatever emotional punches he threw, never standing up to him.

When she contracted her final illness, Arthur did little to comfort her or to help her deal with the reality of her inevitable demise. As she lay on her deathbed with her family around her and the end drawing near, Arthur approached her. "I know I haven't been very good to you, but I beg you to please forgive me. If I could do it all over again, I would behave differently. Really, I would." That was it.

Arthur figured he'd simply ask for forgiveness, erasing his responsibility for decades of his wife's torture. He was in for a surprise. Dina looked at him. In her eyes, he saw a strength and defiance he'd never seen before. "I'm sorry but I *cannot* forgive you," she whispered with her last ounce of strength. "You hurt me so much and so often. I cannot forgive you – not in this world… and not in the World to Come." And then she died.

COMMENT: *Those are not good final words to hear from one's wife. Not good at all. The truth is, it's not good to hear that from anyone at any time. Arthur, you'd better head for her kever with a minyan. Pronto.*

NOACH

"FOR THE LAND IS FILLED WITH *CHAMAS*" (Noach 6:13)

Rashi tells us that chamas *is stealing. The* halacha *is that stealing is stealing no matter how much or how little one has taken.*

I WALKED into the wedding hall and looked around. Not recognizing anyone, I realized I was at the wrong wedding. The one I was invited to was actually at the hall next door. Just about everyone in Israel has had the same experience, as quite a few complexes have multiple wedding halls. After making my way to the right wedding, I found the *baal simcha* and wished him *mazel tov*, mentioning to him that I'd almost gotten comfortable in the wrong hall.

He laughed. "You're not the first one that happened to tonight. A *bochur* came over to me a few minutes ago," he related, "because he also got mixed up. He was supposed to be at the other wedding. He told me he owes me for a cup and a half of Pepsi that he drank here before realizing he was in the wrong hall."

COMMENT: *The* bochur *obviously did not expect the* baal simcha *to charge him for the drink. Still, having indulged in something which was objectively off-limits to him, he couldn't just let it pass without the* baal simcha *being* moichel. *This is the type of person one should look for as a partner in business. Or as an advertisement for Pepsi.*

"AND NOACH DID ALL THAT *ELOKIM* COMMANDED HIM" (Noach 6:22)

This pasuk *teaches us that Noach got busy right away with the difficult project of building the* taiva *and didn't stop until it was completed.*

IT was the middle of the night and the streets were quiet. After several weeks of careful planning, thirty seven year old Hampton J. Dupree attempted to break into the vault of the city's largest bank. He chose the weekend, as it would provide him with the best chance of not being "bothered" while doing his important work. He drilled and bored and drilled some more, all the while being careful not to set off any alarms. Finally, after four long hours of hard work, he managed to crawl in. There he was, all alone with all the loot and goodies. A dream come true. But Hampton had worked hard, something he wasn't used to doing, especially on weekends. So he decided to lie down on the floor and take a well-deserved nap.

He was woken up shortly after by three gentlemen in blue uniforms who accompanied him to a place where he'd have lots of time to sleep. You see, as Hampton lay down for his snooze, his foot inadvertently hit an alarm button, resulting in his rude awakening.

COMMENT: Chazal *say one who starts a* mitzvah *should be sure to complete it. Quitting in the middle is usually the result of laziness, a* middah *we generally must overcome. Of course, there is a positive use for laziness, and that is that we should be lazy when it comes to engaging in sinful activities. Hampton would have done better letting his laziness take over before beginning his criminal activity rather than in the middle, wouldn't you say? Nighty-night Hampton.*

"AND CHAM WAS THE FATHER OF CANAAN" (Noach 9:18)

Chazal *say that due to his lack of self-control, Cham's skin turned black while in the* taiva.

RUDY Bleeltrack's constant hacking cough was driving his wife Francine crazy, as well as causing her a lot of worry. At just under two packs a day, Rudy was considered a heavy smoker. "I'm fine," Rudy would assure her any time she suggested a visit to the doctor, which was every hour or so. Finally, after a ten minute coughing fit one day, which included a little blood, he agreed to go.

"Here are the test results," the doctor said, as he handed Rudy his lung x-ray across the table.

"They overexposed the film, huh?" Rudy Commented, as all he could see was a big black mass.

"Uh, no, Mr. Bleeltrack, they did not overexpose the film," the doctor said. "That black is not a result of overexposure of the film. It's overexposure of your lungs to cigarette smoke, tar and nicotine."

Rudy stopped smoking.

COMMENT: *The trick in life is to find motivation. In Rudy's case, it wasn't the trick in life – it was the trick* for *life. It just took a little black motivation.*

"LET US BUILD A CITY AND A TOWER"
(Noach 11:4)

The mefarshim *explain that the real reason they were building the tower was to become independent so they would have no need to rely on the* Ribbono shel Olam.

THINGS had really been *simchadik* at the *sheva berachos*. The food was good and the speakers interesting… and brief. The *baal habayis* then called upon Yirmiyahu Siegler to say a few words. Yirmiyahu said some nice things about the *chasan*, which he connected to an interesting point of *hashkafa*. As he was speaking, Gedalia Binstock whispered to the person sitting next to the *sefarim* shelves to hand him a *gemara* Berachos. He quickly turned pages back and forth until he found the exact page he was looking for. "Ah ha!" he said to himself. "Oh boy, oh boy, oh *boy* – am I going to give it to him!" Yirmiyahu finished and was greeted with a round of "*yasher koachs*" and "very nices."

"What you said is contradicted by this *gemara* right here," Gedalia barked, practically shoving the *gemara* into Yirmiyahu's chest. "Just look!"

"Why don't you calm down, Gedalia, and give me a chance to breathe?" Yirmiyahu said, taken aback by his brusque manner.

"Breathe? Breathe!? What you said is *kefira* and you're an *apikores*… and I should let you breathe?"

"It's not *kefira*… and you are a total fool."

"Yeah, but I can be counted for a *minyan* and you can't!" Gedalia snapped.

"With your I. Q., you probably can't count at all!" Yirmiyahu retorted. He brushed past Gedalia and headed outside. Gedalia ran out after him, and the shocked room full of people could still hear them yelling and insulting each other down the block.

"I can't believe what I just saw," Naftali Wein said to Lipa Yosef Tanenbaum. Lipa Yosef laughed, which disturbed Naftali. "What do you find funny about all this?" he asked.

Lipa Yosef looked at him in surprise. "You don't know? Those two hate each other. They're in the middle of a huge *din Torah* and each has been spreading all sorts of stories about the other. It's a miracle they were able to sit in a room together for so long before the blow-up happened. It's so pitiful, I find it amusing."

COMMENT: *When people get upset about little things, it's usually something else that's really bothering them. It's uncanny how often this is the case. So don't focus on the complaint – look for the cause.*

"AND A TOWER WHOSE TOP REACHES THE HEAVENS" (Noach 11:4)

The midrash *says that when a human fell and died it didn't bother them, but when a brick fell, they all cried.*

THE terrified crowd looked on with horror, anticipating a gory scene. A man had fainted and fallen on the subway tracks. Another man jumped down to pull him up... but the train was already fast approaching. It really didn't look like either of them had much chance not to be killed. Much to everyone's relief, however, the rescue succeeded and no one was hurt.

The hero, thirty four year old Carlos Rodriguez, was interviewed by the local reporters. "Weren't you concerned about endangering your life?" one of the reporters asked him. "What made you decide to do it?" another one asked.

Carlos didn't seem too interested in his fifteen minutes of fame. He was straight and to the point. "Look, man," he said, "if that guy woulda gotten runned over then there'd be a big delay, cleanin' up the mess and all. That would mean I'd be late ta work, an' I get paid time an' a half on Sundays. So there was no way no how I was gonna let that stop me from gettin' to work on time. So I jumped down an' pulled him away.

Time and a half is a lot of money, ya know?"

COMMENT: *Yeah, we know. We also know that written on the American dollar is something about Whom they trust. Perhaps they ought to add another line right after it in parentheses. It should read, "But it's the dollar we worship."*

LECH LECHA

"AND THEY CAME TO THE LAND OF CANAAN" (Lech Lecha 12:5)

ONCE again madness descended upon the land. It was time for the World Cup soccer tournament. It's that special time once every four years when the world takes leave of its senses, forgetting about economies, starving people, unemployment, health, and other such trivialities. Instead, they focus with unparalleled interest on that which is truly important – groups of eleven grown men in short pants kicking at a ball and once in a while at each other.

It was therefore no wonder that Yigal Horowitz from London found himself trapped in a terrible dilemma. The English team had a game scheduled for Saturday. Being *shomer Shabbos*, Yigal was not going to be able to see it. What to do, what to do? Yigal thought of all the technological possibilities that would allow for Saturday viewing, but he also knew that they definitely weren't acceptable on Shabbos. He could see a delayed telecast on *motzai* Shabbos, but by then chances were he'd hear the final score before seeing the game.

When something is important enough, people become mighty resourceful. Yigal was no exception. He came up with an ingenious solution. He booked a flight to Israel, where Shabbos ended earlier than in the U.K. On *motzai Shabbos*, he sat down to watch the game live. England lost.

COMMENT: *Just imagine there's an unbelievable* shiur *being given in Israel on a* motzai Shabbos *and the only way someone in the U.K. would be able to attend would be if they flew to Israel for Shabbos. Or just imagine that* motzai Shabbos *is the last* sheva berachos *of a dear friend whose wedding you couldn't attend. Yigal, would you fly in for them? Probably not, right? Well, what does that say about your priorities? However, if you are the type of person who would fly in for them, then...* you still shouldn't have flown in for a stupid soccer match!

"AND THE PEOPLE OF SEDOM WERE WICKED AND EVIL" (Lech Lecha 13:13)

HOW it happened is not certain... but the fact is that it happened and was reported by many of the news stations. Art connoisseur Elizabeth Wellington was visiting one of the fanciest art museums in New York. At some point, she tripped or lost her balance and fell heavily to the ground, howling with pain and writhing in agony. Her ankle was bent at a grotesque angle – the pain was excruciating. Unfortunately for her, as she lost her balance, she lunged forward and her finger caught the bottom of an $80,000,000 (!) Picasso, damaging the painting.

All of the people in the immediate vicinity – without exception – gathered around the painting to assess the damage. "Do you think it's reparable?" asked one person in a panicky voice. "How could this have happened?" lamented another. All the while, Elizabeth called for help and moaned with pain… yet the people totally ignored her. They lovingly carried the painting into a special emergency repair room in the museum – and Elizabeth was left alone on the floor.

COMMENT: *The most grotesque angle in this story is the angle these people have on life and its value. Think about it. If the painting was only worth five thousand dollars, they'd all have rushed to help* her. *While hala-cha recognizes a factor called* hefsed meruba *(significant financial loss), it's never taken into considersation when human suffering is involved.*

The conclusion of the story was that the museum spokesman announced a short time later that there was no permanent damage done to the painting. I think Elizabeth was lucky. I mean, if she would've caused serious damage, they would probably have thrown her to the lions… or worse, to the humans!

"AND THE ESCAPEE CAME AND TOLD AVRAHAM" (Lech Lecha 14:13)

Chazal *say this refers to Og, who managed to escape from the four kings. Og had also previously had the good fortune to survive the flood by clinging to the outside of Noach's ark.*

SOME people have a knack for being in the right place at the right time, and some people just seem to manage to always be in the wrong place at the wrong time. Such a person was Yokimo Toshuki. On August 6, 1945, Yokimo was in his home in Hiroshima. That was a *really* bad place to be on that particular day. As a matter of fact, there was probably no worse place on earth to be. Sitting atop an erupted volcano would have most likely been a better choice.

Well, Yokimo was one of the fortunate few who actually survived the atomic bomb dropped on Hiroshima that day. Yokimo then decided to relocate to a city called… Nagasaki. That's right. And as unbelievable as it sounds, he was there three days later when it too was nuked. Unbelievable as it sounds, he survived that one, also. Yokimo died last year at the age of ninety one.

COMMENT: *There is a statement in the* gemara *that a person's feet carry him to where he's meant to be. One can make all sorts of calculations taking different factors into consideration, but at the end of the day he's going to end up exactly where the* Ribbono shel Olam *wants him. Sometimes, it works to his benefit and sometimes it spells his downfall. Yokimo saw how it could've gone either way.*

"ONLY WHAT THE YOUTHS HAVE EATEN"
(Lech Lecha 14:24)

S HNEUR Rabinovich took the *issur* of *chometz* seriously. He came to the U.S. from the old country and had never had much of an education, but whatever he did know he kept to the letter of the law. One of the things he knew was that *chometz* on Pesach is a big no-no. He not only wouldn't dream of eating *gebruchts*, but he was extremely stringent. He barely ate anything the entire holiday, out of concern it might somehow be *chometz*.

"How are you so sure?" was his standard sarcastic reply to anyone insisting that the food in front of him was perfectly okay.

He practically subsisted the entire holiday on roasted almonds, which he insisted on roasting himself, trusting no one else. No one was even allowed in the kitchen while he was preparing them. The funny thing was that not only were his almonds super-kosher, they even had a special taste and crunch. One year, one of his kids tried making the almonds, but they just didn't taste quite the way they did when Shneur made them.

"What's the secret, Tatty?" his son asked him.

Shneur laughed. "There are some secrets one doesn't share," he said. He then went and made the almonds with the special taste. The family just assumed it was one of those instances of special *siyata d'Shmaya* for one who demonstrates uncompromising devotion.

It was only when his daughter-in-law happened to accidentally walk into the off-limits-while-I'm-roasting kitchen that they discovered the secret of his almonds. You see, before Shneur put the almonds in the roasting pan he soaked them in… beer. That's right, beer. Real live beer with a capital "B." That was the secret behind the special taste of the almonds.

"Are you absolutely sure?" he kept asking – this time not sarcastically, mind you – when his family members told him it was as *assur* as can be. It took quite a bit of convincing until he finally understood that beer is uncompromisingly *chometz*.

 COMMENT: *Uncompromising devotion to the cause is certainly admirable. But more admirable still is doing what's right. There are people whose headlong rush to righteousness leads them to trouble. Slowing down – and learning twenty minutes of* halacha *daily – brings more productive results. Much more productive. Crunch, crunch.*

"WHERE ARE YOU COMING FROM AND WHERE ARE YOU GOING?"
(Lech Lecha 16:8)

MY brother lives in Telshe Stone, a beautiful little community situated in the Judean hills about halfway between Yerushalayim and Bnei Brak. One evening, he was coming back home from *maariv* when he noticed a *bochur* standing on the sidewalk with a suitcase in his hand and a bewildered look on his face. "Can I help you?" my brother asked.

"Yes. I'm looking for Eliyahu Hanavi Street," he answered with a thick French accent.

"Uh, there's no street here by that name," my brother told him.

"Yes, there is," the *bochur* insisted. "I'm meant to be at my cousins' home at eight o'clock and he lives at 28 Eliyahu Hanavi Street in Bnei Brak."

"Well, there *is* an Eliyahu Hanavi Street in Bnei Brak, but this is actually Telshe Stone."

My brother invited the now confused and perturbed *bochur* into his home and the source of the confusion was cleared up. It turned out that this fine young man had gotten into a cab in Yerushalayim and told the cabby his desired destination. The Arab driver apparently understood from his accent that the *bochur* was a clueless foreigner, so he dropped him off in Telshe Stone and told him it was Bnei Brak. "He even pointed to a building and told me that it's number 28," the young man lamented. And as if this wasn't enough, when the *bochur* took his suitcase out of the trunk, the Arab took the opportunity to reach into the coat he had left draped over the front seat and pinched his wallet.

COMMENT: *It is important to always know where you're trying to get to. And I don't only mean geographically. I mean in life. Assuming one's goal is to grow as a Jew, which is what should be every Jew's real goal, then everything the person does should be assessed in terms of if and how it will serve him in attaining that goal. All the other things we try to achieve along the way should be seen as means to the ultimate goal – not as a goal in and of themselves.*

VAYEIRA

"AND HE SAID, 'MY MASTERS, PLEASE DO NOT PASS'" (Vayeira 18:3)

There is an opinion that Avraham was addressing Hashem when he said this, in which case the word Masters is actually Hashem's name in the singular. That is to say he was asking Hashem to wait, so to speak, while he attended to the needs of his guests.

IN his later years, it was known that the great Chazon Ish *zt"l* would sometimes miss *davening* with a *minyan*, due to the many people who needed him to answer *halachic* questions. "It's hard to believe so many people have questions of *pikuach nefesh*," someone close to him once Commented, knowing that for *pikuach nefesh* the entire Torah is set aside.

"They aren't all matters of *pikuach nefesh*," the Chazon Ish responded. "As a matter of fact, most of them aren't."

"So why do you miss *minyan* to answer them?"

"Why do I *daven* at all?" the Chazon Ish asked him softly. "Why? Because that's what Hashem wants you to do."

"Exactly. And when there are people waiting to ask me questions, what Hashem wants me to do is answer them as soon as possible. He doesn't want me to make them wait. Since that's what Hashem wants, that's what I do."

COMMENT: *It's important to always stay focused on the fact that we have one job in life – to fulfill* ratzon *Hashem. Sometimes we get so caught up in our performance of* mitzvos *that we forget why we're performing them. Of course, before doing something as drastic as missing* minyan, *one should ask a competent* posek. *Unless, of course, you are a* posek *like the Chazon Ish, in which case you can* pasken *for yourself.*

"I WILL TAKE BREAD AND YOU WILL EAT"
(Vayeira 18:5)

ZILPA and Maimon Emanuel and their six kids were making the move from the U.S. to Israel. Zilpa was a high-level executive, always on the go and constantly involved with big movers and shakers. She needed a contact person in Israel to discuss the details of her move with, so a friend gave her the number of the Blitsteins. They were an American family living in the neighborhood the Emanuels were planning on moving to. Zilpa spoke to Shani Blitstein several times on the phone to find out about schools, stores and other things of that sort.

The night before the Emanuels arrived, Shani made a

meal for the entire family along with fresh-baked desserts and put the food in the refrigerator in their flat. She put up a beautiful welcome sign, knowing that people making this kind of move need to feel that someone cares about them.

"I can't wait to meet you," Zilpa gushed when she called Shani on the phone the next day to thank her. Shani waited a couple of days to allow them to settle in and then went over. The two spoke for a while, and Shani found herself enchanted when she found out about Zilpa's occupation.

"Wow," she kept blurting out as Zilpa described the life of a high-powered executive, something Shani knew she could never in her wildest dreams hope to experience. "I'm so impressed by what you do!" she practically shouted when Zilpa had stopped talking.

Zilpa looked Shani squarely in the eye. "But I can't make welcome meals and make new neighbors feel so wonderful," she answered wistfully.

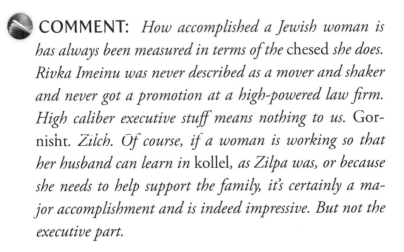 COMMENT: *How accomplished a Jewish woman is has always been measured in terms of the* chesed *she does. Rivka Imeinu was never described as a mover and shaker and never got a promotion at a high-powered law firm. High caliber executive stuff means nothing to us.* Gornisht. Zilch. *Of course, if a woman is working so that her husband can learn in* kollel, *as Zilpa was, or because she needs to help support the family, it's certainly a major accomplishment and is indeed impressive. But not the executive part.*

"AVRAHAM APPROACHED AND SAID, 'WILL YOU ANNIHILATE THE RIGHTEOUS WITH THE WICKED?'" (Vayeira 18:23)

Rashi says that when the pasuk *said he approached, it means, among other things, davening. We see the greatness of Avraham Avinu, that even though these were wicked people, he still cared enough about them to* daven, *and* daven *hard.*

ONE of the most dramatic incidents in recent history was the famous Entebbe rescue in 1976. The successful Israeli raid, defying all odds, was clearly the result of the outpouring of *tefillos* of Jews all over the world. As a matter of fact, an Israeli commando who took part in that mission became a *baal teshuva* and today is a *rosh kollel*. He said in a public talk that the risk they were taking was so great it could only be termed madness.

If an act of madness can turn out so well, it can only be the result of Hashem's willing it to be that way, likely due to *tefilla* or other *zechusim*.

When the Mir *yeshiva* assembled in the *beis medrash* to *daven* when the crisis was at its peak, the *rosh yeshiva* Harav Chaim Shmuelevitz *zt"l* addressed those present. "The lives of those hostages depend on our *tefillos,*" he cried. "If you don't *daven* as if your father or brother is among those in captivity then you have not fulfilled your *chiyuv* of *tefilla!*" Those present *really davened.*

COMMENT: *We don't have to wait for such a dramatic situation in order to really pour out our hearts. So many of* *our friends and acquaintances need* yeshuos *in so many ways. We have to* daven *for them as if they are our father or brother. Wow, would things look different if we did!*

"MAYBE THERE ARE FIFTY *TZADDIKIM*"
(Vayeira 18:24)

It seems ironic that Avraham Avinu would go to bat for the people of Sedom, considering that they lived with values diametrically opposed to his. The mefarshim *explain that having been designated* av hamon goyim, *the father of the nations, he felt responsible for them and therefore had to plead on their behalf.*

FRANKFURT, circa 1930. Police doing their rounds at about 2 a.m. spotted a man climbing a ladder to get into a food factory. Certain it was a burglar, they drew their pistols and called to him to come down the ladder. They were shocked to find it was none other than the elderly Dayan Posen, well-known leader of the Jewish community. At the time, he was in his eighties. He explained that he was the *kashrus mashgiach* of the factory and wanted to do an inspection.

"Well then, why don't you come at a normal time and in a normal manner?" they asked.

"And why don't you patrol looking for burglars at 10 a.m.?" he asked in return.

"At 10 a.m.? At 10 a.m. we won't find anyone doing anything wrong. They save their mischief for nighttime."

"Well, in my line of business, I also won't find anyone doing anything wrong at that hour."

COMMENT: *Hopefully, no* mashgiach *will ever find that anything is wrong at any hour. But the reality is that when there's a lot of money involved, the rules are not always adhered to as meticulously as they should be. A* kashrus mashgiach *carries responsibility for a large* tzibbur, *so he must be willing to do* whatever *is necessary to ensure his products meet the standards expected. Dayan Posen felt he had to make nocturnal visits on ladders. It's a lesson for all of us to climb to the heights of our responsibility.*

"AND HE SAID, 'PLEASE, MY MASTERS, COME INTO YOUR SERVANT'S HOME'"
(Vayeira 19:2)

Although very different than Avraham in many ways, one thing Lot learned while in Avraham's home was the importance of opening one's home to others.

IN her early sixties, Bella Berk decided she'd like to cut down on the amount and frequency of guests she and her husband hosted for Shabbos. Over the years, their home – like the homes of many in *Klal Yisrael* – had always been open to a wide variety of people. There was rarely a Shabbos when there wasn't a potential *baal teshuva* or two, a *yeshiva bochur*, or some friend of a friend at their Shabbos table. Bella was of the opinion that if people were coming, they would have to eat well, so she put a lot of time and energy into the Shabbos preparations.

With age slowing her down a bit and the niggling feeling

that somehow her hospitality hadn't really affected her guests much, she told her husband Eli that she'd like to take a break from having guests for a while. Eli himself was fine with the idea, as he himself felt the need to relax on Shabbos without the pressure of making conversation and entertaining.

And so one Thursday night, Bella found herself with all the cooking for their small Shabbos finished and she herself reading the paper. Suddenly, the phone rang with that ominous Thursday night ring – the one that meant someone needed a last minute Shabbos placement.

"Hi, Mrs. Berk. It's Shalom Kleiner." To make a long story short, Shalom was involved in outreach and needed Mrs. Berk's services. Unable to bring herself to refuse, Mrs. Berk agreed to take two of the boys he was bringing to the neighborhood for a Shabbaton.

"Oh, well, we'll start having those quiet Shabbosim next week," she thought with a sigh.

Half an hour before Shabbos, Shalom brought the boys over. When they entered, one of the boys, looking around the room, seemed astonished. Both Shalom and Mrs. Berk noticed his facial change and wondered what was up.

"THIS IS THE HOUSE, THIS IS THE HOUSE!!" the boy shouted excitedly. "THIS IS THE HOUSE." He didn't wait for anyone to ask what he was talking about. "When I came to Israel three years ago, I was completely irreligious. I went somewhere for my first Shabbos and had an unbelievable time. It was a *major* factor in my deciding to become *frum*. At the time I was clueless about everything and didn't even get the people's names. I always

wondered who those people were. This is the house! THIS
IS THE HOUSE!!"

The Berks dropped their plans to stop having guests.

COMMENT: *In* davening *we say* "zorei'ah tzedda-
kos," *which the commentaries explain means Hashem
"plants" our acts of kindness, so to speak, and then we get
credit for whatever grows out of them. Bella Burk probably never imagined the effects of her hospitality and the
credit she'd get for the* mitzvos *done by this boy and all
the other guests who were positively influenced by her and
her family. I'll bet you hope that your phone rings next
Thursday night.*

CHAYEI SARAH

"GIVE ME A BURIAL PLOT"
(Chayei Sarah 23:4)

EL Al flight attendant Liat Shlevin noticed a woman silently weeping nonstop in her seat. "Is there something I can do to help you?" she asked sympathetically.

"No, there's nothing anyone can do now."

Liat understood there had been a death of some sort. In her line of business, she was unfortunately used to seeing bereaved passengers, but she wasn't prepared for what she heard next. "My father died yesterday in the U.S. and I'm going in for the funeral. He asked before he died that we exhume my mother's remains and bring them from Israel to America. The remains are on this plane."

COMMENT: *It's almost unheard of that someone who dies in Israel will be buried in* chutz la'aretz. *Even more*

57

absurd is it to have an already buried body exhumed for reburial outside of Israel. We can only wonder why Hashem decided this woman had to be removed from the soil of Eretz Yisrael.

"FOUR HUNDRED SHEKELS BETWEEN ME AND YOU – WHAT IS IT?"
(Chayei Sarah 23:15)

The commentaries ask what happened to Ephron. First, he was ready to give the land away for free. Then he does a total about-face and asks for an exorbitant sum. How could such a change have taken place? The answer given is that it had all been talk up until now. At this point, however, Avraham Avinu showed him the coins. When he saw all that money, he lost control of himself and the real Ephron, selfish and greedy, came out.

G ETTING an annual deferral from the Israeli army involves going down to the *lishkat hagiyus* (the recruitment center), waiting in line for a couple of hours and then having an official form stamped by a desk worker. Back in the days when I was young and mischievous, I found myself surrounded by dozens of new secular recruits at the center, all of us waiting in an interminable line for our respective turns.

After a few minutes of trying uncomfortably to learn out of a *sefer* held in my hand, I noticed there was a small table in the center of the waiting room that no one was using and which had no identifiable purpose. I pulled up a chair to it, took out a few *sefarim* and a notebook and started preparing a *shiur*. I must admit that I wanted to be as conspicuous as possible, to show I wasn't impressed or intimidated by the high and holy army. If someone would object, I would move.

I had actually gotten comfortable and had become oblivious to my surroundings when I heard a loud and unfriendly voice addressing me. "What'd you do… turn this place into a *yeshiva*? What are you here for?" It was the commanding officer of the center, a colonel. His head was totally shaven, a small knitted *kippa* the size of a salmon patty perched precariously upon it. And if you think his *voice* sounded unfriendly, you should've seen the look on his *face*.

"I have to get my annual deferral," I answered in the most exaggeratedly sweet voice I could muster. I felt it was the best way I could let him know his gratuitous remark about *yeshivos* didn't faze me in the least.

"Get him outta here quickly," he snapped at the young lady behind the desk.

"Okay, right away, sir," she answered. She continued with the person at her desk and I went back to my preparing, feeling wonderful inside.

About ten minutes later, the colonel walked past again. "WHAT?!" he bellowed. "HE'S STILL *HERE*?! I TOLD YOU TO GET HIM OUTTA HERE! NOW GET HIM OUTTA HERE! HE BETTER BE OUT BY THE TIME I GET BACK!" After he stomped out, she called me ahead of everyone else there, stamped my paper, and I was off on my merry way.

COMMENT: *I can't help but feel that if I was looking at any other sort of printed matter other than* sefarim, *he would not have had such a dramatic reaction. I always chuckle when I tell this story over to my* talmidim. *The* mishna *says one who studies Torah is paid dividends in this world. My dividend was getting out of that recruitment center quickly —and being able to use the story in a book. Sorry, colonel, no royalties for you. After all, I use the stories in* yeshiva.

"FOUR HUNDRED SHEKELS OF SILVER"
(Chayei Sarah 23:16)

Chazal *say this was a vast sum of money, especially for low-grade burial land.*

MESHULUM Bingovich was somewhere between eccentric and strange, probably a little bit of both. Even so, the *gabbai* was surprised when Meshulum insisted on getting the *aliya* for the *tochacha*, which predicts the calamites that will befall the Jews if they don't behave as they should. This *aliya* is usually given to the *baal korei* instead of to one of the congregants, so that it shouldn't seem as if someone is being singled out for the curse.

The *gabbai* didn't know what to do, so he asked the *rav* of the *shul.* The *rav* said to tell Meshulum that he could only have the *aliya* if he purchased it, confident that this would put a stop to Meshulum's nonsensical request.

Both the *rav* and the *gabbai* were in for a surprise. Meshulum agreed to pay whatever the *shul* asked. Seeing it was useless to argue, they agreed upon a price and Meshulum was given the ominous *aliya*.

About three weeks later, Meshulum received word that a very wealthy uncle of his had died in the U.S., leaving him his entire estate and all his holdings. There was no way for Meshulum to take care of matters long distance, so he packed up his family and left his beloved Bnei Brak to go live in America.

Someone went to the Steipler *zt"l* to ask if the two incidents were connected. "How could it be that this is what happened after he intentionally took the *aliya* for the *tochacha?*" the man asked. "Does this mean we should all try to get that *aliya?*"

"I knew he'd end up with a curse," the Steipler answered with a laugh, "but I didn't know it would be such a big one!"

 COMMENT: *We've all heard the horror stories of what happens to some people after they win the lottery, and we know intellectually that the Steipler is right. Yet if we knew that the* aliya *for the* tochacha *would bring wealth, we'd fight over it. Why is that?*

"AND YOU SHALL TAKE A WIFE FOR MY SON" (Chayei Sarah 24:4)

This section of the Torah is the classic guide to shidduchim *and what one should be looking for in a spouse. It also teaches us that a* shidduch *will happen when Hashem wants it to, no matter what the circumstances. Sometimes the husband has to go find his wife, like in the case of Yaakov Avinu. Sometimes, like with Yitzchak, it's the wife who comes to the husband.*

ANYONE who has flown knows how difficult it is to concentrate on learning while sitting in a coach class seat. By the time you get on the plane after all the security checks, you're pretty tired out. Plus, the air is dry and there isn't much leg room. In addition, there are all sorts of inappropriate *yetzer haras* on the screen in front of you.

In spite of all that, Shloimi Hirsh made up his mind that on the flight home from Israel for his brother's wedding he was going to learn. He would give himself time to sleep, but he intended to learn during all his waking hours.

Chazal say, "*Ein davar omeid bifnei haratzon,* Nothing stands in the way of what you really want to do." Shloimi activated his willpower and learned for virtually the entire flight. Basya Bracha Rubinoff was sitting a few rows back and watched Shloimi with amazement. She realized that what she was seeing was just what she was looking for… a husband who would sit and learn and learn and learn.

There was a *frum* couple sitting on the plane. Basya Bracha approached them and explained that she would like to find out about this *bochur* and have a *shidduch* arranged. Shloimi wasn't even thinking about marriage at the time. Two weeks later, Shloimi and Basya Bracha officially became *chasan* and *kallah*.

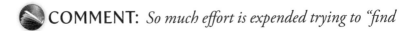 COMMENT: *So much effort is expended trying to "find*

the right one." The gemara *says, "If one is engaged in* Torah *study, Hashem will provide his needs." It really works. And in Shloimi's case, he hadn't even seen it as a need yet. But* being *engaged led to* getting *engaged. Such is the* koach *of* Torah!

"AND I SAID TO MY MASTER, 'PERHAPS THE WOMAN WILL NOT WANT TO FOLLOW ME'" (Chayei Sarah 24:39)

Rashi mentions that Eliezer had a daughter who he wanted Yitzchak to marry.

YOU could hear a pin drop. *Shofar* blowing had begun and no one in the *shul* so much as breathed, each person concentrating intensely on the meaning of *shofar* and making sure to fulfill his *halachic* obligation. All of a sudden, though, there was a ruckus coming from the *ezras nashim.*

"I can't believe people can make noise at a time like this!" was the first thought that raced through Avner Klahr's head. When the noise didn't die down, he realized it was something out of the ordinary.

It turned out that a young lady had passed out in the *ezras nashim.* She was okay. She had just gotten a little lightheaded, due to not eating anything before *shul.* "People who are too weak really shouldn't be in *shul,*" Avner thought to himself.

It was only when he got home that Avner found out it was… *his* daughter who had passed out and disturbed his

religious devotions. Avner told me he learned an important lesson that Rosh Hashana about tolerance in general
and being *dan l'kaf zechus* in particular.

COMMENT: *Rosh Hashana is the ideal time to inter-
nalize the concept of being* dan l'kaf zechus. *We ourselves
are hoping Hashem will give us the benefit of the doubt.
The* gemara *reveals the formula: One who judges others
favorably will be judged favorably in* Shamayim. *But to
really get to the point that you're that type of person, the
work must begin long before Rosh Hashana.*

"AND AVRAHAM DIED" (Chayei Sarah 25:8)

AS Betzalel slept, he saw a soft silvery cloud coming
towards him. He felt warm, overcome by an indescribably sweet sensation. And then he saw his father. His father who had been *niftar* just a few months before. His appearance was hard to describe… he just looked
so *wonderful!* His face was glowing with an other-worldly
incandescence.

"Do you know why I'm so radiant?" he asked rhetorical-
ly. "It's because I just came out of a *shiur* that I heard from
the Rambam. Can you believe it… the *Rambam!* What a
shiur! What a *shiur!* And I was only *two thousand* seats away
from him. That's considered very close up here. What a
shiur! And each seat is not just a seat closer. Each seat is a
new level and an entire *world* of understanding! The more
you learn down there, the better your understanding where

I am. It's so good here. It's *soooo* good here! Now I'm going to another *shiur*, from…" but his father's words faded and his image disappeared.

Betzalel awoke with that relaxed, refreshed feeling one only experiences with a true and meaningful dream. He remembered every detail so vividly. The next day he learned with new energy and vigor, committed to continuing that way in the future.

 COMMENT: *I'm sure he became even more focused when he learned the Rambam on the* sugya.

TOLDOS

"VAYE'ETAR" (Toldos 25:21)
This was tefilla.

BROKEN and forlorn, a man approached Harav Avigdor Miller *zt"l.* "My son was just diagnosed with the *machala,*" he lamented and then started crying bitter tears.

After thinking for a few moments, Rav Miller asked him where he *davens.* "Do the people talk during the *davening?*"

"Yes, they do."

"Well, the talking is blocking the *tefillos* in that *shul* from going up. Switch *shuls* immediately. *Daven* in a *shul* where there is no talking; then the *tefillos* will have a more powerful effect."

The man did as he was told. Three months later, he came back to Rav Miller. "We got the medical report today," he said through his tears. "There isn't a sign of the *machala* anywhere in his body."

COMMENT: *If we really believed in the power of* tefilla, *it wouldn't even cross our minds to talk during* davening. *And by the way, talking during* davening *includes using cell phones.*

"AND THERE WAS A FAMINE IN THE LAND"
(Toldos 26:1)

THE dire financial situation in the Baranovich *yeshiva* forced the *rosh yeshiva*, Harav Elchonon Wasserman *zt"l, Hy"d* to make an extended fundraising trip to the U.S. There was a wealthy clothing factory owner in Manhattan whom Reb Elchonon had known as a child in Baranovich. This man had left many years earlier and did extremely well financially in the land of opportunity. America, however, was also a land that presented the opportunity to abandon *Yiddishkeit*, which this man had also done extremely well. Reb Elchonon made an appointment to see him in his Manhattan office on the top floor of his clothing factory.

"Rabbi Wasserman," the man said after the preliminary pleasantries, "what did you come here for?"

Reb Elchonon lifted the back of his *frock* towards the man and showed him the place where a button had fallen off. "I've come to have a button sewn onto my *frock*," Reb Elchonon said.

The man chuckled. "Really, Rabbi, why have you come?"

Reb Elchonon's normal fiery look remained on his face. "I came to have a button sewn onto my *frock*."

The man decided to beat Reb Elchonon at his own game. "Excellent. Just come with me, and I'll have it taken care of for you." He led Reb Elchonon down into the factory area where hundreds of workers were busy making clothes. He figured that when Reb Elchonon would see how vast his factory was, he'd be overwhelmed by his success and would make his appeal, which was obviously what he had come for.

"Hey, Pete, can you sew a button on the rabbi's coat?" he called to one of the employees. The man took the *frock* and quickly did as the boss requested. "Now, Rabbi Wasserman, you see what I've got going here. Tell me why you've come."

"I told you, and you've done it. Thank you." With that, Reb Elchonon turned and left, and a waiting car drove him back to his host's home.

The next morning, the telephone rang bright and early. "Rabbi Wasserman," the man practically shouted into the phone, "you cost me a night's sleep. WHY DID YOU COME?!!"

"Please come here and we'll talk," Reb Elchonon responded. The man quickly drove over. "You find it so hard to believe that I'd come all the way from Baranovich to the United States just to have a button sewn on a *frock*. But your *neshama* came from underneath the *kisai hakavod* and traveled through seven heavens to get here. *Did it make that trip just so you could own a factory that sews buttons and makes clothes?!*"

The man was shaken to the core by the great rabbi's

words and the sincerity with which they had been delivered. He became totally observant and a loyal supporter of the Baranovich *yeshiva*.

COMMENT: *Once in a while, we really should think about where our* neshama *came from... and where it's going back to. Just close your eyes and think. Spiritual bliss.* Kisei hakavod. Gan Eden. *Total detachment from anything physical. Eternal existence.* Malachim.
  Buttons, anyone?

"DO NOT GO DOWN TO MITZRAYIM"
(Toldos 26:2)

ANYONE who has ever traveled with kids knows they'd rather do just about anything else. Even when we're just talking about short distances. Therefore, on *motzai Shabbos*, when it was time for the Shifrins to return from their cousin's *bar mitzvah* in Ramat Beit Shemesh to their home in Sanhedria Murchevet, Zelig and Meira were not looking forward to the adventure. Sure, it had been a lovely *simcha*, and the Glicks, who had hosted them, were wonderful people. Still, the Shifrins had five children under the age of seven and ... well, you know how it is. Packing all the stuff. Schlepping over to the bus stop. Waiting for the bus. Riding with *kvetchy* kids. Keeping plastic bags within reach just in case... ughhh.

When they finally finished cleaning up and getting their bags packed – having lost twenty minutes looking for Miri's missing shoe – Mr. Glick offered to drive them over to the bus stop. They clambered into his van for the three minute ride up the hill. As he pulled onto the main road, however, he turned right, instead of left towards the bus stop.

Zelig figured there was another bus stop he wasn't aware of. But things became clearer as he saw Mr. Glick head out for the main highway which leads to Yerushalayim. "Wow, that's so nice of him," Zelig thought to himself. "He's going to drop us off at a bus stop on the main highway so we won't have to wait and drive through all the stops in Beit Shemesh."

That wasn't the plan, though. Mr. Glick drove on and on. "What street do you live on in Sanhedria Murchevet?" he asked.

"Oh, please, that's okay. You shouldn't take us…" both Shifrins began protesting.

Mr. Glick cut them off. "I'm taking you to your house and that's that."

They couldn't believe he was giving them over an hour and a half of his time… but boy were they appreciative! When they finally arrived and unloaded, Zelig again thanked him. "How did you do something like that?" he asked with pure admiration in his eyes.

"Look. You're a *marbitz Torah* and your wife is a teacher. If you'd have schlepped home on public transportation, how would you have functioned tomorrow? You'd be absolutely exhausted. So how could I *not* save you the trip?"

COMMENT: *What a great question. We should always ask ourselves any time our assistance is needed: "How can we* not *do it?"*

"MY WIFE" (Toldos 26:7)

NO girl was good enough for Gershon Gavtan. He was talented, smart and handsome. One girl didn't have enough *yichus* and the other wasn't clever enough. One didn't have the right looks and another wasn't dignified enough. Gershon kept rejecting the girls, some after he met them and some just based on the reports.

One day he went to his *rebbe* to ask why he thought he hadn't found his wife yet. "Oh, make my day!" the *rebbe* thought to himself, as he'd been waiting for this moment for quite a while. "Gershon, the problem is *you*. You have a huge ego and think way too highly of yourself. Yes, you have many good qualities, but you really do have to work on humility a little. And perhaps more than a little."

Gershon took the words to heart and started working on himself. Each night at *mussar seder*, his *rebbe* would see him study the subject. He went through one *mussar* classic after another, attacking the problem from all directions.

About four months later, his *rebbe* approached him to suggest a *shidduch* with a girl whose name had actually come up before. "*Rebbe*, I rejected her three months ago," Gershon objected. "Now that I've added humility to my list of qualities, there's even *more* reason for me not to meet her."

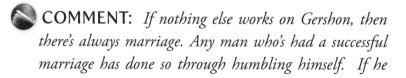 COMMENT: *If nothing else works on Gershon, then there's always marriage. Any man who's had a successful marriage has done so through humbling himself. If he*

doesn't... his wife will. So, Gershon, you'd better start working on yourself – real *quick.*

"LEST I DIE" (Toldos 26:9)

THERE is an apocryphal story that goes as follows: When the *malach hamaves* was put in charge of terminating people's lives, he protested. "I really don't want this job," he complained.

"Why not?" asked a heavenly voice.

"Well, because if I go around killing people, nobody will like me. That's why."

"You've got nothing to worry about," the voice responded. "You see, when someone dies, people will never blame you. They'll say it was a heart attack, a traffic accident, cigarette smoking – whatever. But almost no one is ever going to say it was the *malach hamaves*. Now get to work."

COMMENT: *We certainly believe in cause and effect. The problem is there is a bit of confusion when it comes to determining what exactly the cause is. All of the above mentioned "causes" of death are merely agents – not the causes. The* cause *is man's behavior or, more accurately, misbehavior.*

VEYETZEI

"AND I WILL BE WITH YOU AND I WILL PROTECT YOU" (Vayetzei 28:15)

Hashem promised Yaakov Avinu that He would take care of him and provide for him.

WE all know that the expenditures for Shabbos and Yom Tov are not included in the amount that is predetermined for us on Rosh Hashana. Rather, the rule is that one will be reimbursed for whatever he spends in honor of these special days. With this in mind, we can understand the quaint custom practiced by Harav Shimshon Pincus *zt"l*.

Rav Pincus would take his kids into a grocery store each *erev Shabbos* and tell them to pick out some goodies. But he didn't do it the way most parents would have. No, no – not Rav Pincus. As a true man of faith, he would tell his kids to pick out anything and everything they wanted in the store. "Take whatever you want!" he would tell them. "It's all free, absolutely free. No matter how much you have to pay, the *Ribbono shel Olam* is going to give it back. The whole store is yours, all yours! Just help yourselves!" And he did that week after week.

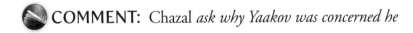 **COMMENT:** *Please don't get into "but all that sugar is bad for the kids" mode. Please just try to absorb the real message here. It's free.*

"IF HASHEM WILL BE WITH ME AND PROTECT ME" (Vayetzei 28:20)

A COUPLE of years back there was a plane crash which killed the president of Poland along with several high-ranking officials, including the head of the military. It was a national disaster. Basically, an entirely new government had to be appointed. The fact that they were on their way to a memorial service in Russia gave rise to speculation and rumors about sabotage and all sorts of interesting things like that. The story was a front pager for quite a while.

Lost in the excitement was what had happened to the chief rabbi of Poland – or rather, what *didn't* happen to him. You see, the rabbi was invited to the memorial service and was under quite a bit of diplomatic pressure to attend. However, he was forced to decline the offer because… the service was being held on Shabbos.

COMMENT: Chazal *ask why Yaakov was concerned he*

would come to harm. After all, Hashem had already promised to watch over him. The answer is that he was worried that perhaps some misdeed might cause him to lose that Divine protection. We see that following Hashem's commands brings with it that much sought after Divine protection.

"AND YAAKOV PICKED UP HIS FEET AND WENT" (Vayetzei 29:1)

The commentaries point out that whereas there are some people who go wherever their feet happen to carry them, Yaakov Avinu was different. He *carried his feet – they didn't carry* him.

SEVENTY four year old Harold Parker of Sydney, Australia got into his car for the short drive to the grocery store. When he didn't return within the hour, his wife became concerned. After an hour and a half, she was downright worried, so she called their married children. Clive, Beatrice and Trevor each drove around looking for him, but without luck. Having no other choice, they called the police.

Much to their relief, Harold was found about eight hours later in Victoria... some six hundred kilometers away! "I got on the highway and started driving," Harold explained. "I was enjoying the drive so much I decided to keep on going. Next thing you know, I found myself in Victoria," he added with a chuckle. His family members were not laughing.

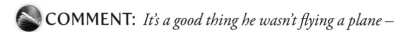 **COMMENT:** *It's a good thing he wasn't flying a plane –*

who knows where he would've ended up. Torah Jews don't "end up" in places. Each step in the course of our day is calculated in advance. Or at least it should be.

"IN THE MORNING, BEHOLD SHE WAS LEAH" (Vayetzei 29:5)

Chazal *say Rachel gave Leah the* simanim *so that she wouldn't be publicly humiliated. At the time, Rachel did not know she would also end up marrying Yaakov. She was, in effect, giving up her husband and all the* Olam Hazeh *and* Olam Haba *that came along with that.*

A SHIDDUCH was made between the daughter of Rav Shraga Feivel Frank, father-in-law of Rav Moshe Mordechai Epstein *zt"l* and Rav Isser Zalman Meltzer *zt"l*, and Aaron Bakst, the finest *bochur* in all of Europe.

Shortly after the engagement, Aaron came to spend a Shabbos with the *kallah* and her family. He noticed that the brothers of the *kallah* were giving him a bit of a cold shoulder. "What seems to be the problem?" he asked one of them.

The brother hesitated for a few moments before responding, and Aaron understood what he had to say was not easy for him. "Before our father was *niftar*, he left instructions that the boy we take for our sister should be *the* top *bochur* in the *yeshiva* world. We heard great things about you, but it came to our attention that there's someone named Moshe Mordechai Epstein, and *he* is the top *bochur* in the *yeshiva* world."

Aaron asked for the *tenaim* document and promptly tore

it up. "I have no *kepaida* whatsoever," he said. "She may carry out her father's wishes and marry the top *bochur*."

Aaron Bakst eventually became Hagaon Harav Bakst, *rav* of a very prominent *kehilla* in Europe. Many years later, the Slabodka *yeshiva* moved to Chevron in Eretz Yisrael. The Alter of Slabodka invited Rav Bakst to join the *yeshiva* in Chevron and serve as the *rosh yeshiva*. Rav Bakst asked the Alter who the *maggidei shiur* were. Upon being told that Rav Moshe Mordechai Epstein was one of them, Rav Bakst turned down the offer. This meant turning down a very prestigious position, a position that would have been the envy of many.

When asked why, Rav Bakst explained, "If I'm the *rosh yeshiva*, imagine how Rav Moshe Mordechai's wife is going to feel every time she sees me. Imagine her pain at the thought that her husband is playing second fiddle to me. No, I just can't do that to her." Rav Bakst later perished in the war along with his *kehilla*.

COMMENT: *When a certain type of car is no longer available, we say, "They don't make that model anymore." I think the same can be said for certain people.*

"AND RACHEL WAS ENVIOUS OF HER SISTER" (Vayetzei 30:15)

ONE of the recent representatives of the anti-Torah camp was the late Tommy Lapid. His never-ending attacks against the Torah community culminated in his forming a short- lived political party called Shinui. The party enjoyed spectacular success for a brief period of time – and then *we* enjoyed its spectacular collapse as it disappeared from the Israeli political scene.

But Lapid's distorted spirit lives on. His son Yair, a newspaper reporter (no, not for the Yated or Hamodia), picked up right where his father left off. However, this book is not about politics so we'll go no further in our analysis of the Lapids. What caught my attention and actually evoked a laugh was a report in one of the *frum* newspapers regarding something that Yair, who has since become the treasury minister, wrote in one of his columns.

The younger Lapid claims that he has discovered the source of *chareidi* frustration. The underlying cause is… *that they are jealous of the secular.*

COMMENT: *We feel bad for all our secular brothers who must live with the results of* prikas ohl *– violence in the schools, rampant drug and alcohol abuse, the unraveling of the family unit, the total nonexistence of morals and decency. In short, it's a picture of misery in all areas. So what exactly is there to be jealous of? The silly notion that unbridled pursuit of pleasure leads to happiness and fulfillment is clearly just that – a silly notion.*

"IT'S NOT ENOUGH THAT YOU TOOK MY HUSBAND?!" (Vayetzei 30:5)

When Leah confronted Rachel with this statement, Rachel could have given a pretty solid response. After all, Yaakov had intended to marry her, *and it was her selflessness that made it possible for Leah to become Yaakov's wife. She didn't respond, though, because she knew Leah would feel bad. Her silence under those trying circumstances is indicative of the very high level she was on.*

THE life story of Rebbetzin Chaya Sara Kramer *z"l*, wife of the *tzaddik* Rav Yaakov Moshe Kramer *zt"l*, is recounted in the beautiful book *Holy Woman*. Rav Kramer's first wife was killed in the war. When the young Chaya Sara came to Israel, he married her. This amazing couple did not have any biological children. An amazing thing that only became known after Rebbetzin Kramer was *niftar* was that Rav Yaakov Moshe and his first wife *did* have a child, a daughter, and she was also killed in the war. In the over forty years of his marriage to Rebbetzin Chaya Sara, he never let his wife know that he had had a child with his first wife. He didn't tell her so that she shouldn't feel bad knowing that their childlessness was "her fault." Did you hear that – over *forty* years?!

COMMENT: *Keeping any secret for a long time is tough. For spouses, to keep things from each other is even tougher. A lesser person, in a fit of anger or frustration, would likely have blurted something out at some point. Rav Kramer, however, was not a lesser person – Rav Kramer was a huge person. Actually, people can be defined through inverse proportion. The bigger the blurter, the smaller the person. And vice versa.*

VAYISHLACH

"SAVE ME NOW FROM MY BROTHER, FROM EISAV" (Vayishlach 32:12)

Yaakov Avinu was concerned about two issues with Eisav. There is Eisav, his arch-enemy who was looking to destroy Klal Yisrael. *And then there is Eisav his "brother," the friendly Eisav who allows us to comfortably enter his world and take a spiritual beating. So many negative influences have been absorbed by* Klal Yisrael *as a result of Eisav's "brotherly" love.*

CELL phones. The very mention of this insidious instrument is enough to make one cringe. The invasion of our privacy and peace of mind, with access to all sorts of forbidden pastures... the list of negative things they bring about is longer than many would like to admit. So many bad *middos* are promoted by this device of destruction, and so many people have been battered spiritually. In addition, medical research has produced some preliminary findings which indicate extended cell phone use can lead to cancer.

However, there's another terrible effect that none of the doctors could have predicted. Thirty seven year old Hosho Nikomo of Japan placed his cell phone in his shirt pocket. Little did he suspect that the device was faulty. Incredible as it sounds, the cell phone blew up in his pocket, killing Hosho instantly.

COMMENT: *When we hear about someone dying in an instant, we're shaken. And even something like the long-term effects of cigarettes frightens us. Why don't the spiritual dangers presented by these instruments over the long-term frighten us as well? After all, we consider spiritual death* worse *than physical death. A good question, if I may say so myself.*

"AND LEAVE A GAP BETWEEN ONE FLOCK AND THE NEXT" (Vayishlach 2:17)

Yaakov Avinu had in mind that by leaving a gap between the flocks, Eisav would have a chance to get used to the idea that he was about to meet up with Yaakov. The gradual conditioning was meant to lessen Eisav's feelings of animosity. A sudden meeting, on the other hand, might leave Eisav feeling his hatred of Yaakov full force.

AFTER his first Shabbos in America, Harav Chatzkel Levenstein *zt"l* was visibly upset. "I must leave, and leave quickly," he said to one of his *talmidim.* "Why is the *rav* so upset?" he asked.

"Why? Because I was *mechallel Shabbos,* that's why!"

The *talmid* waited for an explanation, and it was not long in coming. "You see, I witnessed actual *chillul Shabbos* today, something I *never* saw in Europe, and it shocked me. I was shaken to the core. But the problem is, if I continue to see *chillul Shabbos*, I'll become conditioned to it. The next time it won't upset me as much and the time after that even less. That's why I say I was *mechallel Shabbos*."

COMMENT: Chazal *say the* yetzer hara *works on a person in gradual stages. First he tells him to do one* aveira, *then another, until eventually he tells him to go and worship idols. This is what alarmed Reb Chatzkel, and it's this that we must always be on guard against. Any spiritual backslide must be nipped in the bud, or it can lead to disastrous results.*

"HE SAID, 'SEND ME, FOR THE MORNING HAS BROKEN'" (Vayishlach 32:27)

Chazal *say the* malach *had to go because this was the* very *day that he had to say* shira.

HARAV Yaakov Kamenetsky *zt"l* once had two men come before him for litigation. Shepsel the butcher claimed that Meshulem the *melamed* owed him money, and he had a *shtar* to prove it. Meshulem vehemently denied the claim. He said he never took any loan from Shepsel. As to the *shtar*, he protested vociferously that it was a forgery.

Reb Yaakov looked over the *shtar* carefully. After a few minutes of scrutiny, he asked Shepsel if the loan had taken place either before or after the secular date on the *shtar*, which would invalidate it. Shepsel said it had not. The loan took place on the date written on the *shtar*.

"Are you sure?" Reb Yaakov asked.

"Of course I'm sure," Shepsel answered confidently. "You think I don't know the *halacha* that a *shtar* must not be misdated?"

Reb Yaakov gave Shepsel a very stern look. "In that case... Meshulem doesn't owe you any money."

"What?! Why not?!"

"Shepsel," responded Reb Yaakov, "the secular date on the *shtar* falls out *exactly on Yom Kippur*! That's why."

 COMMENT: *One more thing he'll have to do* teshuva *for next Yom Kippur.*

"AND HIS ELEVEN SONS"
(Vayishlach 32:23)

Rashi points out that Dina seems to have been left out in the pasuk. *As a matter of fact, she actually was there. Yaakov had concealed her in a box so that Eisav shouldn't see her. For this, Yaakov was punished with the Shechem incident. Yaakov should have considered that perhaps Dina would have exerted a positive influence on Eisav and he would have changed his ways.*

AS I was walking through the Ohr Somayach offices, the *rosh yeshiva* Harav Nota Schiller *shlit"a* stopped me. He was reading a letter. Knowing that I'm an obsessive/compulsive story collector, he told me he had a good one.

"This is a letter from a former *talmid*, Peretz Maizer," he began. "Peretz was once at a shooting range for target practice before entering the Israeli army. My brother happened to be there and he told Peretz, then Brent, about Ohr Somayach. Peretz thanked him politely but had zero interest in attending. It seems, however, he made the mistake of telling his wife about the encounter.

"You see, a few months later he had to have his shoe repaired. When the shoemaker gave it back, the shoe was wrapped in newspaper… and that paper happened to have a write-up on Ohr Somayach. 'It's a sign. Now you have no excuse,' his wife told him. So he came to check it out. Today he and his family are completely *frum*."

So saying, Rav Schiller showed me another paper contained in the envelope, Peretz's concrete way of expressing his *hakaras hatov* to the institution that gave him life in this world and the next.

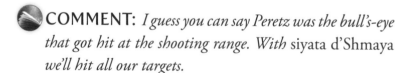 **COMMENT:** *I guess you can say Peretz was the bull's-eye that got hit at the shooting range. With siyata d'Shmaya we'll hit all our targets.*

"AND YAAKOV SAID TO SHIMON AND LEVI, 'YOU HAVE TROUBLED ME'" (Vayishlach 34:30)

Yaakov Avinu criticized Shimon and Levi for having behaved in a rash manner, which put them all in a precarious situation.

J UST as seventy four year old Gideon Golani was about to pull onto the highway, he saw an elderly man standing by the bus stop. "I'm headed for Yerushalayim," Gideon told him. "Can I offer you a ride?"

The man gratefully got in and the two seventy-somethings had a nice conversation. It turned out that the passenger, Ophir Goldman, lived not far from Gideon in Tel Aviv and was actually the *gabbai* in the *shul* Gideon's father used to *daven* in.

As Gideon got close to Yerushalayim, he asked Ophir where he had to get to. "I have to go to Kiryat Moshe," Ophir told him.

"Well, I'd love to take you, and later this evening I have to go there myself. Right now, though, I have to be somewhere else. So I'll leave you off at the entrance to the city and you'll make your way from there. Please forgive me."

"Look," said Ophir, "if you start a *mitzvah* you should finish it. I'd really appreciate it if you would take me where I have to go."

This was not the response Gideon was expecting. Not at all. If anything, he had expected to hear some expression of gratitude. "Look, under normal circumstances I would, but right now I'm in a rush, so I won't be able to," he said with evident irritation.

"You know," responded Ophir, "if a person can't finish a *mitzvah*, he shouldn't get involved with it to begin with."

Gideon lost his cookies. "NO KIDDING!!" he exploded. "YOU'RE ABSOLUTELY RIGHT!!" And with that, he turned the car around and drove… all the way back to Tel Aviv! He ordered Ophir out of his car and the two of them exchanged some, how shall we put it, unpleasant last words.

Gideon then turned back and drove to his destination in Kiryat Moshe, which happened to be his grandson's *eirusin*. It took him a while to calm down from the unpleasant incident. About an hour later, the door opened and in walked ... Ophir, who just happened to be the *kallah's* grandfather. The engagement was broken off.

COMMENT: *Who do you think was in the wrong here? Personally, I think Ophir was wrong. And I also think Gideon was wrong. You think they can't both be wrong? Then you're wrong, too. There are plenty of instances in life where both sides in a feud are wrong. And that's absolutely right.*

VEYEISHEV

"AND YOSEF BROUGHT A BAD REPORT ABOUT THEM TO THEIR FATHER"
(Vayeishev 37:2)

We see from this parsha *and the ones that follow the kind of trouble that comes about when one is not careful regarding what he says.*

WHILE some insist the fuss made over England's royal family is a big waste of money, the truth is that the country benefits from it immensely. The tourism revenue, promoted by all the hoopla and pageantry which surrounds the royals, runs into the billions of dollars.

Regardless of whether you think the expenses of the royal family are justified or not, in England the queen is held in high esteem and is placed on something of a pedestal.

So when T.V. broadcaster Rodney Gleest said in passing that the queen was "boring," there was an uproar in the country. He insisted in his defense that he was only saying what everyone was thinking. Although we suspect the outcry fit the category of "they protesteth too much," there was an outcry nonetheless. Under public pressure (read: fear of loss of revenue), the T.V. station fired Rodney. He really didn't realize how bad a situation he was in until he tried to find another job and found that no one else would hire him. He lost his livelihood and the prestige that went with it… all because he let one careless sentence slip out of his mouth.

COMMENT: *The mishna says, "V'lo matzasi laguf tov mishtika, I haven't found anything better for a person than silence," – and no one's ever been fired for applying it.*

"AND NOW LET'S KILL HIM"
(Vayeishev 37:20)

The brothers felt they would be justified in killing Yosef, but what they did ended up bringing about undesirable results. One of the lessons to be learned from this episode is that one should check with others who are more qualified, in this case Yaakov Avinu, to ensure that the chosen course of action is indeed appropriate.

LEIL *Yom Kippur* brings with it a certain intense holiness simply not found the rest of the year. Even those far removed from spiritual pursuits seem to somehow tap into that extra "something" that Yom Kippur provides.

It was with a mixture of solemnity and excitement that Levi Yitzchak Spiegel embarked on his holy mission. Levi Yitzchak had borrowed the key to the local *shteibel* from the *gabbai* and locked himself in the *shul*, in order to fulfill the custom of staying up all night on Yom Kippur saying Tehillim and learning Torah. Beautiful.

There was only one hitch. Levi Yitzchak's wife Ethel was in her ninth month – actually, three days past her due date. She really didn't want to be left alone at home with their six kids, the oldest of whom was nine.

Levi Yitzchak assured her they would have *siyata d'Shmaya* and she wouldn't go into labor. "Look," she protested, "you went to Uman for Rosh Hashana even though I cried and pleaded with you not to, and we lucked out. What Hashem thinks of you abandoning me at a time like this, I don't know. But tonight I want you home. I'm past my…"

"Relax," he interrupted with a reassuring smile. "Just be *b'simcha* and everything will be okay."

It wasn't. Ethel went into labor at 1:30 a.m. and had to wake up her neighbors and have them send their ten year old to get Levi Yitzchak. Well, the righteous Levi Yitzchak had fallen into a deep spiritual slumber after his fervent supplications, so he couldn't hear the kid banging non-stop for ten minutes on the *shul* door.

Hatzalah had to be called. Somehow, Ethel got through it all and gave birth to a healthy baby boy. I guess that was the *siyata d'Shmaya* Levi Yitzchak had been talking about.

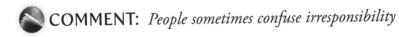 **COMMENT:** *People sometimes confuse irresponsibility*

with bitachon. A Torah Jew must behave responsibly at all times, even if what he wants to do is more fun. As a matter of fact, doing what one wants is often the tell-tale sign that the action is irresponsible. Not always, of course – but often. Mazel tov, *Levi Yitzchak.*

"AND YAAKOV RENT HIS GARMENTS" (Vayeishev 37:34)

Rashi later (38:1) says they hadn't realized the extent of the grief that they'd cause Yaakov Avinu, and they therefore demoted Yehuda. The lesson, of course, is that one must always think about the consequences of one's actions, and not choose a course of action impulsively.

HITLER'S rise to power and his openly anti-Semitic views were cause for concern to Jews all over the world. The leading rabbis of the Reform movement in America held a meeting in a comfortable hotel conference room, accompanied by a delectable lunch, to discuss what they could do to show support for the Jews of Europe. After a couple of hours, they came up with a decision.

The rabbis contacted the media and made a big splash with their official announcement that "the Reform movement, on behalf of American Jewry, officially declares war on Hitler." Their rhetoric was obviously meaningless, as they had absolutely no means of waging that war.

Although silly, their declaration wasn't harmless. Far from it. Very far. When Hitler heard about it, he went ballistic. He threw himself on the floor and had one of his famous temper tantrums. It was while in the throes of that tantrum that he initiated the "final solution."

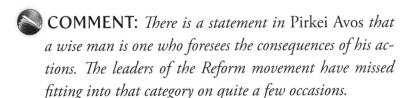 **COMMENT:** *There is a statement in* Pirkei Avos *that a wise man is one who foresees the consequences of his actions. The leaders of the Reform movement have missed fitting into that category on quite a few occasions.*

"AND HASHEM WAS WITH YOSEF AND HE WAS SUCCESSFUL" (Vayeishev 39:2)

This pasuk *stresses that success in life only comes through* siyata d'Shmaya.

OFFICER Wayne Pierce saw the blue Lexus swerving ever so slightly. The untrained eye might not even have noticed it, but twelve years in the force had given Wayne an edge in these matters. He followed the car for a little while, seeing the car swerve a few more times.

"I wonder what that guy is on," he said to himself. He flipped on his blue lights and siren and pulled the car over.

"I haven't had anything to drink in three weeks," insisted the man, forty nine year old Culver Stevens.

"I know, I know," Wayne said in a sarcastic tone of voice. "But you'll take this breathalyzer test anyhow, won't you?"

"You're just wasting your time and mine," Culver said. Still, having no choice other than facing arrest, he submitted to the test. Not a drop of alcohol in his system. He did it a second time. Nothing.

Wayne was embarrassed – and baffled. He had not been wrong about administering a breathalyzer test in the last eight years. "It just can't be. Something is not right," he thought to himself. Then he remembered something he had heard in a first aid course. "I think you ought to get a complete physical to make sure everything is okay, buddy."

"What for?" asked Culver. "You're a cop, not a doctor, remember? Just stop bothering people and everyone will be all right. See ya." With that parting shot, he drove off.

His wife wasn't as easily convinced. "He must have had a reason to say what he said," she insisted.

"Yeah, he didn't want to look like a total fool," snapped her husband.

Alas, like most husbands, he lost the argument. The next day he found himself at his doctor, who did an examination and then sent him for further tests at the hospital.

Two days later, Culver Stevens had brain surgery to remove a malignant tumor. "Five more days and he'd have been dead," said chief surgeon Dr. Ross Malloy Jr. Culver made a grateful call to Officer Wayne Pierce, thanking him for his alertness.

COMMENT: *It's a good idea to think about the things that have gone well in your life and then analyze how much of it was a result of your efforts. An honest assessment will reveal that the* Ribbono shel Olam *had much more to do with it than you did. It's also a good idea to pick up a* siddur *or* tehillim *and make a grateful call to Him.*

MIKEITZ

"PHARAOH GOT ANGRY AT HIS SERVANTS"
(Mikeitz 41:10)

This anger caused two officials to be removed from their positions.

DUDU Ephraim, the maitre de at a fancy restaurant in Netanya, invited his boss to his home for dinner. As they took their seats around the table, the boss had a feeling that something wasn't right, but he couldn't quite put his finger on it. Halfway through the appetizer he suddenly realized what it was. "You thief!" he cried, shocking Dudu and his wife. "I *knew* the cutlery looked familiar! This is the stuff that's been missing from the restaurant. *You're* the one who's been taking it!" Indeed, for quite some time Dudu had been pilfering all sorts of expensive utensils from the restaurant. Poor planning to invite the boss over. The next day, Dudu was looking for new employment.

COMMENT: *They should've used disposables. An even better idea would have been not to steal.*

"AND THE SIGNIFICANCE OF THE DREAM BEING REPEATED" (Mikeitz 41:32)

B ACK when I was a sophomore in high school we had a teacher who taught us English. He was a burly, crude, and mean ex-Marine, with a tattoo on his arm. He didn't like us. Of course, the feeling was mutual and then some. However, unlike other teachers upon whom we ran roughshod, we were terrified of Mr. Wallace. We didn't make a peep in class. Just breathing put us at risk.

On top of all this, Mr. Wallace had some pretty annoying habits, like making us do a lot of busywork during class and reading a newspaper while we did it. There was also the way he would brandish his glasses as he lectured, waving them at us in a way we found demeaning when he wished to make a point.

But as annoying as all that was, it was nothing compared to his practice of periodically pausing and then repeating the last word of a sentence, an obvious attempt at showing himself to be sophisticated. So, for example, he would say something like, "There must be better structure to your sentences… sentences." Or, "It's going to be a very close presidential election… election." This took place on a regular basis, and we all found it quite irritating… irritating.

In any event, what he did one day really took the cake.

He was about to hand back our test papers, but before doing so he paused to make a dramatic announcement. "The trouble with your papers," he began, "is that there is too much repetition… repetition." Honestly, that's what he said. I witnessed it myself. I almost bit my lip off trying to stop myself from laughing… laughing.

COMMENT: *I have often used Mr. Wallace's little habit as an example when I give talks regarding the importance of* chazara. *Certain things in life don't require repetition. However, when it comes to* talmud Torah, *there is no limit as to how many times we must review. To my credit, I don't wave my glasses when I tell this over… over.*

"YOU SHALL BE IN CHARGE OF MY HOUSE" (Mikeitz 41:40)
Pharaoh recognized that Yosef had the ability to run the country, and therefore appointed him to the post.

ELISHA Segal had been on the streets for some time. While the phenomenon of "off the *derech* kids" has turned into a plague in our days, Elisha was somewhat ahead of his time. This was back in the seventies, when the problem was much less widespread.

Elisha worked odd jobs and slept in a rented cellar, headed absolutely nowhere in life. One day, out of a job and out of money, he started looking through the want ads. He saw that Sha'ar Yashuv, the famous *yeshiva* founded by Harav Shlomo Freifeld *zt"l*, was in need of a janitor.

He went to the *yeshiva* and spoke with Rav Freifeld. "Look," the great man said, seeing something in the young man that many others had obviously missed, "I don't want you to be the janitor. I mean, we could use one, but we're not desperate. What I'd really like you to do is be a *maggid shiur*. I see you have the heart and communication skills necessary to be an effective *rebbe*. There is a group of boys here I'd like you to teach. You can come in your jeans and long hair. I don't care. Just come."

Needless to say, Elisha was absolutely speechless. It had been a long time since anyone had said anything positive about him, and certainly the first time *ever* that *anyone* had mentioned he could teach Torah. Overcoming his initial shock, Elisha took Rav Freifeld up on the offer and eventually became a major *marbitz Torah* in *Klal Yisrael*.

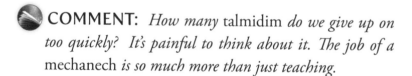 COMMENT: *How many* talmidim *do we give up on too quickly? It's painful to think about it. The job of a* mechanech *is so much more than just teaching.*

"AND HE SAID TO THEM, 'YOU ARE SPIES'"
(Mikeitz 42:9)

DAVE Kahn was in trouble and he knew it, sitting as he was across the table from one very harsh-looking principal. Some of the boys had been involved with illegal substances and somehow the principal had found out that Dave was one of them.

"Look, Dave," began Rabbi Swedlow, "this is very

serious business. We know that there were other guys involved. Dave, I'd like you to tell me who they are."

"I'm sorry," Dave said without hesitation. "There is simply no way I'm going to rat on my friends."

"Look, Dave. You're in big trouble. If you don't tell me who was involved, you're going to be suspended and maybe worse. If you help the *yeshiva*, we can be a little more lenient."

Dave sat there silently for a few moments. He had to think and think fast. This was serious trouble, and he'd need all of his resourcefulness to get out of it. After a couple of minutes, Rabbi Swedlow broke the silence. "Look, even if you don't validate our suspicions, we pretty much know who was involved. We know Mike Cohen and Arthur Karoll were both involved."

"Well, you're ..." Dave began, but then stopped.

"Yeah, yeah, what is it?" asked Rabbi Swedlow eagerly.

"No, I'd rather not say anything because I don't want to get into any more trouble."

"Don't worry," Rabbi Swedlow reassured him, "you won't get into any more trouble."

"After what I have to say, I'm *sure* I'll get in more trouble."

"No, you won't. You can speak freely, I assure you."

"Do you promise that no matter what I say I won't get into more trouble?"

"Absolutely."

"Okay then, here goes. You're a liar!" declared Dave.

"WHAT?! HOW DARE..." but the rabbi caught himself. He realized that he'd just made a promise... and that he'd stepped into Dave's well-laid trap. "And why am I a

liar?" he asked calmly, in a remarkable display of compo-
sure.

"Because you told me you knew that Mike Cohen and
Arthur Karoll were involved, and I know for a *fact* that they
were not."

Rabbi Swedlow spent the next few minutes trying to
respond to Dave's accusation that a dishonest principal
was worse for a *yeshiva* than a few boys doing something
wrong. Being put on the defensive really took the wind out
of his sails, and Dave ended up getting off a lot easier than
he should have.

COMMENT: *I included this story because there is a
very important lesson for* mechanchim. *Never get into
a situation where talmidim put you on the defensive for
doing your job. And never let the* talmidim *sidetrack you
from the real issue at hand, which they often try to do.
Rabbi Swedlow should've laughed and said, "You did that
really well, Dave. You won't get in trouble for what you
said. But you're still in big trouble for your other crime."*

"AND HE SAID TO THEM, 'YOU ARE SPIES'"
(Mikeitz 42:9)

"**A**RYEH, please meet me in my office in ten
minutes." Aryeh knew what it was about. He
had missed most of *shacharis* yet again, and
the principal had told him that the next time it would happen his parents would be called. Aryeh hated to put his

parents through this sort of trouble. They were back home in St. Louis and had had reservations about sending him out of town to *yeshiva* in the first place. Only after he had promised to cooperate fully and follow all the *yeshiva's* rules did they consent.

The principal dialed. "Mrs. Zeldman," he heard the *rosh yeshiva* say after the opening pleasantries, "I'm sorry but we are left with no choice. One more missed *shacharis* and we're going to have to ask Aryeh to leave the *yeshiva* for good."

While trying to stop her head from spinning, Mrs. Zeldman heard what sounded like the door closing. "Mrs. Zeldman, he just left the office," the *rosh yeshiva* said. "Don't worry. He's a good boy and we have no intention of dismissing him. But he's got a weakness in this area and I feel giving him a little fright is what it's going to take to get him to *davening* on time." It worked. Aryeh didn't miss another *shacharis*.

 COMMENT: *There are a couple of problems with this story. First of all, the principal should have told Mrs. Zeldman in advance that that's what he was planning to do. And furthermore, a* mechanech *must ask a* halachic *authority about the permissibility of resorting to a bluff in order to achieve his goals. Just because something is effective doesn't mean it's permissible.*

VAYIGASH

"FOR HOW CAN I GO TO MY FATHER AND THE LAD IS NOT WITH ME"
(Vayigash 44:34)

Yosef saw in Yehuda's willingness to go to any extent to free Binyamin a form of teshuva *for what had been done to Yosef so many years earlier.*

ELUL is the month when we focus on *teshuva*. In the old days, people took this month quite seriously. Two examples. Two of the local ne'er-do-wells in the town of Mir were once fighting with each other one day during Elul. An elderly woman happened to pass by and saw what was going on. "During Elul!?" she exclaimed... and they immediately desisted. They were buffoons to whom just about nothing was sacred – but Elul was Elul.

And then there was the father who was visiting with his twelve year old son in Mir during Elul and wanted to show the boy the famous Mirrer *yeshiva*. "You can't bring him now," someone told the father. "It's Elul! There's a fire in there!" Such was his description of the intensity in the *yeshiva* during this period.

But don't think it's been left behind entirely. In our day and age there are also those who play for keeps during this month. A rabbi was on a night flight to the United States in the month of Elul. Just about everyone on the dark and quiet plane was asleep. Suddenly, they were all startled awake by a frightening sound. It was a *shofar* being blown – loudly. The blower, a young man belonging to a certain religious group known for their somewhat, uh, enthusiastic devotions, was *davening shacharis*. As soon as he saw the sun rising he wanted to carry out the custom of sounding the *shofar* daily during Elul. The people on the plane fulfilled – unexpectedly and most literally – the directive of the *pasuk*, "Arise, o' slumberers from your sleep…"

 COMMENT: *Part of Elul and doing* teshuva *is learning how to determine which actions are appropriate and when. Nowadays, even* breathing *loudly on a plane can cause a panic, all the more so sounding a* shofar. *But just between us… how much would you have given to get a look at the faces of the people on that plane? Can you imagine?*

"I AM YOSEF, IS MY FATHER STILL ALIVE?"
(Vayigash 45:3)

Chazal *say this was a form of rebuke. The Bais Halevi explains how we see rebuke in what seems to be an innocent question. The brothers claimed to be concerned for Yaakov's well-being and therefore could not return home without Binyamin. Yosef pointed out that this hadn't seemed to be a concern when they had sold him. That was the rebuke.*

ALL the seats on the bus were taken, so Rav Rheine had no choice but to stand. As the bus started moving, he noticed Ezra Davidman seated in the row just ahead of where he was standing. Ezra was a former *talmid* of his and was now learning in the *yeshiva's kollel*, and they still had a *kesher*. Ezra would periodically ask him questions on the *gemara* and would also come by for guidance once in a while. Rav Rheine did not want to put Ezra through the difficult *nisayon* of having to give up his seat, so he avoided making eye contact.

A few minutes later Ezra noticed Rav Rheine standing, so he said weakly, "Would the *rav* like to sit?" His offer, though, was not accompanied by his starting to get up, and Rav Rheine could tell he really did not want to, so he simply smiled and said, "No, I'm fine just like this." Ezra nodded with a look of relief on his face and settled back comfortably.

Twenty minutes later, they both got off at the same stop. "Ezra," Rav Rheine began, "for the last twenty minutes I've been thinking that you have to be taught a lesson in *derech eretz*. How could you *possibly* sit while a *rebbe* of yours is standing? If a *rebbe* is standing, you don't *offer* your seat. You *insist* the *rebbe* sits and you get up right away to make sure that he does. I'm sorry to have to say this, but you have to learn. I didn't want to say anything on the bus because I was *nogei'a badavar*. Had I told you then that you should have insisted that I sit I would have benefited, so I had reason to suspect the purity of my motivation. But now that I have nothing to gain, I know that what I'm saying is for your benefit."

COMMENT: *Waiting until he got off the bus is indeed an excellent indication of his motivation. All too often we convince ourselves that our motivation is "the principle of the matter" — with us playing the role of principal. And the fact that Rav Rheine told off his* talmid *is also something we can learn from. A* rebbe *has a responsibility to teach, even if it's not pleasant. If they are not told, they will not know.*

"IT'S NOT YOU WHO SENT ME HERE. IT'S HASHEM" (Vayigash 45:8)

Yosef told the brothers that he bears no grudge against them, because Hashem orchestrated the entire adventure.

HARAV Chaim Ozer Grodzinski was the unchallenged *gadol hador*. People would come to him for letters of recommendation for various causes, personal or community-oriented. Being a soft person, he would usually accommodate them. This was in spite of the amount of time it took to listen to them and then write the recommendation.

Well, a man once came to him with such a request and Rav Chaim Ozer turned him down. Now, if Rav Chaim Ozer turned him down, there was a good reason for it.

The man started yelling at Rav Chaim Ozer and calling him names. After some really good shouts, he turned and stormed out the door. The people in the next room were quite upset at this affront to *kavod haTorah*. "How could you let him yell at you like that?" one of the people asked. "Why didn't you call us? We would have bounced him out good and proper."

Rav Chaim Ozer smiled his sweet smile. "What can I tell you? I just don't know how to get angry."

COMMENT: *What Rav Chaim Ozer knew – lots and lots of* Torah *– we don't know. But what he* didn't *know – how to get angry or upset at people – we know only too well. We have to keep in mind that people who annoy us or rub us the wrong way have been sent by the* Ribbono shel Olam, *so there's really nothing to get upset about. If that's too philosophical, we should just think about the fact that we sometimes annoy others or rub them the wrong way. That should do it.*

"AND THEY TOLD HIM YOSEF IS STILL ALIVE" (Vayigash 45:26)

Chazal *say they broke the news to Yaakov gently through Serach bas Asher, because they were concerned about how he'd handle a sudden shock.*

I T happened every year in the crowded, old Shaarei Chesed *shul*. The *gabbai* would announce *rosh chodesh* Elul at the *rosh chodesh bentching*. Shortly after, there would be a cry for water from the *ezras nashim*. Why? Because each year, old Mrs. Gutmandel would faint when she heard the name of the month which stands for introspection and *teshuva.* Each and every year. Hearing "Elul" had that powerful of an effect.

 COMMENT: *Some of the cynics are probably thinking she should've just looked at a calendar and she would have known* Elul *is coming. Well, it wasn't being taken by surprise that got her. It was what* Elul *means. There are some things which no amount of anticipation can fully prepare a person for. The reality is too overwhelming. Skydiving and alligator wrestling immediately come to mind. No matter how much one prepares for them under simulated conditions, when the real thing happens the participant begins to sweat – and heavily at that.* To a Torah *Jew,* Elul *is – or should be – the same. And if it isn't – one ought to sweat over* that.

"AND HE BROUGHT OFFERINGS"
(Vayigash 46:1)

These offerings were brought out of gratitude that Yosef was still alive. Nowadays, we don't have offerings. We have tefilla *instead.*

THE well-known head of Ezer Mitzion, Rav Chananya Cholek, was once at the *Kosel* with a wealthy man. While standing there, the two noticed a Jew standing by the Wall and crying his eyes out in *tefilla.*

"There can only be one of two things that would make a person cry like that," Rav Cholek said to the *gevir.* "Either he has a medical problem, or he has some sort of financial problem. Let's make a deal. If it's medical, I'll help him out.

If it's financial, then you'll help him."

The *gevir* was intrigued by the challenge and immediately agreed to it. Rav Cholek approached the man. "Hello. My name is Cholek, and if you or anyone in your family has any sort of medical problem I will be glad to try and help you out."

The man smiled through his tears. "Thank you very much, but everyone in my family is well, *baruch Hashem.*"

Rav Cholek went back to the *gevir*. "Okay, it's your turn. He said it's not a medical issue."

"Just tell me how much you need and I'll write out a check right here and now," the *gevir* said to the man.

"Thank you so much. But the truth is, while we don't have much, we don't really need much. We're doing okay."

"So then why were you crying like that?" the two of them asked.

"Last night we married off our twelfth and last child," the man answered. "Each time I had to marry off one of my kids I'd come here and ask Hashem for help, and He has never yet turned us down. Today I just came to thank Him for all of His kindness. That's why I was crying. Doesn't everyone do that?"

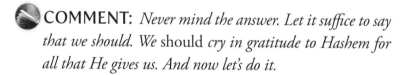 COMMENT: *Never mind the answer. Let it suffice to say that we should. We should* cry in gratitude to Hashem for all that He gives us. And now let's do it.

"TO INSTRUCT AHEAD OF HIM IN GOSHEN" (Vayigash 46:28)

Rashi says this means that he was to instruct how to settle the land.

I T'S the job of all *rebbeim* to instruct their *talmidim*, and that instruction extends far beyond the book learning. The *rebbeim* must provide guidance for how their charges are to behave as well. Sometimes they have to do it in a sharp manner, so that the lesson is fully absorbed and never forgotten.

Rav Verizer was seated at his table looking over the *gemara* and awaiting the arrival of his *talmidim*. None of the plastic chairs they normally used were in the room, as they had all been used at a *simcha* in the *yeshiva's* dining room the night before.

The door opened and Elimelech entered. Noticing there were no chairs, he went out and came back a few minutes later carrying one. As he settled in his seat, Rav Verizer said, "Good morning, Elimelech. Is your back okay?"

"Yeah, fine, *baruch Hashem*. Why wouldn't it be?"

"Well, I know you saw there were no chairs in the room and you went out and got one. I also know those chairs are not at all heavy and you could easily have carried three or four of them so that others would also have a place to sit. Since you didn't, I figured maybe your back was hurting you."

COMMENT: *I imagine Elimelech became a regular "chair bringer" after that. And please don't ask why Rav Verizer himself didn't bring the chairs. He obviously felt the boys should take responsibility for it. And he taught them about that responsibility – in a way they'd never forget.*

VAYECHI

"HOWEVER, HIS YOUNGER BROTHER WILL BE GREATER THAN HIM" (Vayechi 48:19)

A GROUP of boys had a contest to see who could climb to the top of a pole the fastest. One of the boys won by a significant margin. His *zaidy*, who was raising him in place of the boy's deceased father, happened to be watching the contest. He took advantage of a golden opportunity to impart a lesson to his beloved grandson.

"The reason you won," he began, "is because you did something different than all the other boys. As each of them climbed the high pole, they looked down. That made them slower, as their fear and nerves took over. You, however, never looked down – you just kept looking up. If you apply that to your Torah learning, you'll become very big, *im yirtzeh Hashem*. Very, very big."

The *zaidy* was Harav Yitzchak Meir Alter *zt"l*, better known as the Chiddushei Harim, and the grandson was

Harav Yehuda Aryeh Leib Alter *zt"l*, the famous Sfas Emes. To say he became very big is an understatement. A very big understatement.

 COMMENT: *We must always keep our focus upward.*

"YISSACHAR IS A HARD-BONED DONKEY"
(Vayechi 49:14)
Chazal tell us that Yissachar was a Torah learner and his tribe was the tribe of Torah learners. Torah was their life and sole occupation.

WHEN the great Mirrer *rosh yeshiva*, Harav Shmuel Birenbaum *zt"l*, awoke from heart surgery, the first thing he asked for was a *gemara*. Even in his weakened state, he learned for as long as his strength held out. After he could learn no longer, he clasped the *gemara* tightly and held it against his heart.

"You think it's the successful surgery that keeps my heart beating?" he asked those standing near. "It's *this* that keeps my heart beating." And he clutched it even tighter.

COMMENT: *Hearing this should make our hearts beat a little stronger.*

"AND HE INCLINED HIS SHOULDER TO
BEAR THE BURDEN" (Vayechi 49:15)
The "burden" referred to here is the commitment to Torah

learning. Although called a burden, it provides more satisfaction to one who studies it responsibly than any other pursuit in the world.

SIXTY six year old Walter Davenport was driving his wife Carla nuts. He'd retired two years earlier from a high paying position as a senior purchaser for a clothing chain. He still hadn't found something with which to productively occupy his time. Forgetting the rule that wives look forward to their husbands leaving in the morning, he hung around the house.

Predictably, Carla felt her turf was invaded. He was constantly making suggestions, criticizing and getting under her skin. He tried hobbies and he tried entertainment, but nothing gave him a sense of fulfillment.

Finally, one glorious day, Carla got the relief she had longed for. Walter got nailed making some sort of illegal turn and was given a two hundred dollar ticket by the cop. He went to court to contest the ticket but lost. From that moment on he was like a man possessed. He spent every waking minute fighting the fine. Correspondences, e-mails, meetings… the works.

It took over a year and a half and more than fifteen thousand dollars in expenses, but he finally beat the ticket. Walter was ecstatic. He was drunk with glee. He spent about a week busily telling one and all about his tremendous accomplishment. And then he went back to driving Carla nuts.

COMMENT: *Pirkei Avos says a person should grow old with Torah. There is nothing else that can provide an*

older man with the kind of fulfillment and satisfaction
that Torah study can. Of course, it's best if one develops a
taste for it when he's younger, when it's easier. But even if
he hasn't, he could and should still get involved. Of course,
it's important that he also set aside at least a little time
to… drive his wife nuts.

"AND HE EXPIRED AND WAS GATHERED TO HIS PEOPLE" (Vayechi 49:33)

Chazal *say that Yaakov Avinu did not die.*

IT was nothing short of a miracle. While riding his bike, thirteen year old Shlomo turned the corner onto a main street and was hit by a bus. Everyone who saw him lying there unconscious assumed he was dead. And if not, then he was soon to be. There was no way he could have survived such a blow. The Hatzalah guys worked on him and rushed him to the hospital, but they knew there was no hope.

As word of the accident spread, people began saying Tehillim for the comatose boy and his family went to the *Kosel.* Even so, no one harbored any realistic hopes for his survival. The doctors said it was a matter of hours.

The hours, however, stretched on and then became a day. Then a few days. In all, the boy who was now Refael Shlomo was in a coma for three weeks. The doctors said that even if he woke up he would be severely brain damaged.

They were wrong. Slowly, ever so slowly, he began to rally. First he opened his eyes. Then he started to communicate by nodding, and then his speech gradually returned.

After some three months in the hospital, he was fully communicative, though his speech was slow and slurred and he only had use of one arm. He could not move his legs at all.

After six months, his body started to function significantly better. As of this writing, he still has a way to go, but he is alive, *baruch Hashem*, and constantly making progress.

While this ordeal was taking place, there was one thing he said that's enough to send shivers up anyone's spine. As soon as he was capable, he asked that people should learn with him. Although in the beginning he couldn't talk, he would show his participation through eye movements. After regaining the slightest ability to speak, he became more active while learning with his *chavrusas*.

Obviously, while all this was going on, he had grueling physical rehabilitation. At some point he wanted to cut down on the time-consuming rehab and focus more on his learning. His mother, on the other hand, wanted him to enter the top rehab place in the country.

Refael Shlomo protested that it would simply take too much time away from Torah learning. All he wanted to do was go back to *yeshiva*. His mother made it clear that this was not an option, and she was going to pull rank.

Refael Shlomo, however, stopped her in her tracks. "Mom," he said through his tears of frustration, "I've... been... there. I've... seen... it. I'm... not... afraid... to... go... back. I... was... brought... back... down... to... learn... Torah. If... I... can't... learn... I... may... as... well... go... back... up... there."

 **COMMENT:** *!!!*

"I WILL SUPPORT YOU" (Vayechi 50:21)

"I'M sorry, but I won't be giving you anything near what I've given in the past." Rav Kaufman had barely taken his seat in Mr. Halpert's downtown office when he was treated to this declaration. Mr. Halpert seemed to genuinely love Torah and was pretty generous in his support of Rav Kaufman's *kollel*. He'd been coming to Mr. Halpert for years, so he was more than a bit surprised.

"May I ask why?"

"Yes, and I'll be glad to tell you. You see, I now support eight *kollels* of my own in Eretz Yisrael, so I really am somewhat limited."

Rav Kaufman had never heard of this new network of *kollelim*. "What are the names of these *kollelim*?" he asked him.

"Four are called Halpert, one is Cohen, one is Mandlebaum, one is Shrenk and one is Chaimovitz."

"Well, I've never heard of any of them, but as long as you're supporting Torah, that's all that matters."

Mr. Halpert laughed. "Of course you've never heard of any of them. They are my four sons and four sons-in-law who are all learning full time and I'm supporting them. They are my eight *kollelim*."

COMMENT: *It is a tremendous* zechus *for* Klal Yisrael *that there are so many Torah learners today who are being supported by their parents. This shows that people realize what is truly important and what it's worth spending money on.*

SHEMOS

SHEMOS

"AND THESE ARE THE NAMES OF THE *BNEI YISRAEL*" (Shemos 1:1)

GETTING secular college students interested in any sort of activity other than drinking and partying is quite a challenge. When Morris Youngman took the position as an outreach worker in a university town, he hadn't realized just how difficult it actually was. With his engaging personality and friendly approach, he thought he'd be having these young people eating out of his hands. Or at least eating over at his Shabbos table.

After two long months, he found "business" very slow. An experienced campus *kiruv* worker friend suggested he use some sort of gimmick to attract "customers."

Morris decided to implement his suggestion. He set up a table in one of the popular gathering spots with a big sign that read "FREE *KUGEL*." Anyone coming over was welcome to some good old fashioned *lukshen kugel*, which was to hopefully open the door to a relationship.

Students actually came over to nosh on some free food and Morris succeeded in making some connections. The kicker, however, was when one student, obviously not Jewish, came over and asked, "Who's Kugel and what's he incarcerated for?"

COMMENT: *Morris probably should've served cholent instead. No one would ask, "Who's Cholent?"*

"AND THESE ARE THE NAMES OF THE *BNEI YISRAEL"* (Shemos 1:1)

The pasuk *refers to Yaakov by both of his names, Yisrael and Yaakov.*

IN our day and age, the most famous person with both names of Yaakov Avinu was undoubtedly the Steipler, Harav Yaakov Yisrael Kanievsky *zt"l*. It is generally agreed that he had *ruach hakodesh*. But for those of you who are skeptical, you can draw your own conclusions. Here are a few stories. These stories were shared by the people who had been personally involved or who heard the stories from those who were:

There were two *avreichim* from a *yeshiva* in Yerushalayim who went to the Steipler for a *beracha*. When they entered his room, they put a note they had brought with them with their request on the Steipler's table. (The Steipler was hard of hearing, so requests were submitted by the petitioners on prewritten notes.) The Steipler shouted at them to leave.

All the way back to Yerushalayim they tried to figure out what they could possibly have done wrong that the Steipler picked up on. The only thing they could think of was that they had written the note on top of a *sefer*. They then wrote their request again, this time being careful that it should be on the table with no *sefer* underneath.

When they arrived back at the Steipler's residence, they saw a sign on his door that said, "Please do not bring notes that are written on *sefarim*!"

THEN there was the man who entered the Steipler's room for a *beracha* and the Steipler immediately shouted at him to leave. He asked the Steipler's grandson what the problem was.

"Are you *shomer Shabbos*?"

"Yes."

"Do you have a T.V.?"

"No." (The Steipler would not give *berachos* to people who had a T.V.)

"Are you wearing *tzitzis*?"

"No."

"Go put on a pair of *tzitzis* and then come back." The man went home and put on *tzitzis*. When he came back and entered the room, the Steipler didn't say a word and proceeded to give him a *beracha*.

A SIXTY two year old man who had recently been diagnosed with Parkinson's disease came to the Steipler for a *beracha*. "You don't need a *beracha*," the Steipler declared, "you can live for another twenty years!" The man was *niftar* twenty years later *to the day*!

AND of course there was the *yeshiva bochur* who came to the Steipler with a request for a *beracha*. "Tell your *rosh yeshiva* I want to speak to him," the Steipler said. When the *rosh yeshiva* arrived, the Steipler asked him, "Why are you sending me *goyim* for *berachos*?" The *rosh yeshiva* was clueless as to what the great man was talking about. "That boy you sent yesterday – check his *yichus*. He's not Jewish!" The *rosh yeshiva* was sure the Steipler was making a mistake. The boy came from a fine family and had been in the *yeshiva* for quite a while. However, upon investigation it turned out that the boy's maternal grandmother had had a Reform conversion. The boy was indeed not Jewish.

COMMENT: Chazal *say that one who studies Torah* lishma, *which means with no thought of personal gain, merits many things. It was blatantly obvious that the Steipler* zt"l *was a living example of that* mishna *in Pirkei Avos.*

"SHE SAW THE BASKET IN THE REEDS AND REACHED OUT HER ARM AND TOOK IT" (Shemos 2:5)

When Pharaoh's daughter pulled in the basket and saved that baby's life, she had no idea how far-reaching the ramifications of her actions would be.

"**A**RE you Shelly Pritchook?" the stewardess asked politely, hovering over the passenger with a kosher meal in her hand.

"Yes, I am," Shelly answered. The stewardess placed the meal on her tray and carried on down the aisle.

Shelly had not even managed to open her double seal when a woman came up from behind her. "Hi," she began in a slightly embarrassed tone of voice. "My name is Tally. I overheard the stewardess say the name Pritchook. You don't happen to know Zale Pritchook by any chance, do you?"

"Well, actually I do," Shelly said with a laugh. "He's my husband." Shelly and Zale, both having suffered the loss of their spouses, had just recently married. "He's at the back of the plane right now, *davening mincha*. He'll be here in a couple of minutes."

"I would like to introduce him to some people," Tally said, clearly excited.

Zale came back to his seat and saw a woman with three very fine looking *bnei Torah* standing in the aisle. "Hi, Zale," the woman began, tears welling in her eyes. "I'm Tally Schiff. Do you remember me?"

Zale remembered immediately. Over thirty years earlier, he and his first wife had been *mekarev* Tally and her husband Robert, neither of whom knew the first thing about *Yiddishkeit*. "Robert was *niftar* three years ago," Tally said sadly, "but these boys are what he left to carry on. It's all because of you. When I heard the stewardess say the name Pritchook, I just had to find out if you were related. I realized there couldn't be too many people in the world with that name. And," she added, the tears flowing freely now, "in *our* world there is only one."

COMMENT: *When Zale pulled Tally and her husband Robert out of their emptiness many years earlier, perhaps he had assumed that something everlasting might come out of it. Did he envision real live* bnei Torah, *all of whom would go on to build families of more* bnei Torah? *I find it hard to believe. Yet, there they were on a Virgin Atlantic flight, not a likely spot for a* kiruv-of-over-thirty-years-ago-reunion, *seeing the huge dividends from his investment of the distant past.*

"AND THE BOY GREW UP" (Shemos 2:10)

The midrash *relates the story of Moshe pulling the crown off Pharaoh's head. One of his advisors, Bilaam, called for his immediate execution. Yisro, the other advisor, suggested the famous test of the gems versus the coals. The result was that Moshe stayed alive and, some forty years later, became the son-in-law of that very same Yisro who had saved his life. Yisro received a tangible reward for his efforts.*

ANDREA'S parents asked that their daughter, a public school student, be allowed to play in an all-girls baseball league sponsored by the local day school. The request was met with stiff opposition. Parents objected, concerned – and rightly so – that exposure to a public school girl would have a negative effect on their daughters. One of the fathers, Jack Schwartz, knew

Andrea's dad through some business dealings and therefore attempted to get her accepted. No go. The parents simply didn't want it.

Jack convened a meeting and took personal responsibility. "If there is even *one* complaint about her language or about the things she talks about or anything else that someone finds inappropriate, I will *personally* pull her out of the league," he declared. It took some convincing, but the parents eventually relented. There was not one complaint the entire summer, as Andrea was actually a very refined girl.

At the end of the summer, she told her parents she wished to leave public school and attend day school. I'm sure you can guess the rest of the story. Andrea became *frum*, followed by her parents becoming Torah observant. Andrea's dad eventually became the head of the day school's parents' association.

COMMENT: *The question of accepting a girl with such a background into a group of* frum *girls is obviously one which must be asked of* daas *Torah. Regular people's opinions are irrelevant in such a weighty situation. On the other hand, if it is decided that it's the right thing to do, the person who set the ball in motion (I couldn't resist) will be the happy recipient of the reward for all the positive ripple effects.*

"AND HE SAID TO THE *RASHA*, 'WHY DO YOU STRIKE YOUR FELLOW?'"
(Shemos 2:3)

RABBI Chanoch Landsman had only been principal of the day school for three weeks. It was a well-established school with a large student body, and Chanoch knew it would take some time to really get settled in the job. He realized that he should expect some speed bumps at the outset, but what he actually experienced exceeded his worst nightmare.

One morning, he was filling in for one of the *rebbeim* who had called in absent at the last minute. During the first twenty minutes of class, two of the boys in the back were talking, acting as if he didn't exist. Normally, it wouldn't have disturbed him so much, but now he was the principal. He just could not allow such a blatant show of disregard for authority to go unpunished.

He called over Elchonon, the one who was doing most of the talking, and gave him a slap across the face. "It's not my fault!" Elchonon yelled at him through his tears. "Meir's family just arrived in the country from Israel. I was translating for him!" Needless to say, Rabbi Landsman felt absolutely horrible. He apologized profusely to the boy. He even tried to turn it into a *mussar* lesson for the class, blaming himself for what happened.

About forty five minutes later, the door of the classroom was thrown open, and an outraged woman stormed in. "WHY DID YOU SLAP MY SON ?" she screamed. "WHY DID YOU SLAP MY SON?" Before Chanoch knew what happened, she walked over… and slapped him across the face! In front of the entire class! Within minutes, the corridors of the school were filled with students, all talking about how the new principal just got slapped by someone's mother.

COMMENT: *There is much discussion about if and when corporal punishment should be used by educators. There are qualified* talmidei chachamim *who are of the opinion that a* rebbe *may slap a student, and there are other* talmidei chachamim *who oppose it. However, I know of no opinion that a parent may* ever *strike a principal or rebbe.*

"AND HE GAVE HIS DAUGHTER TZIPORA TO MOSHE" (Shemos 2:21)

As we mentioned above, Yisro, as Pharaoh's advisor, saved baby Moshe from being killed at Bilaam's suggestion and later became his father-in-law quite a few decades later.

A GERMAN platoon in WWI captured a bunch of Italian soldiers. The commandant of the platoon did not feel like schlepping the P.O.W.s around, so he gave his men orders to take the whole bunch of them into the forest and gun them down.

There was a Jewish soldier in the platoon who protested. "We can't just shoot them in cold blood. They surrendered and put their trust in us. It's just not right."

"I'm in charge here, Weinroth," the commandant snapped. "And I say we should shoot them, so that's what we're gonna do."

"Well, you'll have to kill me first," Weinroth said firmly, "because I'm not going to let you shoot them." Somehow, Weinroth ended up getting his way and they didn't kill the Italians.

Shortly after WWI, Michoel Leib Weinroth moved to the U.S. He settled in Chicago, where he opened a small glazier business and raised a family. One day, while out riding in his wagon, he passed a building which had had a big fire a few days earlier. Michoel Leib noticed a big pile of windows which had been discarded because they were cracked and blackened from the fire. He pulled up his wagon and started loading them on, as he'd be able to use the glass for his business. After a couple hours of work, his hands were all blackened from the soot, so he went into the building to wash his hands off.

Michoel Leib got one of the biggest surprises of his life. When he turned on the faucet, instead of water out came… beer. Beer! You see, this was during the era of Prohibition. It turned out the building was a headquarters of one of the bootleg alcohol operations then at work in Chicago. The occupants had cleverly hidden their illegal liquid in the building's plumbing system.

As Michoel Leib stared in surprise at the golden juice flowing out of the tap, one of the occupants noticed that he'd noticed. He immediately grabbed Michoel Leib and called out to his cronies, who promptly joined him. "What're we gonna do wit' him?" one of the gangsters asked.

"Well, I don' see that we have any choice but to bump him off," answered one of the others. "I mean, if this boid talks then our entire operation is blown and we go to da klink. Let's get him outta here and get it done."

All in the room were in agreement, and Michoel Leib felt terribly panicked. "Before we kill 'im we better ask da boss," one of them objected.

"Yeah, he's right," said another. "Da boss ain't gonna like it if we do somtin' like dis on our own."

The boss, Vincent "Big Snake" Piruzzo, walked in. "Dis better be important or all you guys is in big trouble," he threatened. "I was in da middle of cuttin' an extortion deal and I don't like to be interrupted fer trivialities." The men gave him a quick summary of what was going on. "Okay, take him out and knock him... hey, buddy," he suddenly said, with a quizzical glance at Michoel Leib, "you look familiar from somewhere."

He started asking Michoel Leib all sorts of questions, and eventually traced the fact that he'd been a German soldier in WWI. "Did your platoon ever capture a group of Italian soldiers?" he asked excitedly. Sure enough, Vincent Piruzzo had been one of the soldiers Michoel Leib had saved. "Boys, he saved my life, so we're gonna let him go. And he aint' gonna talk, right?" All Michoel could do was nod as he made his way out of there.

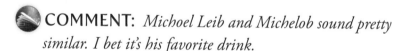 **COMMENT:** *Michoel Leib and Michelob sound pretty similar. I bet it's his favorite drink.*

VA'EIRA

"AND MY MIRACLES" (Va'eira 7:3)

OTAL devastation. The Feigers' new baby was born with a hole in his heart. The medical referral expert, Rav Elimelech Firer, told them their best option was surgery by a specialist in Boston, Dr. Clayton West, at a cost of over $100,000. After all their efforts and phone calls and family contributions, they were only able to come up with $40,000.

The baby's father went to Harav Chaim Kanievsky *shlit"a* to ask him what to do. "I've exhausted all means of *hishtadlus*," the forlorn father lamented.

"If you can't go to the doctor, the doctor will have to come to you," Rav Chaim said cryptically. The Feigers had all the faith in the world in Rav Chaim, but they didn't know what he meant and had no choice but to continue trying to raise more money. Two more days passed and they made no progress.

The next day, they got a call from Rav Firer. "Dr. West

is coming to Hadassah Ein Kerem next week to do three surgeries. This had not been scheduled when we last spoke. I've already made the necessary arrangements for your baby to be number four. Oh, and he's agreed to do it for $8,000."

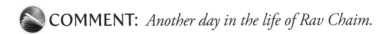 **COMMENT:** *Another day in the life of Rav Chaim.*

"AND HE DIDN'T OBEY THEM"
(Va'eira 8:11)

Pharaoh was a slow learner. It took a lot until the message finally hit home.

HARAV Shlomo Wolbe *zt"l*, the legendary *mash-giach* and *mechanech*, was once invited to give a *shiur* on an army base to a group of high ranking secular Israeli officers. This was at the time when *kiruv* was still a new concept. The army, not realizing the lure an introduction to Torah life would pose for many of the enlisted men, allowed for regular *shiurim* and lectures.

The effect it had was more than the army bargained for, as pilots and soldiers left the military in droves to learn Torah. Unfortunately, after seeing the amount of one way traffic leading from the army to *yeshivos*, most notably Ohr Somayach, they sharply curtailed the lectures.

In any event, Rav Wolbe gave a *shiur* to this very select group. When he returned to his *yeshiva*, one of the people there asked him if he saw any results from the *shiur*. "Yes," he answered, "the generals are all committed to wearing Rabbeinu Tam *tefillin*."

"Really!?" the man asked, indescribably impressed.

"No," snapped Rav Wolbe. "It takes a long time for any type of *chinuch* to have an effect. What do you think – a sudden change is going to take place after one *shiur*?"

 COMMENT: Mechanchim *must have patience. Any expectation of instant results is unrealistic.*

"AND FIRE SHOT EARTHWARD"
(Va'eira 9:23)

AS Rav Moshe Fearman turned the corner in the Har Tzvi neighborhood of Yerushalayim, he saw fire shooting out of the window of an upper floor apartment. There was a woman on the balcony screaming incoherently about a trapped child. A crowd of people stood around, looking on in helpless horror.

Without a moment's hesitation, Rav Moshe ran up the stairs. Throwing a blanket over himself, he yelled to the mother to run down. He then managed to enter the blaze and save the trapped four year old girl. His clothing was singed and he took in a little smoke, but he managed to get the child down, safe and sound.

The hysterical mother hugged her daughter and the relieved crowd gathered around the pair. Realizing he was no longer needed, the unassuming Rav Moshe picked up his briefcase and headed on to his *yeshiva*, where he gave *shiur* and carried on as if nothing out of the ordinary had happened.

The next day, his impressionable friend Nochum Ringle stopped him after *shacharis*. Nochum was *very* excited. "Rav Moshe, did you hear about that incident yesterday in Har Tzvi? There was a fire and a mysterious man came and saved a little girl and then no one saw him after that. They're saying he was Eliyahu Hanavi! I mean, a *real gilui* Eliyahu Hanavi! I mean, how *else* can you *possibly* explain what happened? I mean…"

Rav Moshe started laughing. "What's so funny? I mean…"

"Nochum," Rav Moshe interrupted, "*I'm* Eliyahu Hanavi."

COMMENT: *I heard this story from Rav Moshe himself. Now rumors will spread that I've had* gilui *Eliyahu. But if it helps to sell more books…*

"ONLY IN THE LAND OF GOSHEN"
(Va'eira 9:26)
Living in the land of Goshen, segregated from the natives, provided Bnei Yisrael *with at least a modicum of protection from the negative influences around them.*

"HOW can you, the *bnei Torah*, remain in Eretz Yisrael?" This was the question posed by the Satmar Rebbe, Harav Yoel *zt"l*, to the Chazon Ish *zt"l*. "After all, doesn't the Rambam rule that if one finds himself surrounded by people who have cast off the yoke of Torah, he must leave his civilized dwelling place and go live in a cave? You should all really flee! How do you justify staying?"

"The *batei medrash* and *yeshivos* are our caves," the Chazon Ish answered.

COMMENT: *If this was true over fifty years ago, how much more so is it true now. However, it's not a problem unique to* Eretz Yisrael. *The entire world has become so vulgar and decadent that, wherever one lives, he must take refuge. So, as the old saying goes, "head for the caves."*

BO

"FOR I HAVE MADE HIS HEART HEAVY"
(Bo 10:1)

ET ready for this one. The following story was recorded in the town journal of the city of Lublin about three hundred years ago.

A woman in the town of Lublin was dying and her husband swore that he would not remarry. About a year after she passed away, he decided he did want to remarry. He went to the great *halachic* authority, the Maharshal, and asked him what to do.

The Maharshal released him from his oath, because by swearing not to remarry he was preventing himself from fulfilling the *mitzvah* of marriage, and an oath to neglect a *mitzvah* is not valid.

A woman was suggested as a match and the two got married. Shortly after the marriage, the man died.

His new wife was upset with the Maharshal, because

she felt her husband's death was a punishment for breaking his oath. She said that had she known in advance he'd be punished, she would never have married him.

The Maharshal felt terrible. He decided there was only one thing to do. He wrote a *teshuva* explaining why his position was *halachically* correct. He then went to the cemetery and placed the *teshuva* in the man's grave. Moments after placing the sacred writing in the grave... the man came back to life!

The obvious next step was that the couple married once again. A few days after they did, the wife came to the Maharshal with another complaint. "I don't care for him like I did before he died," she cried. "I don't know why. Maybe it's just knowing he was once dead. I don't know. I only know my feelings are not the same."

Once again, the Maharshal decided there was only one thing to do. He *davened* with great intensity that her feelings should change. Indeed, a few days later, she returned to tell him all was well.

Upon hearing about this incident, the scholars of the generation remarked that the second miracle was greater than the first. Why? Because it's easier to bring the dead to life than it is to change a heart!

COMMENT: *I heard this story in a public drasha given by a prominent rav (no, not the Maharshal). Having been in chinuch for over twenty five years, I have no problem believing the story. It really is hard to change a heart. But truth to tell, I know that from my own life. I myself have been alive for over twenty five years (ahem), and I'm still trying to figure out how to change a heart.*

"GO YOU MEN AND SERVE HASHEM"
(Bo 10:11)

Pharaoh was denying Moshe Rabbeinu's request that all Klal Yisrael leave. He was saying that only the men may go out to serve Hashem.

RECEIVING an invitation from the president of the United States is a big deal. This is especially so if you are the executive vice president of Agudas Yisrael of America, as Rav Shmuel Bloom was. Under normal circumstances he would have been quite pleased, as there were several pressing *klal* issues which an audience with President Bush would go a long way towards resolving.

The trouble was that the *siyum hashas* of the *daf yomi* was taking place that same evening, and over 100,000 people were expected in all the various venues. Rav Bloom was not only one of the main organizers, he was also expected to speak there.

It was one seriously agonizing conflict.

After carefully checking the calendar, he saw that he could attend the morning meeting with the president, which was for a small group of twelve people and which would allow him to have the president's ear. The follow up speech by the president on the White House lawn to three hundred people was something he could afford to miss, so he could just hop on a plane after the morning session and get to the *siyum* that evening.

The meeting with the president went very well. When it ended, Rav Bloom gave the president a brief explanation about *daf yomi*. Mr. Bush was very impressed. Rav Bloom then told him how many people would be attending. "Why only 100,000?" the president asked.

 COMMENT: *The answer, of course, is that's all the venues could accomodate. But don't worry, sir – we'll present the next president with a higher figure,* im yirtzeh Hashem.

"AND THERE WAS DARKNESS OVER THE LAND OF MITZRAYIM" (Bo 10:22)

ONE of the great disasters in recent history managed to shut down air traffic over an entire continent, yet there was not one human casualty caused by it.

Of course, I'm referring to the volcanic cloud which floated down from Iceland and made flying over Europe a hazard. The world saw tangibly how Hashem has unimaginable ways of manipulating things.

Twenty eight year old Daniel Hirschman saw it more clearly than most. In desperate need of a liver transplant, Daniel was number sixty on the international transplant bank list, and he was anticipating a two year wait. Trouble was, the doctors told him he could only live six more months in the state his liver was in.

Well, when the next liver became available, there was no way to fly it out of the country to any of the fifty nine people ahead of him on the list. Daniel was moved to the head of the line and the transplant was performed successfully.

COMMENT: *The shutdown caused incredible amounts of aggravation. We have to remember that just as Daniel's* yeshua *was orchestrated by the* Ribbono shel Olam, *so too was every ounce of suffering that every single individual went through during that period. Stranded passengers at airports, missed meetings, lost baggage – the works.* Hashgacha *is precise to the nth degree.*

"AND EACH MAN SHALL TAKE A LAMB" (Bo 12:3)

WE all know that various groups and movements have made attempts to reform Judaism. They are generally not happy with *halachic* obligations and accountability to the Creator. Well, here's one that takes the cake.

The vegetarian branch of the Conservative movement put out a *haggada* which contained all sorts of amendments to the one we've been using for a couple thousand of years or so. They called it "The Liberated Lamb *Haggada*."

COMMENT: *I wonder if liberating lambs helps stem the tide of assimilation so rampant in the Conservative movement and all other cheap imitations of authentic Judaism. These people have to remember that it's better to eat meat and have Jewish grandchildren than to be a vegetarian and have offspring who we might call "gentle gentiles."*

"AND BLESS ME ALSO" (Bo 12:32)

BARANOVITCH was a small, insignificant town. If not for the fact that the Baranovitch *yeshiva* was there, most of us would probably never have heard of it. But Harav Elchonon Wasserman *zt"l, Hy"d* and his famous *yeshiva* put the town on the map.

The townspeople were poor and the *yeshiva* had trouble providing even a minimal amount of food for the *talmidim*. One of the local women, Mrs. Esther Kaplan *a"h* (my great-grandmother), used to go door-to-door collecting bread and whatever other food the townspeople could afford to part with for the *yeshiva*. Her daughter-in-law Sarah Baila and her sister would also collect for the *yeshiva*.

One day, after they dropped off the food, Reb Elchonon called the two sisters over. "I want to give you a *beracha* that you should both merit to live to a ripe old age." The two passed away on the same date five years apart. Both were ninety seven at the time of their passing, which all would agree constitutes "ripe old age."

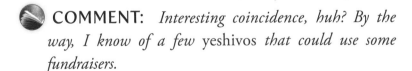 **COMMENT:** *Interesting coincidence, huh? By the way, I know of a few* yeshivos *that could use some fundraisers.*

"AND IT SHALL BE A SIGN ON YOUR HAND AND *TOTAFOS* BETWEEN YOUR EYES" (Bo 13:16)

YISRAEL Gavrilov, a Russian *baal teshuva*, was essentially penniless. However, his lack of material wealth didn't bother him one iota. He was capable of living with very little, as enviably many of the Russian *bnei Torah* are. However, when he took his *tefillin* to have them checked and found out they were *possul* and had been so for some time, he was devastated. He had no means of purchasing a new pair.

Yisrael did something most people would never have thought of doing under those circumstances. He took a *minyan* of *bochurim* with him to *daven vasikin* at the *Kosel* on Purim morning, with instructions that each one should *daven* for him to own a pair of *tefillin*.

The next morning in the *beis medrash*, an *avreich* happened to mention to him that he knew of a wealthy Jew looking to donate an expensive pair of *tefillin* to someone who could use them. He asked him if, by any chance, he knew of someone who could use such a pair and would appreciate their value. He certainly did.

COMMENT: *It doesn't surprise us that his* tefilla *was answered. That he found* bochurim *willing to* daven vasikin *on Purim – now that's a miracle.*

BESHALACH

"THEN MOSHE AND *BNEI YISRAEL* SANG"
(Beshalach 15:1)

Az Yashir *is a glorious declaration of thanks to the* Ribbono shel Olam *and is included in our regular morning prayers.*

A CHASAN once approached his *rebbe*, Harav Mordechai Gifter *zt"l*, a short time before his *chasuna*, requesting advice for his big day. He expected to hear something about *teshuva* and introspection, or perhaps a little about how a husband should treat his wife. Maybe something about thinking over his life's goals and how much he wants to grow and *shteig*.

Boy, was he in for a surprise. "When you are under the *chuppa* saying your *tefillos*, please don't *shuckle* too much," Rav Gifter began. "It's inappropriate for a young *chasan* to make himself look like he's so important. I was once at a *chasuna* where the *kallah* was *shuckling* so hard, I thought she was going to hit her head on the floor."

COMMENT: *It's common for all of us to put our righteousness on display to one degree or another, especially when it comes to* davening. *An excellent way to test whether the externals of one's* tefilla *in public are really a genuine expression of one's* neshama *is to think about whether he would do the same thing if he was* davening *in private. If he wouldn't, then he should cut the theatrics in* shul. *No one is impressed, just as he isn't impressed by anyone else's theatrics. On the other hand, if he would do the same in private, it's probably an authentic expression of his* avodas Hashem *and there may be room to do it in public as well.*

"THIS IS MY G-D AND I WILL GLORIFY HIM" (Beshalach 15:2)

One of the things we learn from this pasuk *is that we should try to beautify* mitzvos *as much as we can and in any way that we can. This is one of the ideas behind putting up decorations in a* succah.

IT was the same story week after week. Yisrael Zev Millstein would not turn up for work on Shabbos, and on Monday he'd be told to look for a new job. No amount of explaining or pleading would help. Many others succumbed to this difficult *nisayon*, but as Yisrael Zev's wife explained to their kids, "In our case it's not even a question. There is no way Daddy is going to work on Shabbos and that's that. If we have to eat bread and onions –that's what we'll do. But *Shabbos?! Work?! No way!*"

The kids admired their parents' *mesirus nefesh*, but it wasn't easy. They only had the bare minimum of food and certainly no new clothing or other basic necessities. When Succos came around, they built a *succah* in the yard, but they weren't expecting it to be a very festive holiday. They could barely afford meat and had no money to spend on decorations.

When Yisrael Zev came home with the boys on *leil Yom Tov*, the family went out to the *succah*. When they entered, they were met with a strange sight. A bunch of pink pieces of paper were hanging in the *succah*. At first the kids assumed that somehow their mother had gotten hold of some pink paper and managed to make some decorations. But then the kids noticed that all the papers had some sort of writing on them.

"What are those papers?" one of them asked.

"Those are called pink slips," their mother answered with tears in her eyes. But they were not tears of deprivation and suffering. No, those were tears of pride and joy. "Each time Daddy was fired, he was given one of those slips. What better way to decorate a *succah* and glorify Hashem's Name than to hang up those slips?"

And they sat down to a *seuda* in the most beautiful *succah* in the world.

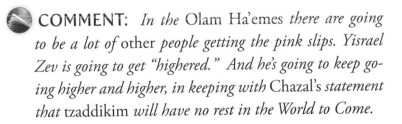 COMMENT: *In the* Olam Ha'emes *there are going to be a lot of* other *people getting the pink slips. Yisrael Zev is going to get "highered." And he's going to keep going higher and higher, in keeping with* Chazal's statement *that* tzaddikim *will have no rest in the* World to Come.

"THE CHARIOTS OF PHARAOH AND HIS ARMIES WERE TOSSED IN THE SEA" (Beshalach 15:4)

The midrash says they were raised high and thrown down, so they got banged up when they hit the water.

THE villa was gorgeous and the view out to the sea was breathtaking. Graham Olsen had worked hard his whole life manufacturing lawn tables. He finally realized his dream by moving out to a remote corner of Australia overlooking the water and the cliffs. So quiet. So peaceful.

He had just settled down in front of his bay window to have breakfast on his first day there when he saw a man walk past and head for the edge of the nearest cliff. "Strange that someone should be around here," Graham thought to himself. "I guess there are other people who like a little peace and quiet." A moment later he screamed in shock… the man had jumped off the cliff! Suicide!!

He had witnessed something worse than his worst nightmare in his new dream home! He couldn't believe it. A few days later, still rattled by what he'd seen, he was sitting facing the window again when he saw another man wandering out to the cliff. Graham ran out, invited the man into his home and actually talked him out of jumping.

It turned out that Graham's home was facing the most popular suicide spot in all of Australia. Graham was recently granted an award by the Australian government in recognition of the fact that he prevents over forty (!) suicides a year by inviting people headed for the cliff into his home to talk. "It's a kettle of tea and two listening ears that do it," says Graham, explaining the secret of his success.

COMMENT: *Stopping people from killing themselves is indeed success. But something is peculiar. I've heard of popular people and popular songs and popular vacation spots – but popular suicide spots?! I mean, no one who made use of the spot can say that one spot is better than another, now can they? On the other hand, maybe I shouldn't jump (eewww) to any conclusions.*

"AND THE ENTIRE CONGREGATION OF *BNEI YISRAEL* COMPLAINED" (Beshalach 16:2)

THE day had been a smashing success. One of the world's leading *kiruv yeshivos* had staged a *yom iyun*, a day of lectures on various Torah topics. The audience left inspired and uplifted, hungry for more. The credit went to Elchonon Schiff, himself a former *talmid* of the *yeshiva*. He was feeling good about the program and had received a steady stream of "*yasher koachs*" when he noticed some trouble brewing at the admissions table. As he drew closer he could hear a middle aged woman saying something about wanting her money back, with the flustered young lady behind the table clearly rejecting her demand.

"What's the trouble, ma'am?" Elchonon asked in his most magnanimous tone of voice.

"I want half my money back," she responded. "You see, the lectures were interesting and everything, but I slept through half of them. Therefore, I think I'm entitled to half my money back."

 COMMENT: *You need a lot more than that.*

"AND THEY DID NOT LISTEN TO MOSHE"
(Beshalach 16:20)
Even in that lofty generation of people who left Mitzrayim, there were those who were uncooperative and had trouble following rules.

YESHIVAS Torah Hamesuka was founded in order to help boys struggling with their *Yiddishkeit.* A warm and caring staff with a high *rebbe*-to-student ratio provided the necessary guidance and support for these vulnerable young men. Predictably, there were forms of behavior in such an institution than one wouldn't expect to find in regular *yeshivos.* For example, it was no surprise to see a boy pull up on a motorcycle for his morning *chavrusa* or to see boys sporting goatees. Sometimes the language was a little rougher than in the mainstream *yeshivos,* and once in a while, there might even be a physical altercation. These were boys who had a lot of pent up anger, after all.

But one clash went beyond the norm, and the reaction of one of the *rebbeim* left a lasting impression on many of the boys.

"Why don't you watch your elbow?" Big Shim barked

at Noam. Noam had turned abruptly with his can of Coke after pulling it out of the vending machine and nailed Big Shim with his elbow in the process.

"Chill out. I didn't do it on purpose, okay?"

"No, it's not okay," Big Shim snapped and then proceeded to treat Noam to a nice shove. Noam shook up his Coke and sprayed some at Big Shim, which stained his freshly washed shirt. Big Shim grabbed Noam, threw him to the ground and proceeded to punch him in the face several times. "*Now* I'm chilled," he said as he got off him. Without another thought, he headed off for the *beis medrash*.

As bad as all that was, it was not terribly out of the ordinary. But what Noam did next was. Perhaps it was the unfairness of Big Shim's reaction or the helplessness at being beaten up by someone bigger. Whatever it was, he became totally irrational. He ran over to the office and grabbed a scissors. He walked over to the *beis medrash*, opened the door and located Big Shim.

"Hey, Shim," he called. As Shim turned, Noam threw the scissors at him. He missed, though, and the scissors flew past his desk… and hit Rav Waldman, one of the *maggidei shiur*, in the forehead!

The scissors made a cut that drew blood and then fell onto his desk. Knowing that whoever threw it would be embarrassed beyond words, Rav Waldman *did not look up to see who threw the scissors!* He calmly pulled out a tissue to wipe his forehead, placed the scissors on the side of his desk and resumed learning as if nothing had happened. *But he did not look up even once!* The boys were very impressed.

COMMENT: *There are several examples mentioned in* Sanhedrin 11a *which demonstrate to what extent one should go to in order to save others from embarrassment. Apparently, Rav Waldman reviewed that* daf *many times. And yes, I'm sure he discussed matters with both boys afterwards in private.*

YISRO

"AND YISRO HEARD... ALL THAT HASHEM DID FOR MOSHE AND YISRAEL" (Yisro 18:1)

The simple meaning of the pasuk *is that Yisro was so impressed with what he heard that he decided to join up with Bnei Yisrael.*

SEVENTEEN year old Riva Clayman was, like, a regular teenage Modern Orthodox girl, ya know, and she wasn't, like, real goal-oriented *Yiddishkeit*-wise. Whatever. She was, like, really into clothes and stuff, and was popular, ya know?

So it's difficult to understand how this girl became the wife of a serious *avreich* and a woman who is serious about her family's growth in Torah and *yiras Shamayim*. Right? Whatever. Well, like, what happened was that Riva and a friend of hers went to her friend's *frummy* brother-in-law's house for a Shabbos meal. They were, like, really giddy, because they saw really *frum* people as whatever, and they, like, didn't know what to expect.

What happened was that when the *frummy* made *kiddush* there was a certain sincerity in how he said it that Riva had never seen before in her life. Not at home and not at any of her friends' homes. This brief moment of inspiration became the impetus for her switching to a very *frum* seminary... and the rest is history. Ya know what I mean?

COMMENT: *It's, like, really awesome how if a person serves Hashem properly, others will be inspired by their example. Whatever.*

"AND I CARRIED YOU ON THE WINGS OF EAGLES" (Yisro 19:4)

AS the Saltzmans exited the Gutnick wedding hall in Yerushalayim, a man standing a few feet away gestured towards them and simultaneously pointed to a van. "Where do you need to get to?" he asked.

"It's okay. We're taking a bus," Mr. Saltzman said.

"Don't worry. I don't charge. I'm not a cab, but maybe I can give you a lift. Where are you headed?"

"We're going to Ramot."

"Great. That's in my direction. Get in." The seven Saltzmans clambered in and settled in the seats, noticing another family of three already in the van. "I'm just dropping them off in Givat Shaul and then we'll head up to Ramot."

The Saltzmans figured the man lived in Ramot and were

very appreciative of the way he went out of his way to find someone to give a ride to. Only when they were getting out in front of their home did they realize there was something out of the ordinary going on. As they thanked the driver, they asked him where he lived. "In Ezras Torah," he answered.

"So why did you take us so far out of your way? We thought you lived here."

The man smiled. "Each night I hang around the Gutnick hall, because I know people are coming out of *simchas* late and public transportation is not great at that hour. An entire enjoyable evening can be ruined by the hassle of trying to get home. So I drive people home from the *simchas* and then come back looking for more. Hopefully, it'll be a *zechus* for me and my family."

COMMENT: *This story really gives me a lift. Another reminder of how it's so true that* chesed *is one of the things about which* Chazal *say there's no limit. A person who truly wants to do* chesed *will find a way to do it.*

"AND THERE WERE LOUD SOUNDS AND LIGHTNING" (Yisro 19:16)

DANNY began asking me in a hesitant voice, "Isn't it true that if you don't know the correct *beracha* for something you make a *shehakol*?" Simcha was standing right next to him and it appeared to me that they were having a *halachic* disagreement. I already know from experience that when a *baal teshuva* asks such a question there's often more to it than meets the eye, but this was really one for the books.

"Uh, yeah, if it isn't possible to determine what the correct *beracha* is," I answered cautiously. "Why?"

"Well, I heard thunder last night and didn't know what *beracha* to make, so I made a *shehakol*. Simcha says that doesn't work."

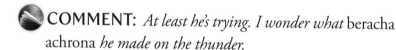 **COMMENT:** *At least he's trying. I wonder what* beracha *achrona* he made on the thunder.

"REMEMBER THE DAY OF SHABBOS AND SANCTIFY IT" (Yisro 20:8)

MR. Fishbein finished his *dvar Torah*. The ladies arose and started clearing off the table, removing the gefilte fish plates and forks in preparation for the next course. Melissa, a secular young lady attending a nearby college, had been sent to the Fishbeins by a local *kiruv* organization and was experiencing her first Shabbos at a *frum* family's home. Seeing all the ladies get up, she got up too and helped clear off the table.

She then put on her coat and said, "Thank you very much for such a wonderful meal." Everyone there was stunned – and then they burst out laughing. They realized Melissa was clueless as to the type of spread that appears at a Shabbos table. Having eaten fish with *challa*, salad and a whole variety of dips, she was certain the evening's festivities were over. Little did she know…

COMMENT: *It's one thing when people openly reject* Shabbos. *But it's something else entirely when people aren't even aware of what they're missing.* Chazal *say Shabbos is called a precious gift. Our job is to share it with others.*

MISHPATIM

"THESE ARE THE LAWS THAT YOU SHALL PLACE BEFORE THEM" (Mishpatim 21:1)

THERE is an apocryphal story told about a prince and princess who were married and lived in a palace. Their marital harmony was marred by the fact that the princess was an incorrigible slob. She never cleaned the palace and the place was a perpetual mess. It was driving the prince nuts. (Why they didn't have servants *is* a great question, but you can't ask questions about stories.)

One day the prince reached the breaking point, and he went over to where the princess was reading a magazine on the couch and took a big cookie out of a bag. "I'm going to give you until I finish eating this cookie to get busy cleaning," he said. "If you haven't started cleaning by the time I finish, then I'm throwing you outta here!"

He ate the cookie slowly, constantly looking to see if

the princess would be intimidated into action. She never budged. He was infuriated. "Guards!" he cried, "throw her outta here!"

The next day the prince regretted his decision. After all, he loved the princess. Trouble was, there was a law in the land that when a prince throws a princess out, he's never allowed to take her back. The prince summoned a wise man and asked him what to do.

The wise man had no solution for him. "The law is the law," he said sadly. A second wise man could do no better.

Finally, the prince called in a wise Jewish man. "Was the cookie a hard cookie or a soft cookie?" the wise man asked.

"Does that really matter?" asked the prince.

"Yes, it does. Please answer my question."

"Umm, it was a hard cookie."

"Good. That means that when you ate the cookie, there were crumbs that must have fallen, so you never really finished the cookie. That being the case, your condition about finishing the cookie was never met, so the expulsion is invalid. You can take your princess back."

COMMENT: *There are a lot of laws with a lot of details in the* Torah. *We have to always keep in mind that* all *the laws and their details, no matter how insignificant they may seem, are of unimaginable importance. Even more than cookie crumbs.*

"AND THESE ARE THE LAWS"
(Mishpatim 21:1)

There are many laws in the Torah. Almost all of these laws are explained in the Oral Torah, the Talmud.

"SCHEINBERG, you're a student of the Talmud, are you not?" It was the first day of the semester, and Mr. Walters, the sociology course instructor, was taking attendance. When he got to Malkiel Scheinberg's name, he looked in the direction of the one student wearing a prominent black yarmulke.

"Yes, I am, sir. Why do you ask?"

"Frankly, because the Talmud has held your people together for two thousand years. There is nothing a course in sociology can add to someone who is a product of that system."

Malkiel was impressed by the man's respect for Judaism and his honesty in expressing it. But Mr. Walters didn't know who he had started up with. "Don't worry about it," Malkiel responded with a smile, "I didn't come here to learn anything. I just need the three credit hours." The two became good friends.

COMMENT: *He's absolutely right, of course. And if we appreciated the value of the Talmud as much as Mr. Walters would expect us to, we'd probably spend more time studying it. Maybe if credit hours were given... hey, they are! And they lead to a much more worthwhile degree.*

"WHEN TWO MEN FIGHT"
(Mishpatim 21:22)

ACHMAD, the *yeshiva* maintenance man from East Jerusalem, came walking in one morning with a bandage around his head, another on his arm and a pronounced limp. He gave the impression that he had been in a car accident or had ridden his bike down a steep flight of stairs.

I saw him talking to Sasson Mizrachi, the man in charge of the hired help. When he left, I walked over to ask what had happened. "Oh, his son beat him up," Sasson answered nonchalantly, as if this was the most natural thing in the world.

"What?!" was all I could manage.

"Yeah, his sons and his wife have been trying to get him out of the house for a while. Apparently, he's got some property worth quite a bit and they want it. It's not a pretty situation. I mean, his son's been in jail a couple of times already. His wife says he's come after her with a knife."

I quipped that they could use some *shalom bayis* counseling, but I was still visibly shaken up. It's not that I cared about that particular individual, but the idea of a son striking a father and violence in the home is just so foreign to us.

"I don't understand what you're so shocked about," Sasson continued. "Last year his daughter-in-law tried to run him over in her car."

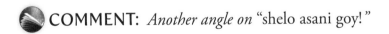 COMMENT: *Another angle on* "shelo asani goy!"

"AND IF A MAN STRIKES THE EYE OF HIS SLAVE OR HIS MAIDSERVANT" (Mishpatim 21:26)

The Torah here is referring to a non-Jewish slave who lives with a Jew.

"**B**'EZRAS *Hashem*, she'll be okay." The Vilners looked up to see who had made that comment. They were in Swedish Covenant hospital with their one year old baby who had fallen and gotten a concussion. Feeling vulnerable and on foreign territory, it was just so good to be in the presence of another *Yid*.

The older lady who had made that Comment sat down next to them and shared some words of *bitachon* and encouragement. A few minutes later she left, and the couple felt so much better.

Their daughter's condition was greatly improved the next morning, and they were able to go home. The next week, they told the rabbi the whole story and what a *chesed* this lady had done for them. "We were so rattled at the time, we forgot to ask her name."

"I have a hunch I know who it is. Can you describe her?" the rabbi asked.

"Well, she was on the tallish side and had pink glasses with little diamond shapes at the corners."

The rabbi laughed. "It's just who I thought. That's Grace Merriwether, my next door neighbor. She does volunteer work at Swedish Covenant. I sell the *chometz* to her every year."

 COMMENT: *When Yosef was sold, the Torah mentions that the Yishmaelim were carrying spices that gave off a pleasant smell. Rashi explains that this was for Yosef's*

benefit. Many ask why this was so significant, considering Yosef had much bigger problems to deal with at the time, like being ripped away from his family, being savagely beaten and being taken to who knows where for who knows how long. One of the answers given as to why Hashem made sure he was surrounded by spices is that when a person is going through an ordeal, it's easy to feel like he's been totally abandoned by Hashem. Yosef was in that type of situation. So Hashem sent him a pleasant little message saying, "I'm with you. Whatever is happening is My plan." That's what happened in the Vilners' case, too. Hashem sent an unexpected kind word to lift their spirits. I guess we could call it a demonstration of Divine "Grace."

"THEY SHALL NOT DWELL IN YOUR LAND"
(Mishpatim 23:33)
The Torah is saying that members of foreign nations will not dwell in the Land of Israel.

UNDER strict orders from my wife not to ride in Arab cabs, I really try to avoid it. However, on this one occasion I got in, thinking the driver was Jewish. It was only after a couple minutes of conversation that I noticed his inability to pronounce the letter "P" – the sure sign that he was not of our tribe. He was a little older, so I wasn't too concerned about anything dreadful happening. Still, I figured if I could keep him talking he'd be too busy thinking about whatever we were talking about and wouldn't be able to contemplate counterproductive behavior. Profound. So I asked him how his *parnassa* was going.

"It's really been a rough stretch," he began. "As a matter of fact, it's been going steadily downhill for the last ten years. You know why? It's because they've brought over a million Russians into the country in the last ten years. And I want to tell you something," he added, the frustration clearly evident in his tone of voice, "ninety five percent of them *aren't even Jewish*!!" He didn't bat an eyelash as he said it.

COMMENT: *I don't know why the influx of people should negatively affect his* parnassa, *and his statistics are slightly off. However, he certainly senses a problem which Jewish political leaders have turned a blind eye to. We are not looking to artificially increase our numbers. We never have, and we never will.*

"AND THEY ATE AND THEY DRANK" (Mishpatim 24:11)

THERE are different *halachic* opinions regarding opening refrigerators on Shabbos while the motor is off (when the inside light will not go on), because of the concern that doing so causes the motor to turn on. Some *poskim* are *machmir* and some are *meikel*. Someone once asked one of the sons of Harav Moshe Feinstein *zt"l* if his father would open a refrigerator on Shabbos. "In my entire life, I never saw my father at the refrigerator," his son answered.

COMMENT: *Or reading a newspaper, or eating popcorn, or hurting someone's feelings, or…*

TERUMA

"AND THEY SHALL MAKE ME A *MIKDASH* AND I WILL DWELL AMONG THEM" (Teruma 25:8)
This is the command to build a house for Hashem.

IT started as a gag. John Flemmington went online looking to trade a paper clip for a pencil. Someone agreed to the deal, more out of looking for something to break the monotony of his life than out of any need for a paper clip. John then managed to trade the pencil for a pen. The pen went for a stapler, which went for a flashlight, which was then traded for a basketball. The ball traded for a fan, which then went for a chair, then for a table, then for a bicycle, then for a moped, then for a motorcycle. That was traded for a role in a movie, and that for a boat, then for a van, and eventually John and his wife ended up trading for... a home in Saskatchewan. The trade-up process took about a year and John ended up in the Guinness book of world records for the most successful trade-up in history!

COMMENT: *I know it's Saskatchewan, but a home is a home. For the price of a paper clip, it's not bad. Of course, better than the home is the mussar lesson John has taught us. We all know that one must always strive to grow. But there is something that we often forget which we can learn from John, and that is that we can strive for unimaginable heights. Of course,* Chazal *put it differently. They said one must always ask himself when his actions will reach the actions of his forefathers.*

"AND THEY SHALL MAKE AN *ARON*"
(Teruma 25:10)

Each of the keilim *in the* Mishkan *symbolized something. The* Aron *was the symbol of Torah and Torah study.*

THE accomplishments of the legendary *rosh yeshiva* of Yeshivas Hanegev, Harav Yissachar Meir *zt"l*, almost defy description. This one man is responsible for an incredibly vast amount of Torah being learned in the world today. He founded *yeshivos*, though told by naysayers that they'd never get off the ground. Those *yeshivos* then led to spin-off *yeshivos* and thousands of *talmidim*. He accomplished all of this while suffering from diabetes most of his life.

No less amazing was his astonishing Torah knowledge. He was as knowledgable about every Torah subject as a regular person is knowledgable about his family members.

It's well known that he slept little and learned with tremendous intensity.

A glimpse into that intensity was mentioned at a *hesped* given about him shortly after his *petirah*. When Reb Yissachar was a young *yeshiva bochur* learning in the famous Ponovezh *yeshiva*, he would shower and dress for Shabbos early in the afternoon and then go to the *beis medrash* to learn until Shabbos began. But that was on *Thursday* afternoon!! You see, he would learn through the afternoon, learn the regular night *seder*, and then do a *mishmar*. But in the morning, he wouldn't crash for the rest of the day, which is what most mortals would do. Rather, he would *daven shacharis*, and then *learn* until Shabbos, only going to sleep after a meager *leil Shabbos seuda*.

COMMENT: *I've often wondered how it is that some people can learn so much on so little sleep. The ability to go on little sleep has a lot to do with motivation and stimulation. The more pumped up a person is, the easier it is to go without sleep. A famous president of the United States is said to have slept only four hours a night. When asked why, he said, "When I'm asleep, I'm not the president." There are some people who have the same sort of motivation when it comes to Torah study, and I envy them. Now, I'd write more about the subject... but I'm a little tired right now.*

"TWO AND A HALF AMOS ITS LENGTH" (Teruma 25:8)

The dimensions of the Aron Kodesh *are all fractions, not whole numbers. The* mefarshim *explain that this symbolizes the idea that one is never finished learning Torah.*

THERE was a small tumult in the corner of the *beis medrash.* "What's going on over there?" the *rosh yeshiva* asked one of the *bochurim.*

"Oh, Yochi Morgenthau just finished all of Bava Metzia."

The *rosh yeshiva* got up out of his seat at the front of the *beis medrash* and made his way over to the *bochur* to give him a "*mazel tov.*" After all, finishing Bava Metzia is a major accomplishment. True, Yochi was a bright boy, but he made it on *hasmada.* He sat and plugged away, staying focused on the goal. That's the reason he was the first one in the *yeshiva* to finish.

"*Mazel tov,*" bellowed the *rosh yeshiva* in his customary manner, the ultimate sign of approval. "It's a great accomplishment." Yochi was smiling and feeling pretty good about himself, but the *rosh yeshiva* wasn't about to let him go on vacation. "Now you have to start *chazering.* You ought to review the whole thing by Shavuos!"

Everyone laughed. Shavuos was ten days away. The boys understood the *rosh yeshiva* meant that Yochi should not rest on his laurels. He should feel good but must keep on going, because the job is never over.

There was only one boy who took the *rosh yeshiva* literally… and that was Yochi. For the next ten days, he basically did not leave his seat. He slept little and ate even less. He learned and learned and then learned some more.

On *erev Shavuos*, he came over to the *rosh yeshiva* to inform him that he'd reviewed the entire Bava Metzia. The *rosh yeshiva* did not bellow this time. Oh, no. He gave Yochi a giant hug and kiss instead.

COMMENT: *And there's even greater reward in store for him from the* Ribbono shel Olam. *Of course, the lesson is that when it comes to Torah, one can accomplish just about anything if he makes up his mind to do it.*

"AND YOU SHALL COAT IT WITH GOLD ON THE INSIDE AND THE OUTSIDE"
(Teruma 25:11)

The mefarshim *explain that inner and outer boxes of gold symbolize that a Jew's behavior should be "gold" in private and in public. Gold under all circumstances.*

IT couldn't happen, it shouldn't happen… but it did happen. Through a careless oversight, the *gabbai* of the *shul* scheduled two *bar mitzvahs* for the same Shabbos. Both Dovid Yosef Scherman and Avigdor Spector had spent months preparing the *parsha* and both had arrived in *shul* fully expecting to *lain* the entire *parsha*.

First there was confusion and chaos, and then anger. Then a hasty meeting was held between the *rav*, the *gabbai* and the two fathers. It was suggested that each of the boys do half, but Dovid Yosef was not happy with that. He had prepared the whole thing and wanted to *lain* the whole *parsha*. He really can't be faulted; it was a major disappointment.

Many full grown adults get upset over much less.

Things were really starting to turn unpleasant when Avigdor suddenly spoke up. "I don't mind if he *lains*," the young boy said. "Life is about learning to handle disappointments, so I may as well start learning now. Anyway, I'm sure I won't lose out. One who is *mevater* never loses out. I'll *lain* a different time."

At first, there were objections to that as well, because everyone knew he'd be bitterly disappointed. But when they came to the realization that there really wasn't another alternative, they took him up on his offer. Everyone in the *shul* was impressed with Avigdor's gesture. Ironically, he ended up with much more *kavod* for his selflessness than did Dovid Yosef for his *laining*.

Fast forward two years. Avigdor's mother was in the hospital one Shabbos with a life-threatening problem. That same Shabbos, Harav Elyashiv *zt"l* was in the hospital, and a *minyan* was held in his room. His attendants had not arranged for a *baal korei*, and they started asking around if anyone knew the *parsha*.

Avigdor said he did, because it was his *bar mitzvah parsha*. So he ended up *laining* for Rav Elyashiv in his private *minyan*! But the story isn't over. After the *minyan*, Rav Elyashiv asked Avigdor why he was in the hospital. Upon hearing about his mother's problem, Rav Elyashiv asked his private doctor, a specialist in the field, to examine her. He did so, told the doctors to change the treatment, and she had a full recovery.

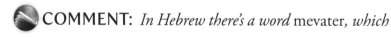 **COMMENT:** *In Hebrew there's a word* mevater, *which*

translates roughly as "to give in." You always hear moth-ers saying to their children, "Be mevater *to your sibling." Harav Chaim Kanievsky has said, "One who is* mevater *never loses out." In Avigdor's case, not only did he not lose out – he gained quite a bit… his mother's life. Indeed, it is a worthwhile policy to always be* mevater.

TETZAVEH

"AND YOU SHALL DRESS AHARON YOUR BROTHER AND HIS SONS"
(Tetzaveh 28:41)

One of the reasons that the kohanim *wore impressive uniforms was to engage the visitors' sense of sight when they came to the* Bais Hamikdash, *thus increasing their awe and respect of the place.*

I WAS in the middle of a private conversation with a student when, all of a sudden, one of my eyes went black for a fleeting second. I realized right away that it wasn't a good thing. When it happened again about five minutes later, I went over to one of the *rebbeim* who had attended medical school before switching careers and becoming a *talmid chacham*. After a quick examination, he told me he thought it was a torn retina and that I must get to an eye doctor ASAP.

The doctor confirmed the diagnosis and told me to come to the hospital the next day for laser surgery. Now,

I pictured lasers the way they always showed them in the movies, you know, guys holding bazooka-looking things and unleashing laser beams that knocked down fortified enemy positions. After explaining the procedure, which basically entailed about one minute of light being flashed into my eye, I was somewhat more relaxed. But a laser is a laser, right?

The next day I went to the outpatient clinic and entered the room where the surgery was to be done. It turned out to be no more than a regular eye doctor's examination room. The doctor instructed me to put my chin on a base and told me he would flash the laser into my dilated pupil. "Now, once you see the flashing light make sure not to move," he warned me. "Okay, here goes," he said and proceeded to push a pedal with his foot which shined a bright light into my eye.

"You moved!" he barked, and quickly turned off the machine. My first thought was, "What got fried in there? Is there now a hole in the back of my head?" Responding to my thoughts, he said, "Nothing happened. Just don't move so we can do this properly, okay? This requires precision." *Baruch Hashem*, he completed the surgery successfully without my moving… or breathing, for that matter.

COMMENT: *More than any other sense, the sense of sight is vulnerable. The* gemara *says that even if a person is made up totally of eyes, like the angel of death, he mustn't look at that which is forbidden. The idea here is that one may find himself in situations where he is surrounded by inappropriate sights. Even so, he is required* *to avoid sinning. It's tough, but he must remember that one false move...*

"AND AHARON SHALL CARRY THE MISHPAT OF BNEI YISRAEL"
(Tetzaveh 28:30)

The kohein gadol carried the responsibility for the spiritual level of Bnei Yisrael. This is one of the ideas alluded to in this pasuk.

THE tension in the room was palpable. Earlier in the week a patient had died due to a mysterious infection. Dr. Sanderson called the surgical team together to see if they could figure out what went wrong. On each of the three occasions that Dr. Sanderson had lost a patient, he called this kind of meeting and managed to figure out who had messed up. One time it was the anesthesiologist, and one time it was the assistant surgeon. The last time it had happened, he had been given the wrong information regarding the patient's history.

The nine people in the room knew that Dr. Blake R. Sanderson was at the top of his profession and that he demanded top performance from his hand-picked team. When he asked each one in turn if they'd done their job perfectly, he meant *perfectly*.

Each in turn said he had done what was expected. No one could explain why the patient had died. "If that's the case, then I will hand in my resignation immediately," Dr. Sanderson said in a soft but firm voice.

"Why?" cried out nine voices almost in unison.

"Because when I began my career as a surgeon, I realized I was taking on a tremendous responsibility," he began. "I made a vow that if a patient ever dies and the fault is mine, I will quit immediately. Well, since none of you are at fault, the fault must be mine. Therefore, I must stop performing surgery." With that, Dr. Sanderson stood up and walked out of the room.

The news spread around the hospital rapidly, leaving everyone shocked. Dr. Sanderson's reputation was well known throughout the medical establishment. The next day, the assistant in charge of the surgical equipment came to Dr. Sanderson's office. "You're not resigning, doctor. It was my fault. I arrived at the hospital late on the day of the surgery and didn't sterilize the equipment the way I was supposed to. The infection that killed the patient was the result of my negligence."

COMMENT: *Unfortunately, there's an awful lot of "unsterilized" equipment out there. All it takes is one little spiritual "infection" and the patient can die. We have to be on constant guard against it and do our jobs responsibly. And* daven. *Hard.*

"AND HIS SOUND SHALL BE HEARD"
(Tetzaveh 28:35)

One of the ideas behind having bells that made noise hanging on the kohein gadol's *coat is to teach us that one should give advance notice before entering somewhere. It is a basic act of consideration to knock on a closed door before entering the area so that the person inside isn't taken by surprise and caught in a compromised situation.*

IT was infrequent that Alter and Henna were apart from each other. Married over sixty years, they rarely went anywhere without each other. So when Henna made a trip to Europe with a tour group, Alter counted the hours until her eight day excursion would be over.

Their married children knew that he was anxious for her to return and that he'd be going to the airport to pick her up. Three days ahead of time, he'd already analyzed all the routes to Lod airport and chosen the best one, as well as figuring out what time he would have to leave to be there on time.

So it was a pretty big shock when he told his son Tzvi that he wouldn't be going to the airport to meet Henna. "Why not, Dad?" Tzvi asked. "Do you feel okay?" Tzvi thought that perhaps the trip to the airport was a bit much for his father at his age.

"Well, I don't think Mom wants me to come," he said.

"Why not?"

"Do you know her friend Rose Morgenstern? Rose went with her on the trip and they're coming back together on the same flight. I asked Rose's husband Yomtov how he's planning to get to the airport and he told me he isn't going. He told me it's too difficult for him with all the riding and schlepping and waiting. So I really don't think Mom would want me to come, because then Rose would feel bad that Mom's husband was able to make it but her husband couldn't."

COMMENT: Bein adam l'chaveiro *requires a willingness to forgo what you would* really *want to do.*

"AS A PLEASANT SMELL, A FIRE OFFERING FOR HASHEM" (Tetzaveh 29:41)

There is no more pleasant "smell" to Hashem than when the Jewish people behave in a way that demonstrates why it is that we are the chosen ones among all the nations.

RABBI Zemble was visiting a school in another city. As the principal of a growing day school, he was always looking to find new ways to improve. He therefore regularly made trips to other schools to see if he could learn from them. During a visit to one school he spent the morning observing classes, and then he went out to the schoolyard to watch the kids during their recess. Nothing out of the ordinary was taking place, just the usual running around and games that little girls play to burn off some of their energy.

"*Oy*, that poor kid," he thought to himself, noticing a little girl sitting alone on one of the swings. She had thick glasses and buck teeth. He could tell at a glance that she was regarded by the others as a *neb*. He'd seen it plenty of times in his own school, but that didn't make it any easier. Each time he saw a child like this it broke his sensitive heart.

After about ten minutes he turned to enter the building, but immediately turned around when he heard crying. A little girl had her face in her hands and was surrounded by a few other girls who were picking on her. "You always mess up when you jump rope," one of them was yelling, and the little girl just sobbed louder.

Rabbi Zemble was about to walk over to break it up when he heard a loud, "Hey, you guyth – quit it!" The little girl whom he'd noticed earlier was running towards the group and kept yelling, "Thtop it, thtop it!"

"*Oy*, on top of it all she has a lisp," was Rabbi Zemble's first thought, but what he heard next blew him away.

"Why are you picking on her?" the *nebby* little girl hollered. "Inthted of picking on her – pick on me! Here I am! Pick on me ath much ath you want. Jutht leave her alone!!"

COMMENT: *A throwback to the* shotrim, *the Jewish leaders who took the beatings from the Mitzriyim so their fellow Jews wouldn't get hit. Whether or not Rabbi Zemble found a way to improve his school, I don't know. But he certainly found a way to improve himself. And we have to, as well.*

"TO DWELL AMONG THEM"
(Tetzaveh 30:46)

NISSI and his wife Elka had a serious *shaila* regarding the *shidduch* of one of their children. They decided to ask Rav Gelbhart, a man known for his wisdom and perception. They knew he was decisive and would give them complete clarity on the issue.

The *rav's* wife answered the door, radiating pleasantness, and led them down the hall into the living room. Elka had to exercise every ounce of self-control she possessed in order to hold back a gasp. Just about every surface in the living room was covered with *sefarim* – the table, the ledges of the breakfront and even one of the chairs. It was unreal. There wasn't a surface that didn't have at least one *sefer* on it. Even the walls were covered from floor to ceiling with shelves packed with *sefarim*. Elka thought of her own living room which was generally spotless and furnished tastefully with furniture that was actually visible to the human eye. She certainly wouldn't tolerate *sefarim* left out.

The couple sat with the *rav* for about twenty minutes. Sure enough, he cut right through to the crux of the issue and rendered his decision. "There is something else I just have to ask before we leave," Elka said. "Forgive me for asking, but why do you have *sefarim* all over the place?"

"I think my wife is more qualified to answer that," the *rav* said, and called the *rebbetzin* to come in. The *rav* told Elka to repeat her question.

"Well, this is a living room," began the *rebbetzin* with a smile from ear to ear, "so I guess it's for *living*. Regarding Torah, the *pasuk* says, '*Ki heim chayeinu*, Torah is our *life*.' So this is what we do in here – we *live*."

COMMENT: *Many attempts have been made using all sorts of substitutions to achieve the elusive state of feeling "alive." But, as the old advertisement goes, "often imitated, never duplicated." There is no substitute for authentic, unadulterated Torah.*

KI SISA

"MAKE FOR US A GOD" (Ki Sisa 32:1)

The sin of the golden calf showed the ultimate lapse in faith. There are thirteen articles of faith enumerated by the Rambam, and every Jew must believe in each one of them with a full heart.

INE year old Brachi was upset. Her brothers still had a few days left to their Succos vacation, whereas the girls had to go back to school. And, of course, her brothers made sure she was aware of her bad luck. "Oof, I wish Moshiach would come already," she lamented, "so then I wouldn't have to go through the suffering of going to school."

Her father, who had had more than his fill of having her around the house during vacation, put things in the proper perspective. "Look," he began, "when Moshiach comes it's going be a deliverance for the parents too. So not only will there be school – it'll probably be for longer hours. Now off you *go*."

COMMENT: *Brachi, my daughter, has the right idea. It's not enough to believe in Moshiach conceptually and to sing pretty songs about his coming. We must live with the belief that Moshiach can come at any time. Thanks for the reminder, Brachi – but you're still going to school.*

"AND HE BUILT AN ALTAR IN FRONT OF HIM" (Ki Sisa 32:5)

Chazal explain that Aharon saw Chur who had stood up to the people at the expense of his life.

THE mayor of the town of Koznitz was a *meshumad*, a renegade Jew who had turned his back on his religion and his people by embracing a foreign religion. When the Nazis invaded the town, they rounded up all the Jews and set the *shul* on fire in front of their eyes. Before doing so, however, they had taken out all the *sifrei Torah* so that they could have a little "fun."

"Here, Kurt," they called to Velvel the *meshumad*, using his new name, "you do the honors of throwing the first Torah scroll into the fire."

"Fellows, I must turn you down," he said. "I renounced my Judaism for the sake of material gain and happiness, and, quite frankly, it was a disappointment on both fronts. So, actually, I've been waiting for an opportunity like this. I'd like to thank you for the chance to make a public declaration of my loyalty to *Yiddishkeit*." So saying, he proceeded to take a long and exaggerated bow in the direction of the Nazis. The enraged Nazis grabbed him, hacked off pieces of his body and then threw him, still alive, into the fire.

COMMENT: *There is a* midrash *about a man named Yosi Meshisa who was given the opportunity by the enemies of the Jews to take something from the* Bais Hamikdash. *He chose the* Menorah. *They told him he couldn't have that, and that he must choose something else. He refused to enter a second time, saying, "I've antagonized my Creator once. I will not do it again." The* midrash *says they sawed him to death. The* midrash *is emphasizing how even Jewish renegades are on a high level.*

"AND YOU SHALL SEE MY BACK BUT MY FRONT SHALL NOT BE SEEN" (Ki Sisa 33:23)

One of the explanations of this pasuk *is that sometimes we don't understand certain events when they take place. But when we look back after time has passed, we get some inkling of the good there was in what happened.*

"IN my opinion, the only realistic option is hip replacement surgery." This was Professor Melnek's conclusion after doing all the tests and seeing the x-rays and MRIs. Rav Seitzer was obviously not happy about having to face surgery. The next two weeks were filled with tension in the Seitzer home.

Then, one morning Rav Seitzer woke up with pain in his foot. "What now?" he groaned. It turned out he had a bad toe infection. It was so bad, he could barely walk. The family doctor put him on antibiotics and told him to put some sort of lift in his shoe. A few days later the toe infection was cured, and Rav Seitzer noticed there was less pain in his hip. Over the next few days, the pain continuously decreased, until it went away completely. In the end, he did not need the hip replacement surgery.

He also had a new insight into how toe infections can be a good thing.

 COMMENT: *"Gam zu l'tova," recognizing that everything is for the good, is something we should live by without needing proof from surgeries canceled due to toe infections. But it's so hard.*

"I WILL REMOVE MY HAND AND YOU WILL SEE MY BACK BUT MY FRONT SHALL NOT BE SEEN" (Ki Sisa 33:23)

As mentioned above, Hashem is telling us here that His ways are incomprehensible to man. No man can understand at the time why Hashem does what He does. However, after the fact, when one sees how events have turned out, he can sometimes get an idea of what the Divine plan was.

HARAV Yekusiel Yehuda Halberstam *zt"l*, the Klausenberger Rebbe, was one of the *gedolei hador* and one of the greatest builders of the Torah world in our generation. The amount he suffered in the war is mind-boggling. His suffering included the loss of his wife and eleven children, incarceration in the death camps for five years and participation in what was known as the death march.

A secular Jew once asked him how he could still believe in Hashem after all he'd been through. Answered the *Rebbe*, "A G-d Who I can understand, I don't need."

COMMENT: *A person who makes his observance contingent on understanding everything might as well quit right now. We don't know why Hashem does what He does. We can't even really understand how shaking a lulav accomplishes anything or why a goat should be pushed off a cliff on Yom Kippur. One can certainly try to understand, but he shouldn't have his entire commitment riding on it. Understand?*

"AND MOSHE DID NOT KNOW THAT THE SKIN OF HIS FACE WAS GLOWING"
(Ki Sisa 34:29)

ONE of the goals that Rav Yitzchak Hutner *zt"l* had for American boys was to learn the meaning of *kavod haTorah*. Any time a *talmid* left his study, he had to back out slightly bowed in deference to his *rebbe*. Rav Hutner had a buzzer by his desk and the door was locked. If any *talmid* walked away in a less respectful manner, Rav Hutner would not buzz him out until the *talmid* would assume the slightly bowed position and back away. While on a personal level he shunned honor, he felt this was something he must do to drive home the lesson to his *talmidim*.

One of his *talmidim* left the Chaim Berlin *yeshiva* to go learn in the Mir in Yerushalayim. When he arrived, he went to speak to Rav Nochum Pertzovitz *zt"l*, the famous *rosh yeshiva* whose wondrous *shiurim* drew hundreds of *talmidim*.

After speaking to Rav Nochum, the *bochur* took leave by bending over and backing out, as he was taught to do whenever leaving the presence of Torah greatness. Rav Nochum, whose humility was legendary, turned to one of his close *talmidim* who happened to be present and asked him, "What's wrong with that *bochur's* back? Is it something temporary or does he have a permanent condition?"

COMMENT: *Anyone who saw Reb Nochum saw genuine, almost tangible humility. That someone should bow when leaving him — what could it be other than a back problem?*

VAYAKHEL

"AND MOSHE GATHERED THE ENTIRE CONGREGATION OF *BNEI YISRAEL*"
(Vayakhel 35:1)

A CROWD had slowly gathered outside the *shul*. The security guard was an hour late, due to one of his regular hangovers, and the doors were locked. Of course, it also started to rain. Finally, the guard arrived and the soaked congregants were able to enter and begin *davening*. The rabbi, as was his custom, spoke before *mussaf*. "I know many of you were inconvenienced this morning," he began, "and I'd like to apologize. I also want to apologize to those of you who wanted to be late but were forced by the delay to be on time."

COMMENT: *The truth hurts. Especially when you're still wet from the rain.*

"ANYONE WITH A GENEROUS HEART"
(Vayakhel 35:5)

"**W**HY don't you spend two weeks in Eretz Yisrael?" Mrs. Shulman asked her husband. "It would really revitalize you, especially after working so hard during tax season. I'm sure they'd be happy to have you back in the *yeshiva* for a couple of weeks."

So off Kalev Shulman went for a two week learning vacation. His plan was to stay in his grandparents' empty flat. He was also planning to visit their graves on Har Hamenuchos for the first time.

When he was there, he went to the cemetery and looked around for the graves for over an hour, but he could not find them. Apparently, the instructions for finding their plot that he'd been given were incorrect. Two days later, he went again and another forty five minutes ended in frustration. Another hour on his third trip brought no more success, so he decided it was just not meant to be.

He got into a cab in the parking lot of the cemetery and told the cabbie to take him to Bayit Vegan. As they drove off, the driver asked him which street he had to get to. "Thirty seven Hachida."

"Which apartment number are you going to?"

Kalev had no idea why he was asking. Then again, this *was* Israel, where no one has any compunction about asking personal questions, from how much you earn to how much you paid for your apartment. "Number fourteen," Kalev answered.

"Why do you want to go there?" the driver persisted.

"Well, I'm staying there," Kalev said, a touch annoyed. The questions were only adding to his frustration.

"Did you know the couple who used to live there?"

The driver's use of the past tense was not lost on Kalev, and he was now quite curious. "As a matter of fact, they were my grandparents. And as another matter of fact, I am now returning from a third failed attempt to find their graves and am headed back to their apartment."

The driver made a sudden U-turn and started heading back towards the cemetery. "What are you doing?" Kalev snapped.

"Your grandparents were *mekarev* me," the driver said with emotion. "I met them when I drove them home from a wedding. They were the sweetest, warmest people I have ever known in my life. I used to be their guest for a Shabbos meal every week. My family is religious because of them and I visit their graves once a month. I'll show you where they are."

COMMENT: *The funny thing is that people who live in Israel take this sort of thing for granted. It happens all the time.*

"AND ALL OF THE WISE-HEARTED WOMEN" (Vayakhel 35:25)

"BYE, Mom, I'm going to Yanky's house."

Twelve year old Avi was almost out the door when his mother hollered, "Avi, get over here! Why are you always going to your friends' houses? You never bring them here. I can't *remember* the last time you had a friend over." Avi was quiet. "Answer me!" his mother screamed.

He looked at her for a long moment and then burst into tears. "It's because of all your yelling and screaming," he answered through his sobs. "You're always raising your voice – to me and to Dad and to everyone. That's why Shuli never brings her friends over and why Baila never brings her friends. When Yitzy gets older, he won't bring his friends either. I'm embarrassed to have my friends come over, so that's why I always go to them. *Their* moms don't scream."

 COMMENT: *It's enough to… make you scream.*

"AND ALL OF THE WOMEN WHOSE HEARTS WERE SO INCLINED" (Vayakhel 35:26)

ALONE as a stone. Eleven year old Greta Weisz had no one left in the world. Her entire family went to the gas chambers and she alone had miraculously survived. What she didn't know was that her father's youngest brother had emigrated to America years before and was now living in Seattle. Rescue workers somehow located him and he paid to have Greta come over, raising her as a family member and eventually marrying her off.

Although herself not observant, Greta's six children all became *shomer Shabbos*. Greta and her husband Marv fully supported their children, both financially and with their constant encouragement. Two of them even learned in *kollel* for a number of years.

In her mid-eighties, Greta contracted a terminal illness. On her deathbed, her son Yoel tried to convince her to be buried in Eretz Yisrael. Knowing his mother's absolute respect for *Yiddishkeit*, he didn't anticipate any sort of objection.

Well, she did raise an objection, but not for any reason he could've possibly imagined. "I am well aware of the fact that it is better for my *neshama* that I be buried in Eretz Yisrael," she explained. "However, when I had absolutely no one, Uncle Shimshy brought me here. He took care of me as well as any father in the world takes care of his child. As you know, he's buried here in Seattle. I feel a debt of gratitude to him, so I don't think it's right for me to abandon him. No, I'm going to have to deny your request. I'll be buried right here near Uncle Shimshy." Yoel made no further attempt to convince her.

COMMENT: *There are different levels of hakaras hatov. I think the bar has just been raised to a new height.*

"WITH WISDOM AND UNDERSTANDING"
(Vayakhel 35:31)

"CORPORAL punishment is a no-no. Never, ever, *ever* spank your children. *Ever, ever.*" Well known psychologist Dr. Bancroft P.

Duddlypoop, Phd., was in the middle of a lecture to doc-
toral candidates on family education and child raising.

He had just made his position on *potching* children
clear and was about to proceed when a hand in the back of
the room went up. "Do you mean you've never, ever, *ever*
raised your hand to your children?" the student asked in
disbelief.

"That's correct," Dr. Duddlypoop answered with a
smug smile, "except, of course, in self-defense."

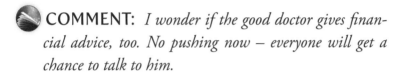 **COMMENT:** *I wonder if the good doctor gives finan-
cial advice, too. No pushing now – everyone will get a
chance to talk to him.*

"AND HE GAVE HIM THE ABILITY TO TEACH" (Vayakhel 35:34)

THERE was a brilliant boy in the famous Ponovezh
yeshiva who had some severe character flaws. He
was haughty, inconsiderate, loud and selfish. His
character was so bad that the famed *mashgiach*, Harav Ye-
chezkel Levenstein *zt"l*, would have nothing to do with
him. He never said a word to the boy.

One day, Reb Chatzkel was walking towards the *yeshiva*
holding a package. The boy happened to be walking behind him and noticed the *mashgiach* up ahead. He ran
over and took the package out of Reb Chatzkel's hands and
carried it for him until they reached the *yeshiva*.

Reb Chatzkel took the package from the boy and then

gave him one of his penetrating looks, a look that had melted many students before him. "You've just done something for me, so I now have a debt of *hakaras hatov* to you," Reb Chatzkel began. "I must do something for you, and so I will." He paused for a moment. "*You are no good!*" he said harshly. "*You are a* mushchas! *You are a* baal gaava! *Nothing good will ever come of you! A person like you is an abomination and an embarrassment to the* yeshiva!" With that, Reb Chatzkel turned and walked away.

The boy was frozen. Paralyzed. The *mashgiach's* words penetrated his heart and he underwent a complete change. He became one of the most conscientious boys in the *yeshiva.*

COMMENT: *People unfamiliar with the* yeshiva *world in general, and Reb Chatzkel Levenstein* zt"l *in particular, may be slightly disturbed by this story. Don't be. Just as a doctor sometimes must resort to drastic measures in order to cure a very sick patient, so too drastic measures must sometimes be resorted to in education. Not often – but sometimes. And those subjected to Reb Chatzkel's drastic measures were usually cured. And quickly.*

PEKUDEI

"ALL OF THE GOLD" (Pekudei 37:24)

"**D**O you wanna borrow a buck?"

"No, I never borrow. Just do it without me this week . I haven't got any singles on me and I don't feel like getting up to get one from my coat pocket."

The seven office workers had been buying a joint lottery ticket each week for the past four years. Mike Kosko was in the middle of reading the newspaper on his lunch break and didn't feel like going downstairs to the coat room. He was also dead set against borrowing even a penny, thus his declining Craig Staple's offer.

Needless to say, the six who went in on the ticket that day ended up winning 319 million dollars. This meant that after taxes, the six would split about 140 million dollars. That's about 23 million bucks a piece. Not a bad day at the office. Mike, though, had had better days.

COMMENT: *I had two thoughts about this story. The first is that the news report mentioned that there was some talk among the coworkers of giving Mike a million dollars each. I'm skeptical. I mean, do they* really *care about the guy that much? Coworkers in an office usually have at best a nice working relationship and then don't see each other until the next day. Most of them are probably going to quit anyhow, so that they can run around spending their millions and never have to see him again. I mean, would* you *give away a million dollars to a casual friend, just like that? I don't care how much money has been won – most people simply would not give away a million bucks.*

Sure, their first reaction would be "let's include Mike," but then they would go home and sleep on it – and the next day things would look different. They'd probably all chip in for a twenty five dollar gift certificate. Remember, if it was just oh-so-simple to give money away, then most yeshivas' *budgetary problems would not exist.*

My second thought concerns Mike. Just imagine how he felt. The disappointment. The constant nagging thought of what would've been had he not been lazy. It was right there, *just waiting for him. And he* blew *it! The shame. The pain. Am I right or not? Now think about the future. The* sefarim hakedoshim *describe* gehenom *as the intense experience of disappointment and shame when one is shown what he could have achieved during his lifetime. It was right* there. *Some*

Torah learning. More generosity in the area of tzedaka. *A little work on the* middos. *And he blew it. The disappointment. The shame. The pain. And there's no one there to give him a little bit of the good that they've got.*

"THIS IS THE ACCOUNTING OF THE *MISHKAN"* (Pekudei 38:21)

ONE of the great Torah builders of our generation, perhaps even the greatest, was Harav Nosson Tzvi Finkel *zt"l,* the *rosh yeshiva* of the Mir empire.   Countless stories came out after his passing describing what he had accomplished and what kind of person he was.   The following story was told over by another *rosh yeshiva* at one of the memorial gatherings for Rav Nosson Tzvi.

"I was headed to downtown Manhattan for an appointment with a very wealthy donor who had an office on the eighteenth floor. When I got there, the Mir *rosh yeshiva* also arrived, as he had an appointment for around the same time. Someone then informed us that there was a problem with the elevator and that it would be out of commission for a while. One of the people standing there immediately volunteered to go up and call the donor down, knowing that there was no way Rav Nosson Tzvi could climb the stairs with advanced Parkinson's disease.

"'Please don't call him down,' Rav Nosson Tzvi said. 'I will go up.' No amount of protesting from those around him helped. 'For Torah, nothing is too hard,' he explained with a smile. And then he painstakingly climbed up eighteen flights of stairs."

I later read that it took him forty five minutes, and yes, he received a very generous donation from the shocked-beyond-words *gevir*.

COMMENT: *There is very little doubt that in the World of Truth Rav Nosson Tzvi is constantly rising to higher levels. Only now, it's on a fast moving escalator.*

"AND BETZALEL THE SON OF URI"
(Pekudei 38:22)

EXCRUCIATING pain sent Rabbi Amos Betzalel to the local emergency room. A specialist diagnosed the problem as a kidney stone, and Rabbi Betzalel was admitted to the ward and put on medication to dissolve the stone. Some time later, in spite of the fact that the pain had eased up somewhat, he started feeling an intense wave of depression wash over him. It got so bad that he started having suicidal thoughts.

He called for a nurse and she told him to wait a few minutes, as she had to look something up. Sure enough, she found that one of the rare side effects of the medication they gave him was intense depression. It affected one in a hundred thousand patients.

They gave Rabbi Betzalel another medicine and the problem was taken care of.

About a week after being released from the hospital, he

was sitting in his office at the *shul* when a man knocked and entered. It turned out the man was seriously depressed and was on the verge of suicide.

Rabbi Betzalel later told a confidant that he then understood why he had to go through what he did. "I would never have been able to empathize properly had I not felt his pain myself. I would have nodded sympathetically and offered some advice. There was no way, though, that I would *really* relate to what this individual was experiencing. *Baruch Hashem,* I was able to help him in a way which otherwise I would not have."

"AND THE FIRE SHALL BE ON IT AT NIGHT"
(Pekudei 40:38)

The fire at night is symbolic of how during the pain of exile, the night, there is a flame of devotion that burns in the Jewish people. It is often more powerful than the devotion when things are going well, the day. On the other hand, one of the tragedies of the exile is Jews being lost to their people.

NO Shabbos candles, no Pesach *seder*, no Yom Kippur, no nothing. That's how Donna Levvo, shortened from the original Levovic, was raised by her parents in suburban Portland. There was absolutely nothing Jewish in their home.

Donna was in her second year of university, headed for a degree in communications, when she, like so many before her, somehow ended up on a trip to Israel and the *Kosel*.

The rest is history. Two and a half years and many family

battles later, Donna got engaged to a *bochur* who planned on learning a good few years in *kollel*. She had never been happier in her life.

Her parents, who had for the most part come to terms with Donna's lifestyle, made the trip to Israel to participate in her wedding. It was a beautiful *simcha* and everything had gone smoothly. That was until the Shabbos *sheva berachos*. There were religious cousins on her father's side of the family and they graciously hosted the Friday night *seuda* for about sixty people. After the first course, her father's cousin Mendel started singing *zemiros* and all the men joined in. It was really lovely.

Donna glanced over at her father and was shocked to see him singing along – without looking in a *zemiros* book. He was really getting into it and at some point even did a bit of a solo. This went on for about twenty minutes, and all the while a volcano of anger and hurt began erupting within her. "You knew about *Yiddishkeit* all along?" she yelled at her father. "You didn't teach me any of it! You robbed me! How dare you?! *How dare you!*" By this time Donna was crying. "I will never speak to you again! *Never!*" And as of this writing, she never has.

COMMENT: *We can't judge Donna. Her words were spoken in pain, deep and intense pain that will probably never dissipate completely. However, the objective Torah view is that one may never yell at or be disrespectful to their parents for any reason. Baalei teshuva must remember that they have no concept of the world their parents grew up in, with its lack of authentic Yiddishkeit. Baalei* teshuva *would be wise to* thank *their parents for having instilled in them truth as a value, which they were then fortunate enough to take to the next level.*

"AND THE OPENING OF THE ME'IL" (Pekudei 39:23)

Chazal *tell us the* me'il *atones for the sin of* lashon hara. *The commentaries explain that there are several different ideas alluded to in the* me'il *which teach us how careful we need to be before opening our mouths.*

Z EVY was visiting his friend Ovadia at a Sefardic *yeshiva* for modern boys who would hopefully turn into *bnei Torah.* Zevy sat in on the daily *halacha shiur* and was shocked silly when he heard the *rebbe* begin by announcing, "Today we'll learn the correct *beracha* to make on pot."

"What in the *world* is going on?" he thought to himself. "I mean, there's catering to the mentality of modern boys… but this is *absolutely* ridiculous." He was even formulating what he would say to the *rebbe* after the *shiur* when one of the boys asked how many times it must be dipped in salt. "Why would someone dip…" he started thinking, but then laughed, realizing what was going on. The Hebrew word for bread, pronounced *pas* by Ashkenazim, is pronounced *pot* by Sefardim. All they were doing was talking about the *beracha* on bread.

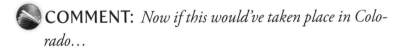 COMMENT: *Now if this would've taken place in Colorado…*

"THEY BROUGHT THE *MISHKAN* TO MOSHE" (Pekudei 39:33)

A YOUNG lady once came to Harav Moshe Feinstein *zt"l* with a weighty *halachic* dilemma. "My mother was married to an American G.I. stationed in England," she began. "Their marriage had a rabbi officiating and kosher witnesses. After a couple of years, she asked for and received a civil divorce from him without receiving a *get* and then married another man. I was born from the second marriage. I became a *baalas teshuva* a few years ago and am now engaged to a fine young man. My friends said I might have a problem marrying him due to the fact that my mother never had a *halachic* divorce. They said I should ask you."

Reb Moshe thought for a few minutes. "Please come back in twenty four hours," he said quietly. The next day, the anxious young lady returned. "There is no problem," Reb Moshe began with a warm smile, "you can marry the *bochur.*"

After the young lady left, those in the room voiced their confusion. "We heard what she told you yesterday. How could it possibly be permissible for her to marry him?"

"After the young lady left yesterday, I asked someone to contact the United States Pentagon," the *posek* of *Klal Yisrael* explained. "Sure enough, their records showed that there was such a man stationed in England. But the records also showed that he was already married to another woman in America and had two children with her. The young lady's mother clearly did not know about that or she would never have married him. Therefore, her marriage to him was an absolute *mekach ta'us*, a mistake from the start, so no *get* whatsoever is needed. She was never married to the man by any stretch of the imagination."

COMMENT: *Reb Moshe would have never rendered a* psak *that compromised* halacha *even in the minutest detail. It was because he cared so much that he thought to contact the Pentagon, which then cleared the way for his* psak. *Amazing what can be accomplished when a person really cares. And no one cared – about* everyone *– as much as Reb Moshe* zt"l.

VAYIKRA

VAYIKRA

"WHEN A MAN BRINGS
A *KORBAN*" (Vayikra 1:2)

R ABBI Fink was leaving the *Kosel* after having *davened shacharis* there. He had just finished backing away and had turned to head for the bus when a woman who was obviously not Jewish approached him. "Excuse me, are you a rabbi?" she asked with a thick Dutch accent.

"Uh, yes, I am. Is there something I can help you with?" he asked pleasantly.

"Yes, I was wondering if there are going to be any sacrifices here today."

The normally quick-witted Rabbi Fink was caught off guard. I mean, it's not a standard question, right? He thought for a moment. "Well, as of now, no," he began, "but there may be some later in the day."

COMMENT: *When he told me the story, I was caught*

off guard as well – but more by his answer than by her question. Maybe I must work on my Dutch accent. More likely, my emunah.

"A KORBAN TO HASHEM" (Vayikra 1:2)

Although the word korban *really means drawing close, it is often translated as a sacrifice because it involves giving up something.*

DO you remember what it was like going into a bank in Israel back in the old days and trying to determine who was ahead of whom in line? Someone would cut in, and when people would yell and scowl, the guy would say, "I was here before. I just ran out to buy bourekas. He was saving my place." Someone might answer, "I was here *yesterday* and left," and then a fierce debate would ensue as to when exactly one may claim to have already "been there." Such fun.

I once spoke to the manager of the bank about the problem and suggested they put in a number system. He told me it would only cause more *balagan*. He actually said that. Well, after many years of arguing and bickering amongst their customers, the bank finally installed an electronic numbering system. (Somehow it didn't result in the anticipated *balagan*.)

One day, Rabbi Leibenstein walked into the bank and took a number, which happened to be forty seven. A look at the board showed they were on number thirty one. Not terrible, but not great, either. Rabbi Leibenstein preferred working with a teller because he had a few questions to ask, but, being in a hurry, he decided not to wait. He threw his number into the wastebasket and went out to try the electronic banking machine.

Alas, the machine was not working. By the time he came back to the main waiting area, he noticed another few people had come into the bank. Rather than take a new number, he started walking over to the wastebsket in order to retrieve his first number.

Suddenly, he stopped. He thought to himself that if anyone would see him take a number out of the wastebasket without knowing that he had already been there, it would result in a *chillul Hashem*. "Look at the sneaky *chareidi* rabbi cheating on the numbers," he could just imagine someone saying.

He also had some question as to the *halachic* permissibility of retrieving his number. After all, when he threw it away he had fully intended not to use it. Who said he was allowed to change his mind and rob other people of their time? He decided to take another ticket and wait his turn, which took an extra twenty minutes after his original number was called.

When he finally got to the counter, the teller answered his questions and told him the electronic machine had just been fixed that minute. "If you do the deposit through the machine, you'll save yourself the bank charges," he advised him. Rabbi Leibenstein went to the machine, which saved him thirty five shekels in bank charges – money he'd have lost if he would have gotten to the teller earlier by using his original number.

COMMENT: *That Hashem rewards the righteous is well known. That a person is willing to forgo his original number due to halachic concerns is something of a novelty. That the electronic numbering system in the bank was working is the biggest novelty of all.*

"IF HIS *KORBAN* IS A BURNT OFFERING"
(Vayikra I:3)

It's well known that nowadays davening *is a substitute for the* korbanos.

IT had been an exhausting day. Rav Spiegleman had gotten off the plane after a seven hour flight and immediately went from one potential donor to the next. By the time he got back to his lodging, it was late at night. He collapsed into a deep sleep, without even eating dinner. At about three thirty a.m. he awoke, having dreamt that he hadn't *davened maariv.*

Sure enough, he hadn't. He pulled himself out of bed, *davened* with *kavana* as he always did, learned for a few minutes and then went back to sleep.

COMMENT: *The average person would probably have dreamt about not eating dinner and then would have gotten up to eat. Dreams are an indication of what a person is truly focused on and longing for. Rav Spiegleman's "food" will taste pretty good in the World to Come.*

"AND THE SONS OF AHARON SHALL PLACE FIRE ON THE *MIZBEI'ACH*"
(Vayikra 1:6)

IT was the fulfillment of every kid's dream. As Bill Stapelton staggered home from his regular bar one Friday night, delightfully drunk, he passed by the fire station. There were no firemen in the front area where the fire engine was parked. Some of the firemen were upstairs and some were in the back room.

Bill noticed a rack with hats and uniforms, so in his inebriated state he figured "why not?" and decided to try them on. He was in full uniform and was putting on the second boot when the piercing scream of the fire alarm sounded. Firemen seemingly came out of the woodwork, throwing on uniforms and jumping on the truck. No one took notice of the fact that one of the people in uniform was a drunken buffoon.

Realizing this was the chance of a lifetime, Bill jumped on the truck and joined them. No one stopped to check who he was, and when they arrived at the site of the blaze he took a hose and started spraying. He hadn't had so much fun in years. Only after they had the fire under control did the regulars notice that this guy was an imposter.

COMMENT: *It's a pretty funny story, and it applies to us more often than we think. Don't we regularly see externalities and overlook the real person inside? And then it's not so funny.*

VAYIKRA 203

"AND IF HIS OFFERING IS A *SHLAMIM*" (Vayikra 3:1)

"**W**HAT a nice kid," Mr. Abrams thought to himself. He had just seen one of the Zingbaum children in *shul*, and the boy had given him a warm smile along with a sweet "good morning." He saw the Zingbaum kids all the time and always walked away thinking this same thought about them. "I really should call their mother and tell her," he thought to himself.

By the time he got home, he had made up his mind to actually make the call. He took the phone book and looked up the number. After four rings, he heard a tired voice answer. "Mrs. Zingbaum?" he asked. "This is Mr. Abrams. I just wanted to tell you that you have wonderful kids."

There was silence on the other end. *It can't be that I heard what I think I heard*, Batya Zingbaum thought to herself. "What did you say?" she asked him.

"I said you have really terrific kids. And I want to tell you that it's not only a reflection of all the time and energy you put into them, it's because of your husband, too. I see him at *avos u'banim* and I see him with them in *shul*. The *kesher* they have is not that common. It's really quite impressive."

After another short silence, Mrs. Zingbaum spoke, but this time it was a totally different tone of voice. She sounded... choked up. "I can't tell you how much I appreciate this call. Here it is, *erev Shabbos*, and I didn't have any energy or motivation. It's been a long week. Hearing what you think of my family has just infused me with a fresh desire to prepare

Shabbos for them. I don't know how to thank you."

"Don't thank me," Mr. Abrams responded. "Just keep up the good work and have lots of *nachas*."

Sunday evening, Mr. Abrams's teenage daughter Leah came home from school. "Daddy," she cried excitedly, "you've got to hear this. Pnini Zingbaum is in my class. She said that because of your phone call they had an unbelievable Shabbos. She said her mother was in a fantastic mood and her parents got along so well. She said it's never like that, since the financial pressure the family is under always makes the atmosphere tense. But this Shabbos was *me'ein Olam Haba*. All because of your phone call."

COMMENT: *All because of his phone call. Think about it – but not for too long. Quickly pick up the phone and make a call.*

"FOR THE SIN WHICH HE HAS SINNED" (Vayikra 5:13)

HUNDREDS of girls from Odessa were being housed in an old Jerusalem building. Due to purely beauracratic considerations, the Ministry of Education would not give approval for the facility to become officially recognized as a dormitory. This meant the girls wouldn't be able to stay there for very long and they had nowhere else to go.

Gad Gavish, a former air force pilot who had become a *baal teshuva*, was the administrator of this program. After numerous appeals were rejected, he was left with no choice but to pull out the heavy artillery. He walked into the main office of the Ministry and sat down with Mr. Sasson Tamari, the guy in charge. "Look," Tamari began in his usual condescending tone of voice, "I can't give approval because we're past our quota." Of course, it was unclear what quota he was talking about. He put down his cup of coffee and took a big bite out of his potato bourekas.

Gad fully anticipated this standard "Please-don't-bother-me-because-I'm-important-and-I-want-to-eat-and-relax" response, but he came prepared. He reached into his attaché case and pulled out a picture of all the girls standing in front of the school building. Tamari looked at it for a moment and grunted through another mouthful, "What about it?"

"Mr. Tamari," Gad said quietly as he looked Tamari straight in the eye, "if you don't give approval, these girls are going to be on a plane tomorrow and flown back to Odessa. You will be held accountable for all eternity for any and all of them that end up intermarrying and raising their children as *goyim*." Tamari almost choked on his bourekas… and the school got the approval.

 COMMENT: *No missile fired by Gad in the air force ever hit a target with as much force as this shot.*

TZAV

"THIS IS THE TORAH OF
THE *OLAH*" (Tzav 6:2)

Tefilla *nowadays is in place of the* korbanos, *which we are
unable to bring.*

THERE is a story which has not been confirmed, but it's
pretty well known and carries an important message.
During WWII, England was being bombarded daily
by the Germans. Prime Minister Winston Churchill met a certain major *Chassidic Rebbe* and asked what advice he could give
him about the situation, known as "the blitz." The *Rebbe* said
he could resort to either the miraculous approach or he could
use the natural approach.

"What would the miraculous one be?" Churchill asked.

Answered the *Rebbe*, "The miraculous way is to rely on
your military strength. You see, the Germans have a better
army and are better equipped. To fight them and emerge
victorious would require a miracle."

"And what is the natural way?"

"The natural way is to pray."

COMMENT: *The most "natural" law that exists is that when one has a problem he should resort to prayer. History shows the English defeated the Germans. Obviously, someone did some serious praying.*

"COMMAND AHARON AND HIS SONS" (Tzav 6:2)

AS the *zman* wound down, I started asking the boys about their plans for the next year. Of course, I was interested in them learning for at least another year, hopefully more. However, it came as no surprise when Shimmy Feivelson told me he wasn't planning on returning. Shimmy had had some highs and lows during his time in *yeshiva,* but the lows far outnumbered the highs. His motivation level was near nil, and the feeling among all the staff members was that he would be better off getting involved in something which he could do wholeheartedly.

So it was something of a surprise when I saw him on the first day of Elul the following year. I didn't have a chance to speak with him the first week, though I did notice that he was learning with an energy that he had never shown before. "Shimmy, what's the story?" I asked him one evening when I was finally freed up.

"Well, it's really not that complicated," he began. 'You

know that I was outta here. We all knew it. But during the last week of the *zman*, Rav Zeltzer gave us a *vaad*. At one point, he said with tremendous feeling, 'You just have to sit down and *do it!*' I thought about that all summer, just that one comment. So I decided to just 'sit down and *do it.*' And, *rebbe*, let me tell you… it feels really good!"

COMMENT: *Our job is to keep shooting the arrows. Even if most miss – one bull's eye wins the "competition." Of course,* siyata d'Shmaya *is needed to have the* zechus *to shoot the winner.*

"AND HE SHALL REMOVE THE ASHES"
(Tzav 6:3)

THERE are quite a few stories floating around about Harav Beinish Finkel *zt"l*, the legendary *rosh yeshiva* of the Mir in Yerushalayim. There are three which share a common theme and an important lesson. There may be other versions of these incidents, but this is the way I remember hearing them.

The first story is about a man who approached Rav Beinish with a proposal. In the old Mir building, back in the days when people smoked in the *beis medrash*, the floor often carried telltale signs of that habit, in the form of butts, ashes and used matches. This man offered to donate money to the *yeshiva* to purchase ashtrays to be placed all over the *beis medrash*, thus eliminating the mess. "If you'd like to donate money to the *yeshiva*, I'll be glad to take it," Rav Beinish replied with the usual twinkle in his eye. "But as far as *what* to do with the money, I alone will decide that." The man gave the money.

The second incident was very much the same, only this time it involved the bathrooms. The condition of the bathrooms in the old days rivaled the condition of the bathrooms back in the original town of Mir, not a good situation. A *very* not good situation. So another man proposed giving a donation for bathroom renovations. And again Rav Beinish said that he'd gladly accept the money, but that *he'll* decide if and when he wants to do renovations. Again, the man gave the money.

The third story, though, is my favorite. Many of the *avreichim* were disturbed by the smoke in the *beis medrash*, which was indeed quite significant. A foggy day in London might describe the picture. They called a meeting of all the *avreichim* and put the matter of smoking in the *beis medrash* to a vote. The majority voted against smoking, and a sign was put up that from then on there was no smoking allowed in the *beis medrash*. The next day, in the middle of the morning *seder* when the *beis medrash* was at its fullest, Rav Beinish walked in… smoking a cigar. The message was clear. The *yeshiva* was his home and no one can vote on policy in someone else's home. The next day Rav Beinish put up a sign that said… smoking is forbidden in the *beis medrash*.

 COMMENT: *No matter how worthy a cause, one must always recognize the limits of his jurisdiction.*

"AND ANY *MINCHA* WHICH IS BAKED"
(Tzav 7:9)

I DON'T know what it was that Motti had done, but it was severe enough that the *rosh yeshiva* had grounded him for a week. He was not allowed to leave the Mattersdorf neighborhood for any reason whatsoever. When Friday came around, all the boys went to play ball in Gan Sacher, as is common in American *yeshivos*.

Motti decided to throw away all his pride and beg. He approached the *rosh yeshiva*, a man known for his unbending consistency, knowing that his chances of getting a reprieve were slim at best. Mustering up his nerve, he put forward his request to go play ball outside the neighborhood. "I really shouldn't," the *rosh yeshiva* began, "but *ha'ahava mekalkeless es hashura* (love muddles one's clear thinking). Go… but play well."

After a good few hours of solid ball playing, Motti returned to his dorm room and found… a freshly baked cake waiting for him on his bed, made by the *rosh yeshiva's* wife.

COMMENT: Chazal *say one should distance* talmidim *with the left hand and draw them near with the right. The* posek hador, *Harav Elyashiv* zt"l, *said success with* talmidim *means almost* exclusive *use of the right. Apparently, the* rosh yeshiva *is a righty.*

"IF AS THANKS HE OFFERS IT" (Tzav 7:12)
A korban todah, *a thanks offering, is brought by people*

who have been in various life-threatening predicaments but have been saved.

BEAUTIFUL scenery was visible on both sides of the bus as Yochi and his wife Sima headed out for one of the settlement towns. A friend living there had told them how wonderful the place was, and they thought moving there might just fit their needs and budget. As they came around a turn on the highway, Yochi noticed many of the people on the bus whispering something. Then some of the people started whispering again a few minutes later. Then it happened yet again. "What are they whispering about?" he asked the person in the next row.

"Oh, these are places where there were terrorist attacks. The people are making the *beracha* one makes when he passes the place where a miracle was done for him." Yochi and Sima settled elsewhere.

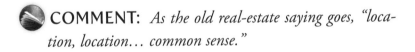 COMMENT: *As the old real-estate saying goes, "location, location... common sense."*

"HE POURED FROM THE ANNOINTING OIL ON AHARON'S HEAD" (Tzav 8:12)

One of the reasons Aharon was chosen for the position of kohein gadol *was his incredible humility.*

SHABABNIKIM. The word strikes fear in the hearts of residents of just about any *frum* neighborhood in Eretz Yisrael. It's a description of kids who have, for whatever reason, ended up on the streets and have no fear of authority, including the police. Their mischief results in burglaries and vandalized public property. Shattered beer bottles in public areas attest to their presence. In the worst scenarios, people are beaten up – in some instances quite badly.

One of the *yeshivos* in a *frum* neighborhood was feeling the effects of these delinquents, with broken windows on a regular basis, eggs thrown at the building, break-ins and, once in a while, a rumble with some of the *bochurim*. When things had gotten out of hand and a number of the *shababnikim* were arrested, a meeting between these boys and the *rosh yeshiva* was arranged by the *frum* activist who works with them.

While everyone appreciated the activist's efforts in dealing with such a difficult problem, there was quite a bit of damage done to the *yeshiva*, running into hundreds of dollars. Some settlement would have to be reached or the *yeshiva* would press charges. Of course, the *shababnikim* had grievances against the *yeshiva* boys for things such as looking at them on the bus and other trivial claims, the standard immaturity of teenagers.

The boys came to the *yeshiva* and sat in a room with the *hanhala* members, awaiting the arrival of the *rosh yeshiva*. When he walked in, even the *shababnikim* couldn't help being impressed by his regal bearing.

It was understood by all the adults in the room that the *rosh yeshiva* was going to lay down the law for these boys and that it would be a final warning. He was under financial pressure as it was, and he'd had about enough. He was also known as a man who spoke his mind in a very forceful way when the situation called for it. The tension in the room was palpable.

The *rosh yeshiva* opened his mouth to speak… and boy, were the people there in for a shock. "First of all," he began, "I would like to apologize for anything the boys in this *yeshiva* have done to wrong you. As the *rosh yeshiva*, their actions are my responsibility, and I will do my best to see that the offending behavior is not repeated." The *rosh yeshiva* continued on in a contrite and apologetic tone. He did mention that the *shababnikim* would be held responsible for any further damage, but he did it in such a gentle way that they never felt threatened. The meeting concluded with a *niggun* and a *rikud*, and the trouble stopped for a long time.

 COMMENT: *A true* talmid chacham *knows what to say, when to say it, and how to say it.*

SHMINI

"AND THEY DIED" (Shmini 10:2)

Different reasons are brought down by Chazal *why Nadav and Avihu died. One reason is that they taught a* halacha *in the presence of their* rebbe, *which in this case was Moshe Rabbeinu. One of the fundamentals of Torah is that one must negate himself totally in the presence of his* rebbe.

HARAV Shach *zt"l* was once walking with the Brisker Rav *zt"l*. Someone came over to Rav Shach, handed him a letter and informed him that it was from the Chazon Ish. Although Rav Shach was certainly extremely curious about the contents, he put the letter straight into his pocket without looking at it. There was simply no way he was going to open it and read it in front of the Brisker Rav. When they arrived at the Brisker Rav's home, Rav Shach took out the letter... and gave it to he Brisker Rav to read.

 COMMENT: *The Brisker Rav himself is said to have*

been impressed by Rav Shach's understanding of protocol. Compare this with the outrageous behavior of answering cell phones in the presence of – and sometimes in the middle of a conversation with – a rav or rosh yeshiva. Help!

"AND AHARON WAS SILENT" (Shmini 10:3)

A PROMINENT *maggid shiur* who was suffering from D.P.S. – Distorted Perspective Syndrome – once approached the great Brisker Rav *zt"l*. "What's the difference between me and you?" he began. "I mean, I say the same things you do in my *shiur*. Why is it that you get far more recognition than I do?"

"My friend," the *rav* answered, "it's true that indeed you say the things that I do. However, the difference is... *I* don't say the things that you do."

COMMENT: *It's not enough for a* maggid shiur *or teacher to know what* to *say. They must also know what* not *to say.*

"DON'T GO OUT LEST YOU DIE" (Shmini 10:7)

IN the early days of Bnei Brak, there was a regular security patrol. The residents were on edge because of the constant Arab attacks, and the security people were somewhat trigger happy. One morning, barely after the crack of dawn, the armed patroller saw a lonely figure walking around outside. Thinking it suspicious, he fired at the figure.

Fortunately, he missed. The man he had shot at was none other than… the Chazon Ish *zt"l*, who was on his way to *daven shacharis.*

When they took out the Torah, the Chazon Ish requested that he be given an *aliya.* Everyone there was sure he was going to *bentch goimel,* but he didn't. One of the people asked him why he'd wanted an *aliya* if he didn't *bentch goimel.*

"As I was walking," explained the leader of *Klal Yisrael,* "someone shot in my direction. At the time, I was saying *birkos haTorah.* The sound of the shot disturbed my *kavana.* On days that I don't have proper *kavana* during *birkos haTorah* I don't learn as well. So I wanted an *aliya* in order to be able to say *birkos haTorah* with full *kavana.*

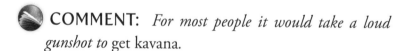 **COMMENT:** *For most people it would take a loud gunshot to* get kavana.

"WINE AND INTOXICATING BEVERAGES YOU SHALL NOT DRINK" (Shmini 10:9)

FIRST came a loud holler. Then a chair went flying across the room. Then a shoe was thrown hard against the opposite wall. Everyone in the family knew what was coming. Congressman Blair Hundley had had too much to drink and was on a tirade. After the flying projectiles there always came a vulgar rant that would last anywhere up to two hours. He was loud and he was filthy. All his family could do was wait it out behind locked doors until he collapsed somewhere on the floor out of sheer exhaustion. They were used to it, but they certainly didn't like it.

His seventeen year old stepson Shawn, who hadn't liked the Congressman from the day he married his mother, decided to pull a teenage prank. He grabbed his digital camera and filmed the entire tirade. He then put it online, where all would be able to see and hear who it was that was taking care of them on Capitol Hill. The ensuing publicity forced the honorable Congressman to resign from his prestigious position ten days later.

 COMMENT: *Ah, the blessings of modern technology. I'll bet the tirade* that *day was quite a sight.*

"BECAUSE THEY ARE AN ABOMINATION"
(Shmini 11:42)

ALVIN Goodman was engaged to Cathy Winthrop, and the marriage was planned for three months away. While the couple was happy and looked forward to their future together, the same could not be said for the rest of *Klal Yisrael.* Unfortunately, this would be yet another marriage which would be the end of a Jewish family line.

During semester break, Alvin flew off to Israel to visit his brother who was spending time in some sort of Jewish program called "*yeshiva*," and he popped in for a look. Being an adventurous free spirit from Oregon and possessing a healthy dose of self-confidence, he had no problem sitting in on one of the beginner *shiurim* at this *yeshiva*, which happened to be Ohr Somayach. This particular *shiur* was a Chumash *shiur* given by Harav Uziel Milevsky *zt"l*. His *shiur* was known for its clarity and depth, and those who attended always came away shaking their heads in marvel at the beauty of his presentation.

Alvin stayed around the *yeshiva* for a couple of weeks, all the while attending classes and meeting people. He had a pretty good time. When he returned to the States, he told Cathy he wanted to push off the wedding for a while because there were a few things he needed to think about.

To make a long story short, he ended up back in *yeshiva*, married a *baalas teshuva* named Bracha, and has raised a beautiful *frum* family.

I once asked him what did it, what it was that hooked him and made him come back for more. "It was that first Chumash *shiur* I attended," he explained. "I didn't understand much of what Rav Milevsky was talking about, because I was totally unfamiliar with the concepts. But I could see there was incredible depth to it and absolute truth. That's what did it."

COMMENT: *"Hama'or shebo yachazireno l'mutav, The light in it will bring him back to be good,"* is how Chazal *have put it. In the area of* kiruv, *so much energy is*

wasted on gimmickry. Instead of resorting to largely inef-
fective tactics, kiruv *workers would be wise to employ the*
methodology recommended by Chazal. *Introduce the un-*
initiated to Torah and allow the Ribbono shel Olam *to*
speak to His wayward children. It works. It really works.

"AND YOU SHALL BE *KADOSH*"
(Shmini 11:45)

A MAN once came to see Harav Hutner *zt"l* in regard to a question he had about learning a certain *kabbala sefer.* "Have you ever ridden on the A train?" Rav Hutner asked him.

"Yes, of course," the man replied.

"Then due to the sights you've seen there you are disqualified from ever learning that *sefer.*"

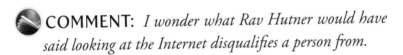 COMMENT: *I wonder what Rav Hutner would have said looking at the Internet disqualifies a person from.*

TAZRIA

"AND IT SHALL BE IN HIS FLESH A *NEGA TZARA'AS*" (Tazria 13:2)

It is well known that tzara'as *was visited upon a person as a punishment for* lashon hara. *There were other causes as well, but* lashon hara *is the one that's best known.*

PERHAPS it was the warmth and the smile. Perhaps it was the accessibility. Perhaps it was the incredible consideration for others. Most likely it was no one individual factor. Whatever it was, *Klal Yisrael* saw in Harav Sholmo Zalman Aurbach *zt"l* a man who was pure goodness. Anyone who knew him loved him. So it was a bit surprising when one of his sons related the following: "Our father was the sweetest of fathers. He was a joy to be around. However, if anyone ever said something inappropriate, there was fear of *middas hadin* (the attribute of strict justice) for two weeks. We walked around on tiptoes until the fear abated."

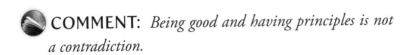 COMMENT: *Being good and having principles is not a contradiction.*

"WHEN A MAN HAS IN HIS FLESH A *SE'AIS* OR *SAPACHAS*" (Tazria 13:2)

There are few personal problems quite as big as tzara'as. *It was uncomfortable, embarrassing, lonely, and more.*

THE dedication that Harav Shach *zt"l* showed his *talmidim* was virtually unmatched. He was in the *beis medrash* with them most of the day, and available at almost all times when he was outside the *beis medrash*. However, when his fame spread as the unchallenged leader of the generation, more and more people began coming to him with their personal issues. At some point, he set aside time each day which was designated for people outside of the Ponovezh *yeshiva*, and they flocked to him in droves. One day, as people came and went after receiving *berachos*, advice, or, in some cases money, a *bochur* learning in the *yeshiva* awaited his turn. When his turn came, he entered and told Rav Shach that he doesn't understand a certain Tosfos.

"Why are you coming to me now?" Rav Shach gently reproved him. "You know that you can come to me any time in the *beis medrash*. This time is specifically for people with problems."

"But *rebbe*," the boy exclaimed, "this Tosfos is *my*

problem! Why is my problem any less urgent than anyone else's problem?"

Rav Shach smiled... and sat with the boy then and there and explained the Tosfos until it was clear to him.

COMMENT: *The fact that we don't see lack of knowing and understanding Torah as a problem is... our* biggest *problem! Bigger than health,* shidduch *and* parnassa *problems. Furthermore, if we viewed Torah as our main problem we wouldn't* have *as many of those other problems.*

"IT IS TZARA'AS" (Tazria 13:8)

The commentaries explain that tzara'as *is a demonstration of Hashem's* hashgacha. *An individual says a few forbidden words and then gets a Divine punishment –* hashgacha *doesn't get much clearer than that.*

A VERY Skolnik decided to use his vacation to go to Israel and look for a *shidduch*. He had been trying for a while in the U.S. without positive results, so it was off to the land where funny things happen. His return ticket was for six weeks later.

Now there's funny and there's funny. On the second day there, he met a young lady through a *shadchan*. After a week, they were engaged. They arranged a wedding in her native South Africa for three weeks later. Immediately after the *chasuna*, they flew back to Israel. Avery returned home on the same round trip ticket, only this time he had some extra baggage.

COMMENT: *If you ever feel a need to strengthen your belief in* hashgacha, *ask anyone how their* shidduch *happened. There is such blatantly visible* hashgacha *in this area of life. And it's really funny.*

"IT IS TZARA'AS" (Tazria 13:8)

As was mentioned in the previous story, the theme of tzara'as *is Hashem's precise* hashgacha.

IT was heartbreaking. Rav Binyomin Rothner had stopped to see a friend before he left to the airport for his flight home. He was just on time to witness the drama. There was a young lady there who was crying and trying to say something, but she could barely get the words out of her mouth. Rav Rothner managed to figure out the problem. She was recently engaged and was very poor. Her tears were the result of her inability to purchase a gold watch for her *chasan.*

Without a moment's hesitation, Rav Rothner took off his gold watch and handed it to the young lady. After the overjoyed *kallah* left, his rabbi friend asked him how he could part with such a valuable item just like that. "Nothing to worry about," Rav Rothner said. "I'm sure Hashem will make it up to me."

When he arrived at the airport and finished check in, one of the staff members of the airlines he was flying on called him aside. He assumed it was some sort of extra security search, but as the guy was smiling broadly he wondered if it was something else. "Congratulations, rabbi," the over-friendly official began in a loud voice, "you are our one millionth customer! And here's your prize – a brand new *gold watch*!"

COMMENT: *Beautiful. But it doesn't explain why* chasanim *need gold watches. Or, for that matter, any other exaggeratedly expensive gifts.*

"IT DID NOT SPREAD" (Tazria 13:53)

THERE'S spreading and then there's spreading. A group of people in Indiana decided to make a demonstration for some environmental cause or another. So they made a chain of pennies placed on the ground which spread out a long way. How long? Forty miles. That's right – forty miles worth of pennies, which adds up to 33,000 dollars. That's a *lot* of pennies and also a Guinness book world record.

COMMENT: Chazal *say that the* tzedaka *we give adds up. Each coin we part with becomes a piece of a suit of armor that will protect us in the World to Come. So, as the old saying goes, it's worth it to "save" those pennies.*

METZORA

"AND I WILL PLACE A NEGA TZARA'AS IN YOUR HOMES" (Metzora 14:34)

Rashi points out that this was a way for them to find the treasures that had been hidden in their homes. When the nega tzara'as *was discovered and the house broken, the treasures hidden inside became visible. One of the lessons here is that Hashem's help can come in many ways.*

G EDALIA had had a terrible morning. As the person in charge of the *yeshiva* kitchen, whenever anything went wrong he was on the receiving end of the complaints. On that particular morning, the milk delivery never came, so breakfast was an unhappy affair. And then the ovens stopped working, so the chicken served for lunch reminded the *bochurim* of *fleishig* sushi and they let Gedalia know it. Then one of the workers called in sick.

Gedalia counted the minutes until his lunch break so that he could go home and take a nap. With each step closer to home his mood became progressively worse. All it would take was one small thing not to his liking to set off a volcanic explosion. But the explosion never happened.

As he passed the building next to his, he noticed a towel hanging on the line to dry with three words printed on it – "RELAX, RELAX, RELAX." To this day, Gedalia sees it as a sign from Heaven. Why? Because never before or since has he seen the towel hanging there.

COMMENT: *I would love to find out that one of the kitchen workers called Gedalia's wife to let her know he was coming home in a foul mood, and that she called the neighbor to hang out the towel.*

"A NEGA TZARA'AS" (Metzora 14:34)

As mentioned in the previous story, this was a way for them to find the hidden treasures.

IT started by the Japanese Minister of Agriculture. As he opened the door of his office one morning, he found an envelope full of cash with a note that said, "Best wishes." Later in the day, a junior clerk in the Ministry of Transportation found a similar envelope stuffed with cash in her desk drawer. The next day it was the chief assistant of the Minister of Health. This pattern of cash envelopes delivered anonymously to various government offices continued for about two weeks. It was major news in Japan and took up much of the space in the print media and television news. It was the main topic of discussion on television talk shows, as everyone speculated as to who was so good-hearted and generous. However, in spite of all their best efforts, they never discovered the identity of the person.

COMMENT: *There is probably no Torah Jew who is terribly impressed by this story. For us, anonymous giving is a way of life. There isn't a* frum *community anywhere that doesn't have some sort of* tzedaka *fund to help needy families anonymously. And then there are the families who receive without even knowing that they're receiving. So, no, it isn't a major topic of discussion by us. Oh yeah, there's another difference between us and the Japanese donor. We* give to those who *need.*

"TZARA'AS IN A HOUSE" (Metzora 14:34)

One of the causes of house tzara'as *is selfishness. The classic example is of one who won't lend his possessions to others, using the excuse that he doesn't own that which has been requested. This results in his home being destroyed and everyone seeing that he did, in fact, own the things he claimed he didn't.*

THE tragic passing of Harav Shimshon Pincus *zt"l* was a big blow to *Klal Yisrael.* The stories of his *tzidkus* abound and never cease to amaze. However, there is one story which seems unremarkable, yet I feel is the most remarkable of all.

One of his sons related that he never in his life saw his father close a window that someone else had opened or open a window that someone else had closed.

![icon] COMMENT: *This is one of the most amazing examples of not being selfish I've ever heard.*

"AND HE SHALL BREAK DOWN THE HOUSE" (Metzora 14:45)

I T was a beautiful *chanukas habayis* celebration. Really beautiful, with fancy flowers flown in from some country in Europe. Everyone "oohed" and "aahed." Of course, there was a vast selection of food and lots of expensive alcoholic beverages. It had to be this way. After all, it's not every day that a *chanukas habayis* is made for a five million dollar home, and the Vesters' home had cost just that. That's right – five million smackers. It had a gym in the basement, a music room, and an entertainment room complete with a fully stocked bar and all sorts of other things that could *really* help a Jew grow in *ruchniyus*. Lester and Esther Vester really did it right.

This party took place on Sunday. Two days later... the home was no more, as Hurricane Sandy totally destroyed it. Five million bucks down the drain – just like that.

![icon] COMMENT: *Just imagine how the Vesters felt. Terrible. Really terrible. And we feel terrible for them. But just imagine how they would've felt had they only lost an average house, after giving away that five million – or at least a healthy chunk of it – to support Torah or some other tzedaka. Maybe then their average house would even have*

been spared. Who knows? One thing, however, is clear. Poverty, Chazal *tell us, is a revolving wheel. One never knows when he'll go down, even if currently he's at the top. Best to take advantage when one can, rather than regret the lost opportunities which get... washed away.*

"WHEN A MAN BECOMES A ZAV"
(Metzora 15:2)
There are various causes of becoming a zav, *one of which is overindulgence in food.*

"**W**HAT kind of food does the *rav* eat?" asked the young lady of Rav Nissim Karelitz's *rebbetzin.*

The *rebbetzin* smiled. "Many years ago, when we were *chasan* and *kallah,* I asked the *rav's* mother which type of food he enjoys. After all, I wanted to please him, as any wife would. She said, 'In this house, we never discuss food at all.' So for the last fifty plus years, I've been serving him food and we don't discuss it. Whatever I serve him, he eats, and he *always* thanks me. But we never discuss it."

COMMENT: *I was hesitant about including this story, because I figured there would be people who would say, "But what if his wife wanted to talk about it?" and, "But wouldn't she feel unappreciated?" and so on. However, aside from the well known fact that there are no women in the world who feel as appreciated as the wives of* talmidei chachamim, *I wanted to share an example of the level some reach. Bon appetite!*

"AND THEY SHALL NOT DIE"
(Metzora 15:31)

"I NEVER get mad," my cabbie said. A car had just carelessly cut us off in traffic and he had remained uncharacteristically calm for a cab driver.

I smelled a story coming. "Why not?" asked curious me.

"Because I used to be the head of an air conditioning installation company and it was a tension-filled job. I smoked heavily – four and a half packs a day. That's right – ninety cigarettes a day. I lit the next one off the one that I'd just finished. Used one match a day. I got real sick one day and started coughing up blood. I quit smoking immediately, cold turkey, but shortly after I became very ill and almost died. Had a two hour surgery which turned into twelve. I realized nothing in life is so important that it's worth getting angry over. So I switched jobs and am a much more pleasant person to my family and everyone else."

COMMENT: *Including the people he spends time on the road with.*

ACHREI MOS

"AFTER THE DEATHS" (Achrei Mos 16:1)

Causing another person embarrassment is tantamount to killing him.

RAV Ploni, a popular *maggid shiur* whose taped *shiurim* are listened to by many, was driving with some of his family members. He reached a light, signaled that he wanted to turn left, and then waited for the oncoming traffic to clear. A *frum* guy behind him honked, but Rav Ploni felt it was unsafe to race the cars, so he waited. The guy honked again, but still Rav Ploni wouldn't risk it. He shrugged his shoulders in the internationally recognized "what can I do" gesture and waited.

In the meantime, the light turned red. The guy pulled out, drew up alongside him and glared at him angrily. Rav Ploni heard his own voice coming from the guy's tape deck in his car.

He was going to identify himself, but then he thought

better of the idea. The guy would be very embarrassed to find out that the man he honked at was the man he regularly learned Torah from.

 COMMENT: *I wonder if the topic of the* shiur *on the tape was patience and self-control.*

"AFTER THE DEATHS" (Achrei Mos 16:1)

AS the people left the cemetery after the burial, a tearful Yaakov Blum, who had flown in from the U.S. the day before due to his father's *petirah*, walked over to the head of the *chevra kadisha*. "Are you new to this job?" he asked the Yerushalmi Jew.

"No, I've been doing this for years. Why do you ask?" The Yerushalmi was worried that perhaps he had done something that had offended the man.

"Well, you showed so much sensitivity and care, I figured you must be new to the job. Generally, people become insensitive when they're involved in things for a long time."

 COMMENT: *It's true. People like* tzedaka *distributors, rabbanim, doctors, and principals who are constantly exposed to people's* tzaros *sometimes become slightly desensitized to the suffering. Part of the job is to make sure that doesn't happen. It's not easy.*

"FIERY COALS" (Achrei Mos 16:12)

A FIRE broke out in the large residential building where Harav Avraham Genechovski zt"l lived. The panicky residents grabbed whatever they could salvage and ran out into the night. Amidst the total chaos and confusion, Rav Genechovski sat in a corner of the courtyard and occupied himself with... writing *kesubos*. He realized many of the couples would not have the presence of mind to take their *kesubos* with them and save them from the fire. The couples would be forbidden to live together until new *kesubos* were written.

🐚 COMMENT: *The thoughtfulness of a truly thoughtful person has no limits. Even under the most extreme circumstances, he still thinks of others. Fires, destructive tornadoes, earthquakes... and even when making a family simcha.*

"AND FROM THEIR SINS"
(Achrei Mos 16:16)

IN a horrific mental lapse, Anshel rang the doorbell. It was *leil Shabbos*, and Anshel was the regular *chavrusa* of Harav Avraham Genechovski zt"l on Friday nights. He quickly realized his mistake and then knocked as he normally did. There was no answer. He knocked again and still no answer. *Strange*, he thought to himself, *the rav usually answers right away*. He knocked again.

Finally, the door opened and a bleary-eyed Rav Genechovski stood before him in his pajamas. "I'm sorry.

I forgot about our learning session and went to sleep after the *seuda*. I heard the knocking and remembered it must be you."

It was only some time later that the real story came out. See, the possibility of Rav Genechovski, who was known for his incredible love of learning, forgetting he had a *chavrusa* was about as likely as a fish forgetting he needs water. He *was* awake and waiting when he heard the doorbell ring. He immediately realized that his *chavrusa* must have done it, and that he'd be extremely embarrassed if Rav Genechovski knew. So he immediately changed into his pajamas and pretended that he'd been sleeping and was only awakened by the knocking at the door.

COMMENT: *Remember how after reading the previous story you thought it couldn't get any better?*

"FROM ALL OF YOUR SINS"
(Achrei Mos 16:30)

There are sins that are bein adam laMakom *and there are sins that are* bein adam l'chaveiro. *Both need atonement.*

"CLOSE the window," Chezky snapped, "it's freezing in here."

"I want it open," Josh snapped back. "It's boiling hot in here and the window *must* stay open. Wide open."

The two roommates could not come to an agreement regarding the room temperature and window-related status, and the argument went on for a while. Finally, Chezky got out of bed and closed the window and the lights. He knew that Josh, almost asleep, would not get himself out of bed to open it again.

Indeed, he didn't. Instead, Josh rolled over, picked up a shoe and threw it through the window to the sound of shattering glass. Chezky resigned himself to his fate and pulled his blanket over his head due to the now frigid temperature. Josh, for his part, really enjoyed the fresh air.

It was something of a surprise to both – and a very telling insight into human nature – when they saw in the morning that Josh had actually thrown his shoe through… the mirror. The window was completely closed and intact.

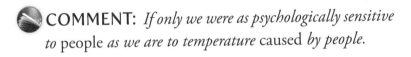 **COMMENT:** *If only we were as psychologically sensitive to* people *as we are to temperature* caused *by people.*

"FOR ON THIS DAY HE SHALL ATONE FOR YOU" (Achrei Mos 16:30)

IT was Yom Kippur in the death camp. "We've *stolen*? We've *stolen*?! *Rebbe*, what has any one of us stolen in this place? Why are we saying in the *vidui* that we've stolen?" one of the inmates of the concentration camp asked.

"I know how much you've suffered," the great Klausenberger Rebbe *zt"l* said softly. "I know how much we've all suffered. There is no question that the thought of suicide has sometimes popped into our minds. To take one's life would be 'stealing' the *neshama* Hashem has placed in this world. For that thought of stealing we have to do *teshuva*."

COMMENT: *I didn't fully understand this story when I first heard it and I don't fully understand it now. But it certainly opens up new avenues of thought as far as what some of the* al chaits *could be referring to.*

KEDOSHIM

"YOU SHALL NOT STEAL" (Kedoshim 19:11)

WAYNE Wagner and Perry Pratt were always up to no good. This time, they decided to "liberate" some cell phones and cameras from a department store. Alas, this time it was not to be. They got nailed by the store's security cop. When they were released after being processed at the police station, the dejected pair returned to their car in the parking lot, where they found... it had been broken into and all their valuables "liberated." They were soon filing a report with the very same cop who had filed one on them just a few minutes earlier.

 COMMENT: *A classic case of the nailed getting filed.*

"DON'T STAND ON YOUR BROTHER'S BLOOD" (Kedoshim 19:16)

This pasuk *teaches us that one must do whatever he can to save another Jew's life.*

AS he crossed the main intersection, Velvie let out a sharp involuntary, "OIYSH!!" He saw what was about to happen an instant before it did. The two cars crashed when one ran a red light. It was a bad smash. Trained as an E.M.T., Velvie dashed over and started applying emergency life-sustaining measures to one of the young crash victims, a seventeen year old girl. He escorted her in the ambulance to the hospital, where she was hooked up to a life support machine.

About a week later, the telephone rang in his home. "Is this Yitzchak Zev Pelz?" asked the caller.

"Uh, yeah," said Velvie, unaccustomed to being called by his full name.

"My name is Ben Appel. I got your name from the hospital where you signed the forms last week when my daughter was admitted. Thank G-d, she's regained consciousness and the doctors say she's going to have a full recovery. I just wanted to thank you for your efforts. According to the doctors, if you hadn't done what you did, she never would've made it to the hospital alive."

"Listen, it was not a big..." Velvie started to say, but the man cut him off.

"You're *frum*, aren't you? I could tell by your name. You know, I used to be in *yeshiva*; my family was *frum*. But I always felt *frum* people only cared about other *frum* people. I see from what you did that that's not true. My family has therefore decided to give Shabbos observance another chance."

🌑 **COMMENT:** *Mr. Appel was obviously using his claimed perception of* frum *people as his noble excuse for dropping out of Torah observance. All he'd have had to do was give a quick look around and he'd see* frum *organizations galore that help anyone and everyone, regardless of race, color or gefilte fish preference. But something about the incident with his daughter* did *make an impression on him. For that, Velvie will be credited with saving* another *life.*

"LOVE YOUR NEIGHBOR AS YOURSELF" (Kedoshim 19-18)

ZELIG Zeigler was frustrated. He wanted to add on to his apartment and had all the city permits. All he needed was for his neighbors to sign that they had no objection to his plan and he'd be all set. What he was planning on doing did not affect any of them in any way, yet there was one unreasonable man (isn't there always?) who refused to sign. Even his wife was okay with it, but Yigal Yeager would not budge.

On *erev Shabbos*, Zelig decided he would make one more appeal to the obstinate man. He would go over to him on *motzai Shabbos* and plead his case. If Yigal wouldn't agree to his plan, he'd have to consider moving. Zelig then started to listen to one of Rav Yitzchak Zilberstein's *shiurim* while he did some running on the treadmill before Shabbos. The *rav* told a story about a man who had built a home, but had inadvertently gone over the boundary onto his neighbor's property by about half a foot. The neighbor, a wealthy man with a vast estate, told him to "remove" his house from his property. The man offered to pay full compensation, but the neighbor said no. "But I'll have to knock down my whole house," he lamented. "You know I'm not affecting you in any way. I'll pay you even more than the value of the land. Just please don't make me knock it down." The neighbor wouldn't grant permission – he insisted on demolition.

So the man went to consult with Harav Shimon Shkop *zt"l*, one of the *gedolei hador* and author of Sharei Yosher, to ask what could be done. Rav Shimon told the man that the next time he was in *shul* and they do *hagba*, he should look intently at the words of the Torah and then approach the obstinate man again. The man had no idea why this should help, but Rav Shimon said to do it, so he did it… and the neighbor inexplicably dropped his complaint without even demanding compensation.

Zelig perked up. That Shabbos in *shul* he made sure to buy *hagba* and he looked *intently* at the words. *I-n-t-e-n-t-l-y*. On *motzai Shabbos* he went over to the difficult neighbor… who immediately agreed to sign.

The delighted Zelig returned home and had just sat down to a cup of coffee when the doorbell rang. It was his friend Wolf Wolbe. "Hi, I owe your son a *bar mitzvah* gift," he said as he handed over a gift-wrapped *sefer*. Zelig's son wasn't home, so he took the liberty of opening it up. It was… the *sefer* Sharei Yosher.

COMMENT: *It says in* halacha *that one who looks at the letters of the Torah during* hagba *draws a great light upon himself. Maybe that's why it helps with troublesome neighbors – they see the light.*

"AND YOU SHALL LOVE YOUR FELLOW AS YOURSELF" (Kedoshim 19:8)

"HEY," Meshulum cried, "there's Avner swimming in the lake! Let's hide his shoes and then watch his reaction when he comes out of the water and can't find them!" The boys were walking around the camp looking for something to do and this seemed like the perfect activity.

"I have a better idea," said Eliyahu. "Let's each donate a dollar and put the money in his shoes with a note that he can keep the money as a gift, and let's watch his reaction to *that*."

COMMENT: *I remember that the man who told me this story was clearly excited about Eliyahu's suggestion. I also happen to know that that man won the class* middos tovos *award in day school. Putting the money in the shoe is something that he himself would most likely have done at that age. I wonder what it says about someone if he's excited by the shoe-taking suggestion.*

"DO NOT TAKE REVENGE"
(Kedoshim 19:18)

LIKE all brothers, Yechiel and Ranan roughed around a little. One day, Ranan was sitting at the table eating an orange when Yechiel walked past and flicked his ear hard. Ranan immediately jumped up to retaliate. Yechiel ran and Ranan ran after him. When he finally had him cornered, Yechiel told Ranan that he couldn't hit him.

"Why *not?*" demanded Ranan.

"Because it's *revenge*," explained the righteous Yechiel.

Ranan hesitated for a split second. "It's not *revenge*," he hissed, "I'm starting *fresh.*"

COMMENT: *Great argument, but not true. Revenge is revenge no matter how skillfully you couch it in other terms. Good thing Ranan and Yechiel were only goofing around. For those who aren't, such as businessmen who feel they've been burned by competitors, employees who feel they've been taken advantage of by the boss, or people who weren't invited to other people's simchas and feel they should have been, a review of the halachos of the issur d'Oraisa of revenge and grudge-bearing is in order. Perhaps an order is more accurate.*

"DO NOT RAZE THE POINTS OF YOUR
BEARD" (Kedoshim 19:27)

This command is the source for the prohibition of shaving with a razor. While it is technically permissible for Jews to shave provided the shaver doesn't function as a razor, it has been the widespread custom for Jews throughout the ages to have beards.

ONE of the ugliest stains on the stained-filled flag of the State of Israel is its treatment of the Yemenites who came to live in the land that was no less theirs than those who were running it with all sorts of strong-armed tactics. These Yemenites were incarcerated in camps under horrible conditions and every effort was made to tear them away from Torah observance. Their *peyos* were forcibly cut (remind you of anyone?) and job opportunities were directly linked to their willingness to drop Shabbos and *kashrus* observance.

There were young activists sent by *gedolim* to try and infiltrate the camps to do whatever they could to improve the situation. Two *avreichim* in their early twenties were once sent by the Chazon Ish *zt"l* on such a mission. When they arrived at the Atlita camp, they couldn't find a break anywhere in the fence to sneak through. There was also an armed patrol, so they couldn't dig under the fence, something they'd done quite a few times in the past. They paced back and forth for a couple of hours and then returned to the Chazon Ish, thoroughly frustrated.

"You've done your *hishtadlus* and that's all that's asked of you," said the great man in his usual composed manner.

Over twenty years (!) later, one of these *avreichim* was attending a *simcha*. Somehow, he and an elderly Yemenite man got into a conversation. "You know why I'm still *frum* today?" the man began. "When we were locked up in the Atlita camp, they told us there were no longer any people with beards, so it didn't make any sense for us to keep ours. In the beginning, I held out because I knew that if the beard goes, then everything else is going to go, too. But they wore down my resolve and I was on the verge of giving in.

"But then one night I was out for a walk and I saw these two guys with beards pacing back and forth right outside the fence for a couple of hours. I decided then and there that my beard was staying. And here I am today, and all of my children and grandchildren are *frum*. *Yishtabach Shemo!*"

COMMENT: *It was indeed a close shave (sorry). Yet another in a long line of reminders that our job is to do our* hishtadlus *and let the* Ribbono shel Olam *take care of the results.*

"YOU SHALL NOT ROUND OFF THE *PEYOS* OF YOUR HEAD" (Kedoshim 19:27)

"...BUT no *peyos*," Ahuva emphasized yet again. Ahuva was starting *shidduchim*, so she and her parents sat down to talk about exactly what she wanted and didn't want in a husband. Her final statement, repeated a few times over the course of the conversation, was the one clarifying her sentiments towards *peyos*. Learning – definitely. *Avodas Hashem* – absolutely. But no *peyos*.

A short time later she met a wonderful *peyos*-free *bochur* named Yisrael Yaakov. After three meetings, the two became engaged. Yisrael Yaakov then returned to his hometown. The two would meet again at the *chuppa*.

So it came as quite a surprise to Ahuva when she looked up at her *badecken* and saw her husband-to-be with... *peyos* tucked neatly behind his ears. She had the brains not to bring up the subject until the next day, but she was *not* a happy camper. She couldn't accuse him of deceiving her, as she had never said a word to him about the subject, but she did feel deceived.

"Oh, my *peyos*?" Yisrael Yaakov asked with a laugh. "It's such a *funny* story. You are not going to believe this. I'm telling you – you just *won't*. See, the day before our first meeting, I went for a haircut. The barber didn't get my instructions clear and really messed up my *peyos*, so I had no choice but to have him remove them completely and start again. Isn't that *hilarious*?" Ahuva had heard funnier stories.

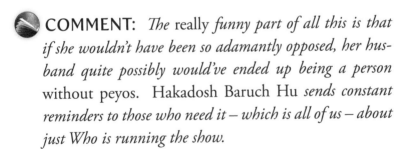 COMMENT: *The really funny part of all this is that if she wouldn't have been so adamantly opposed, her husband quite possibly would've ended up being a person* without peyos. Hakadosh Baruch Hu *sends constant reminders to those who need it – which is all of us – about just Who is running the show.*

EMOR

"TELL THE *KOHANIM* THE SONS OF AHARON AND SAY TO THEM" (Emor 21:1)

From the fact that the Torah repeats the directive "and say to them," Chazal derive that this is teaching that adult ko-hanim have the responsibility to keep minor kohanim away from tumah. This is a lesson for all parents. They must take responsibility for their children and take it seriously.

A T about four in the afternoon Israeli time, Dovi Jaffe's father called. "Yeah, Dad, I'm having a blast. The learning is really great and everything is great." Dovi was lying in bed at the time reading a novel instead of sitting in the *beis medrash.* Meanwhile, his *chavrusa* was once again awaiting Dovi's belated arrival.

Dovi's dad was a sharp cookie. He'd had reservations about sending Dovi to Israel where he'd be away from his watchful eye. Hearing Dovi saying his learning was great sounded awfully suspicious. He had spoken to Dovi's *rebbe,* who had sounded pareve at best about Dovi's involvement in his studies.

Mr. Jaffe decided to act. He booked a flight out of New York that night and arrived in Israel the next day. He came into the *beis medrash* looking for Dovi, but he was nowhere to be found. He went up to the dorm and knocked on the door. "Yeah," called a tired voice.

"Dovi, it's me, Dad." Surprise, surprise, surprise! To say Dovi was shocked is an understatement. Frozen is more like it. *No way*, he thought to himself. *It's gotta be my* chavrusa *playing games.* It wasn't. There was little Dovi could say after being caught red-handed in bed at ten thirty in the morning.

Mr. Jaffe read Dovi his rights, making it very clear what was expected of him if he was going to remain in Israel. Dovi really got his act together and had a productive two years in *yeshiva*.

COMMENT: *A father must be careful before resorting to such tactics, because he runs the risk of embarrassing his son terribly, which is bad enough. Worse is that it could also lead to a severing of any relationship between the father and son. On the other hand, I* am *impressed by how much Mr. Jaffe* cared.

"AND I SHALL BE SANCTIFIED"
(Emor 22:32)

AS the German war machine got closer, the Telshe *yeshiva* community made desperate attempts to figure out some way to survive. Aside from the concern for their lives, they also had another issue on their minds. After all the years of Torah and *avodah* – now there would be a *churban*? "How could it have come to this?" they lamented.

The *rosh yeshiva*, Harav A.Y. Bloch *zt"l*, put it all into proper perspective and set the people straight. "If it is decreed in *Shamayim* that we die *al kiddush Hashem*, then we will gladly accept our fate. However," he added through his tears, "you must know that to die *al kiddush Hashem* is not a *churban*!! To the contrary, all the years the *yeshiva* has been in existence have been leading up to this point! Do you understand? They've been a lead-up! This will not be a *churban*! This will be a *binyan*!"

COMMENT: *We never know what our true* avodah *is. A person can live seventy years or more, as a lead-up to the test or* mitzvah *for which he was put into the world.*

"AND YOU MUST NOT DESECRATE MY HOLY NAME" (Emor 22:32)

IT was one of those moments you just dread. I was giving a *shiur* to raw beginners at Ohr Somayach on the subject of *tefilla,* and we were dealing with the subject of concentration. Gary said he'd like to ask a question. "How is it that people answer their cell phones during *davening*? Doesn't that interfere with their concentration?" He was asking in innocence, without a trace of antagonism or condemnation of the *frum* community.

I responded to his question instead of focusing on his attitude, as I would have done had he been in the latter category. I told him that some have legitimate reasons, like Hatzalah people, doctors, or even *kollel* students whose wives may be in the ninth month of pregnancy and can go into labor at any time. I added that there are those who do not have legitimate reasons and really shouldn't be doing so. Being human, they have weaknesses and this is one of them.

He heard the answer, then thought about it for a few moments. He then threw an unintended verbal punch to my solar plexus. "I guess they just don't really believe what they preach," he said, more to himself than to me.

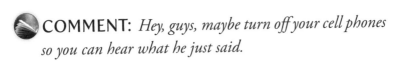 **COMMENT:** *Hey, guys, maybe turn off your cell phones so you can hear what he just said.*

"PESACH FOR HASHEM" (Emor 23:5)

EVERYONE loves the *seder*. Different generations sit together in an attempt to relive the miracles Hashem did for our ancestors. There are all sorts of creative ideas people employ to interest kids and adults alike. Some act out the plagues, others bring props to the table, and one man I know says over almost the entire *haggada* in rhyme. Whatever works is great.

But what Shmuel Shneid did at his *seder* absolutely takes the cake (*kosher l'Pesach* of course). Now Shmuel, a very serious *ben Torah* and intense learner, is also blessed with an excellent sense of humor and a zany personality. When the family reached the plague of frogs, Shmuel lifted the top of a cage in which he had placed a live frog, releasing it into the room. Of course the women started shrieking and jumped on chairs as the little critter hopped around and the men split their sides with laughter. "And that's only *one*," Shmuel cried out. "Imagine what it was like in Mitzrayim with *millions* of them running around!"

COMMENT: *The family had no choice but to allow Shmuel back at the next year's seder – he was one of them, after all. But certain preconditions were made by his mom and the other womenfolk.*

Note: There are certain halachic *problems that could arise using such a technique. Although memorable, it's not a good idea to use living creatures on* Yom Tov.

"AND YOU SHALL TAKE ON THE FIRST DAY FRUIT OF THE *HADAR* TREE, DATE PALM BRANCHES" (Emor 23:40)

CARS were honking and traffic wasn't moving. A bus was blocking the Kikar Shabbos intersection, the main intersection of the Geulah/Meah Shearim neighborhood in Yerushalayim. It was two days before Succos, and this part of town is the main hub for selling the four species. People didn't know why the bus wasn't moving. The driver ignored their shouts, looking eagerly out the window. After a two or three minute delay, a man came running up to the driver's window and handed him a *lulav* and *esrog*. "Oh good, now all I need is to get my *hadasim*," the driver said, as he paid the dealer for his wares and drove off.

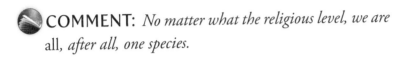 COMMENT: *No matter what the religious level, we are all, after all, one species.*

"IN *SUCCOS* YOU SHALL DWELL SEVEN DAYS" (Emor 23:42)

"OH no, you don't!" squealed Mrs. Kreetch. "What do you think this is, the *shtetl*? We're not gonna have any of that nonsense here!" It was a few days before Succos and Gershon Greishman had gone out to the parking lot of the Winston Towers housing complex in Chicago to build a *succah*. Although populated almost entirely by Jews (it was even nicknamed "Caprini Greenberg" – a reference to the rough inner-city housing complex called "Caprini Green"), many were not sympathetic to the Orthodox cause. Thus the threat from Mrs. Kreetch. This was the same lady who had blocked the building of a *shul* in the cellar of the building and objected to the putting up of a *mezuzah* on the front door.

Of course she got her just desserts, as two of her children became full-fledged *baalei teshuva* and were raising *frum* families.

True to her word, she called the city authorities, and they told Gershon he may not erect any sort of hut in the parking lot or anywhere else on the shared premises. Mrs. Kreetch was sure to be present when the city people were there, a nasty smirk plastered across her face. "You fanatics are an embarrassment to us normal people," she ranted. "I'll show you what the twentieth century is!" she cried, stalking off with the smug look of victory.

But Mrs. Kreetch had overlooked the fact that Gershon was a former college wrestler who prided himself on never having lost a match. He called a truck rental company and made the necessary arrangements. The next day a flatbed truck pulled up and Gershon had them park it in the parking lot, which of course was perfectly legal. He also made sure it was in as clear a view of Mrs. Kreetch's window as possible. He then built a *succah* on the truck, also something the city had no right to prevent, because the structure was not built on the parking lot grounds. Ahhhh, *zman simchasainu!*

COMMENT: *Mrs. Kreetch did* not *enjoy Succos. Hopefully in the future she will — the way the rest of us do.*

BEHAR

"SIX YEARS" (Behar 25:3)

EIGHT years. That's how long Rabbi Briesh had been serving as the camp director and he had a well-earned reputation for total dedication to the campers. Some would call him a workaholic. I call him responsible. But there's responsible and there's responsible – and then there's Rabbi Briesh. You see, in his eight years as director, not once during the two month summer program did he go swimming. *Not once.* Why? "I don't have time for it," he would explain. "There are too many campers and too much to do in order to ensure their constant well-being and safety. I just haven't got the time." Eight years!

COMMENT: *If I had to choose one characteristic that differentiates children from adults, it would be responsibility. An adult is – or at least should be – someone who* *realizes life means taking responsibility. And it's entirely possible for someone to be in their forties or fifties or more and still be considered a child.*

"PROCLAIM FREEDOM
IN THE LAND"
(Behar 25:10)

ONE of the biggest causes of our loss of freedom nowadays is the blasted cell phone. One can hardly think or breathe without that little annoying instrument interfering. Truth to tell, things were not great back in the days of the regular phone either. Meals were disturbed and important matters interrupted due to the ringing of the phone.

Listen to this interesting historical fact. There was one man who refused to allow the phone to interfere with the important things he was doing, and so he did not have a phone in his home. His name: Alexander Graham Bell.

COMMENT: *I don't know what Mr. Bell was involved in that was so important, but whatever it was it didn't hold a candle to Torah or* tefilla. *After all, most people reading this spend thousands of dollars on an education that will instill in their children the importance of Torah and* tefilla. *So maybe we could take a lesson from Mr. Bell and distance the thing that interferes with our priorities instead of being... a bunch of ding-a-lings.*

"AND YOU SHALL NOT HURT THE FEELINGS OF ONE ANOTHER" (Behar 25:17)

DERRICK Domb now goes by his Hebrew name Doniel. He learns in *kollel* and keeps all the *mitzvos*. He once explained what it was that moved him closer to *Yiddishkeit*. "I was at the *Kosel* one day and I did something – I don't remember what it was – that caused some Chassidic guy to start yelling at me. I mean, he was really heated up. It was like an instant *ulpan* of angry Yiddish expressions. At first I was upset, as any normal person would be. But then I started thinking, *If he is so upset, it means he really cares.* Being raised in a society where the only thing people cared about was to have a big screen T.V., I decided to investigate why it was that it mattered so much to him. And here I am."

COMMENT: *I'm not recommending that we should go around yelling at people in the hope that it'll be* mekarev *them. It's usually not a great technique for achieving the desired goal. However, unlike the ultra-pacifists among us, there* are *times when yelling is justified, regardless of the results. Remember, Pinchas used a spear when it was necessary. I know, I know, none of us are Pinchas – but a yell isn't a spear either.*

"FOR *BNEI YISRAEL* ARE MY SERVANTS" (Behar 25:55)

ATRUE servant wants to serve his master at all times and under all circumstances. Such a person was my dear friend Rav Dovid Speyer *zt"l*. All those who knew him saw that he had the singular goal of serving *Hakadosh Baruch Hu* to the fullest, regardless of difficulty or inconvenience.

The story which I felt captured his essence best took place while he was hospitalized, suffering from the illness which cut his life short.

He had a tube in his arm and one day the tube came out. This meant that it would have to be inserted higher up on the arm, causing a lot of pain in the process. "Oh good," was his reaction, "now I'll be able to put on my *tefillin* without anything interfering."

COMMENT: *Unfortunately, it often happens that we truly appreciate the greatness of a person only after he's gone.*

"MY SERVANTS" (Behar 25:55)

As mentioned in the previous story, a true servant is singularly focused on serving his master and is horrified by the idea of letting him down.

HARAV Dovid Beharan *zt"l* was one of the legendary *masmidim* of old Yerushalayim. He would sit in a *beis medrash* virtually the entire day and night studying Torah, not even coming home for meals. His daughter would bring his food to the *beis* *medrash* and then return to remove the dishes. Along with his daily bottle of milk came a bottle of paraffin fuel for the heater he used on the frigid winter days. One day his daughter came to remove the dishes and noticed that the milk bottle was full. She realized that due to his total absorption in his learning her father had inadvertently drank the bottle of fuel. "Oh no," he exclaimed when she pointed it out to him, "I made a *beracha l'vatala!*"

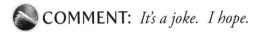 **COMMENT:** *Not quite the reaction most of us would have, right?*

"MY SERVANTS" (Behar 25:55)
A true servant does the job right.

THERE were twenty computer programmers on a plane. Right before takeoff the pilot announced, "The computer program for flying this plane was designed by the Clampton Creations Company." Nineteen of the programmers immediately got off the plane.

The pilot asked the remaining passenger why they got off. "They all work for that company you mentioned, so they thought it best to disembark."

"So why didn't you get off?" the pilot asked.

"Because I work for the company that designed the program that gets the plane off the ground."

COMMENT: *It's a joke. I hope.*

BECHUKOSAI

"IF YOU FOLLOW MY STATUTES"
(Bechukosai 26:3)

Rashi says this refers to toil in Torah. True Torah study requires devotion and exertion.

"**R**EBBE, I'm just not *chapping pshat* in Tosfos," Azriel lamented. Rav Bellow knew that it was a hard Tosfos and most of the *bochurim* would not be able to figure it out. He also knew that his prize *talmid* Azriel, with his extraordinarily sharp mind, would be able to get it – but only if he'd sweat a little.

Rav Bellow chuckled. "You should *fast* in order to get *pshat* in this Tosfos. You're really going to have to work on it. It's one of the most difficult Tosfos in all of *Shas*."

Two days later Rav Bellow noticed that Azriel did not look good. His eyes were watery and he looked drained. "Are you feeling okay?" he asked him.

"Yeah, fine. I'm just a little weak, though, because

I haven't eaten since you told me I should fast over this Tosfos, and that's what I plan on doing. I'm gonna fast until I figure it out. You were right, *rebbe*. This really is a hard Tosfos."

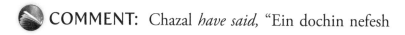 **COMMENT:** *I'm sure Rav Bellow will be more careful next time with his choice of words, but it is good to know there are talmidim who follow instructions to the letter.*

"AND IF YOU DON'T OBEY ME"
(Bechukosai 26:14)

I T was heartbreaking, and unfortunately it was the heartbreak shared by so many others nowadays. Chanoch Cheshin and his wife Chanita had devoted their lives to outreach, living on or near various college campuses and always having an open home. It was rare indeed that they didn't have a Shabbos table full of secular youth as their guests. So it was especially painful to them when their sixteen year old son Chananya began straying from *Yiddishkeit* and within a year was totally off the *derech*.

They tried to be patient, but one day Chanoch could take it no more. He confronted his son. "What went wrong?" he asked. "Was it a bad experience in school? Is it bad friends? Is something bothering you? Tell me – what *is* it?"

"Dad," Chananya said, choking back his tears, "it's the girls *you* brought into the home!"

COMMENT: Chazal *have said,* "Ein dochin nefesh

mipnei nefesh, *You can't choose one life over the other.*" *In the literal sense, it refers to actual life. But it's used in the vernacular with regard to the spiritual realm as well. The primary responsibility of parents is their children. If a couple saves the world at the expense of their own children — or even one child — they've missed the mark. Decisions such as whether to do campus* kiruv *or not, and who to bring into the home and when, are something that must be discussed with* daas Torah *before embarking on the mission. A person can be well meaning in their effort to do right, yet still end up doing it wrong. Those who have succeeded in outreach have done so by following the directives and guidelines set out by* gedolei Yisrael.

"AND IF YOU DO NOT OBEY ME"
(Bechukosai 26:14)

From this pasuk *on, the Torah describes the suffering that will befall* Klal Yisrael *if they do not follow Hashem's commands.*

UNFORTUNATELY, life involves suffering. There will come a time, hopefully very soon, when suffering will cease. Until that time comes, a person must learn how to deal with ordeals and pain. Harav Avraham Genechovski *zt"l* suffered the tragic loss of a sixteen year old son, one of the most painful experiences in the world. His response was to put a portrait of his son on the wall with a sign underneath that said, "*Ve'ahavta es Hashem Elokecha ...uvechol me'odecha,*" a reference to the obligation to love Hashem even when He subjects a person to difficulty.

COMMENT: *A person is supposed to live with the attitude of* gam zu l'tova, *that all is for the good. Now, this doesn't make the pain go away. Things hurt, and some hurt badly. However, adopting this attitude serves as a reminder that the pain isn't for naught, which helps to take out some of the sting. I think this is what Rav Genechovski was doing. He was using the sign as a reminder that there was purpose in the loss, as painful as it was.*

"AND IF YOU LOATHE MY STATUTES"
(Bechukosai 26:15)

"THAT'S really nice, but I definitely do *not* want a guy who's going to be learning in *kollel.*" This was Bella's firm declaration, made in response to her friend Mindy's statement that she wanted a husband who would sit and learn.

"But why not?" asked Mindy, alarmed that her friend was so adamantly opposed to having a husband who would engage in the most important *mitzvah* in the Torah.

"*Why? Why?* I'll *tell* you *why,*" answered Bella with what was clearly pain and resentment in her voice. "My father learned in *kollel* for many years. He's *still* learning in *kollel.* Any time I want anything, my mom tells me I can't have it.

'We can't afford it because Daddy's in learning,' she always says. No way! No *way* is my husband going to be in *kollel*. *No way!*"

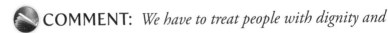 COMMENT: *Kids growing up in a Torah home which has a restricted budget must not feel deprived. Limited, yes, but not deprived. One might say, "We'd love to get it for you but it's not within our budget right now." Why blame the* learning? *Have you ever heard anyone say, "We can't afford it because Daddy's in computers?" My guess is that Bella's mother isn't so thrilled about the idea of her husband learning, and that's the attitude that filtered down to Bella.*

"THOSE THAT HATE YOU SHALL RULE OVER YOU" (Bechukosai 26:17)

A PROMINENT Jewish businessman had a meeting with the leader of a certain country known for its virulent anti-Semitism. This particular leader, though, was uncharacteristically good to the Jews. The businessman, with his somewhat brash personality, took the liberty of asking the leader why he had shown such benevolence.

"I grew up poor," he began. "My mother cleaned people's homes, and she wasn't treated well at all. But there was one family she worked by that was Jewish, and they treated her with dignity and respect. For that I am grateful."

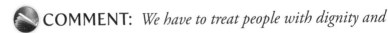 COMMENT: *We have to treat people with dignity and*

respect because they are a tzelem Elokim, *in the image of G-d. But there* are *benefits to doing what's right. In this case, the behavior of* one *family benefited* countless others. *And they'll be rewarded in the* Olam Ha'emes *for* every single *ounce of suffering that they prevented.*

"I WILL SCATTER YOU AMONG THE *GOYIM*" (Bechukosai 26:33)

JUST about the most common picture postcard of Israel has a panoramic view of Old Jerusalem. Most prominent in the picture is the Dome of the Rock, a holy site for Muslims. When one sees it, his first reaction is usually, "Wow, that's so beau…" But then we catch ourselves and quickly remind ourselves that in our eyes it's really not very beautiful at all.

We were all a bit surprised, more than a bit actually, when we heard in a *shiur* given by Harav Avraham Chaim Feuer that Harav Yaakov Kamentsky *zt"l* once said the dome is actually a good thing. Reb Yaakov explained that Jews often forget they're in *galus*. Seeing the dome is a poignant reminder that we still are. And Harav Mordecai Gifter *zt"l* said that when undesirables move into Jewish neighborhoods, forcing Jews to move, that too serves as a reminder to us that we are in *galus*, no matter how comfortable the situation is.

COMMENT: *There is nothing that can compare with the outlook of an* adam gadol.

BAMIDBAR

BAMIDBAR

"TAKE THE SUM TOTAL" (Bamidbar 1:2)

The Torah goes on to report the number of people in Bnei Yisrael. *The commentaries point out that we learn from here that every single Jew is important and has inherent value.*

WEALTHY Willy Wiser was not impressed. "*You* made the choice of bringing them into the world, so it's *your* responsibility to marry them off – not mine."

Kalman Kiegel, the father of twelve who had made the appeal on behalf of his kids, was not to be put off so quickly. He'd made the trip all the way to the U.S. to appeal for funds and he would at least have his say. "Can I ask you something?"

"Sure," Willy answered smugly as he folded his arms. He had already decided this irresponsible *frummy* wouldn't get more than a token eighteen bucks. He actually wanted to hear what he'd say so that he could really lay into him and present *his* worldview on the first *mitzvah* in the Torah. Little did he know that he'd never get his chance.

"Would you want to become a partner with Warren Buffet if the opportunity arose?" asked Kalman.

"Yeah, of course."

"Why?"

"Why? Because it would be a big honor. Even more than that, it would give me credibility in the financial realm. Not quite your area of expertise, huh? People would see *he* trusts me, so *they* would trust me too. And then I'd be into the *really* big bucks." Willy widened his mouth into an even more cynical smile. "And why, may I ask, do you ask?"

Now it was Kalman's turn to wear the smug smile. Willy had stepped right into the trap. "Because the *gemara* says there are three partners in every child – the father, the mother and Hashem. Hashem has been *my* partner *twelve* times. That's a little more impressive than Warren Buffet, don't you think?"

Willy gave a lot more than he had intended.

 COMMENT: *An interesting way to view our children, isn't it?*

"BNEI YISRAEL DID EXACTLY AS HASHEM HAD COMMANDED MOSHE"
(Bamidbar 1:54)

All that had happened here was that Moshe instructed Bnei Yisrael *where they would be encamped. Therefore, the commentaries ask, what is the* pasuk *referring to when it says* "Bnei Yisrael *did what Hashem commanded?" The answer is that they vacated the place by the* Mishkan *where the* levi'im *were to be encamped.*

THE band started playing the lively *"yamim al yemei melech"* tune generally reserved for prominent *rabbanim*, although sometimes it's played for people of lesser stature. Nobody prominent entered the middle of the circle and people started looking around to see who the band members had spotted.   Another minute passed and still nothing. Seizing the opportunity, one of the *bochurim* jumped into the middle as *shtick* to entertain the *chasan*. Suddenly, he felt a shove as a man pushed him out of the way. "That's *my 'yamim!'"* he whispered angrily.

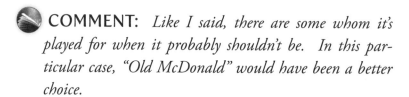 COMMENT: *Like I said, there are some whom it's played for when it probably shouldn't be.   In this particular case, "Old McDonald" would have been a better choice.*

"BUT NADAV AND AVIHU DIED"
(Bamidbar 3:4)

"I'VE bought *chasan Beraishis* for the last twenty years," the man began dejectedly, "but this year I was outbid. It's so painful for me."

"I feel bad for you. *Im yirtzeh Hashem*, you'll get it next year," responded Rav Yisrael Yaakov Fisher *zt"l*. After all, what could possibly be done? Someone else had bought it and had every right to.

"But I so much wanted it. I have no *simcha* now."

"*Im yirtzeh Hashem*, next year," Rav Fisher said again.

"But I'm so sad," the man repeated.

"*Im yirtzeh Hashem*, next year."

The man left as unhappily as he'd arrived. About three weeks later the man had a heart attack and was *niftar*. One of those who had been in the room at the time asked Rav Fisher what happened. "I heard you say '*im yirtzeh Hashem*' three times. What went wrong?"

"He didn't answer *amen*," Rav Fisher said matter of factly, while sadly shaking his head.

COMMENT: *The Ramban says Sarah Imeinu was taken to task for not answering* amen *to the* malach *when he said she'd have a child the next year. This one little word needs to be taken seriously.*

"BUT NADAV AND AVIHU DIED"
(Bamidbar 3:4)

IT was a story reported in the news all over the world. Authorities in South America found the body of missing forty one year old Fernando Gutierrez and the bereaved family arranged a funeral. Sometime during the eulogies, everyone in attendance got the surprise of their life – actually, the surprise of their death. From the back of the crowd a man started calling out, "*I'm here, I'm here! I'm alive, I'm alive!"* Sure enough, it was the "deceased" man himself – who had never died.

The authorities thought the body they found was that of Fernando, while in fact they had mistaken another body for his. And in an absolutely incredible turn of events, he returned from wherever he had been on the very day of "his" funeral.

He said later that at first he didn't realize it was *his* funeral, but when he understood what was going on, he actually enjoyed listening to the nice things people said about him. His mother's reaction was even more interesting. She said, "We're very happy. This sort of thing doesn't happen that often."

COMMENT: *Speaking of understatements. That aside, there's an important lesson here. One must* never *give up hope, because* anything *can happen. And even if the person in question had truly died, which is usually the case, there will be* techias hameisim. *And it can happen at* any *time.*

"AND YOU SHALL TAKE THE *LEVI'IM*"
(Bamidbar 3:41)

I T was *sheva berachos* for Yehuda Yitzchaki and Yehudis Yakabovich. Yehudis's father Yekusiel got up to say a few words. "I would like you all to know why I took this young man as my son-in-law," he began. "A few months back, I had to go from Yerushalayim to Bnei Brak. It was a blistering hot day and I was in a hurry, so I went to a hitchhiking spot to hitch a ride. A car stopped, and it was driven by none other than my new son-in-law Yehuda. We started driving and hit a real bad traffic jam. The trip took close to two hours, it was hot, and the car didn't have air conditioning. Yet not once," here he paused for dramatic effect, "not once during this frustrating trip did Yehuda honk at anyone. Not once. When I saw his self-control, I decided this was the young man for my daughter." Yekusiel finished with a few words of *beracha* and sat down.

Yehuda leaned over towards him. "My horn wasn't working that day," he explained with an apologetic smile.

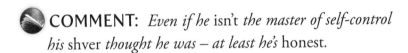 **COMMENT:** *Even if he* isn't *the master of self-control his* shver *thought he was – at least he's* honest.

NASO

"TO DO WORK" (Naso 4:23)

AMERICAN Pie. Two words recognized by just about anyone who lived in America in the seventies. It was not only the song of the year in '71 – it was the song of the *decade*. I'll bet you're already humming it. Right? Right? Even adults who were cynical about pop and rock music enjoyed it. But it wasn't only the tune. The cryptic lyrics written by singer/songwriter Don McLean succeeded in making us feel there was some deep hidden meaning to it all. Faith, the death of music, whiskey and rye – what can it mean? What can it *mean*? An interviewer once asked McLean to shed light on the topic. "Please tell us, tell us – what *does* it mean?"

McLean smiled. "It means… I'm never going to have to work for the *rest* of my life."

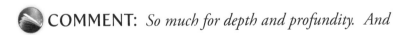 **COMMENT:** *So much for depth and profundity. And*

if this is how empty that society's "deep" things are, imagine what could be said for the rest of the attractions they have to offer. So we say… bye-bye.

"THIS IS THE WORK OF" (Naso 4:24)

Each family of Levi had a different assignment of what to carry.

"**I**S this the chief rabbi of the Jews?"

"Yes, of the community of Gateshead." So began the phone call received by Harav Shraga Feivel Zimmerman *shlit"a*, the Gateshead Rav.

"My name is Dale Daley, and I'm calling from Scotland. I have a confession to make." "Uh, I don't take confessions," Rav Zimmerman said. "Perhaps you should contact a Catholic priest."

"No, this has to do with the Jews. May I speak to you in person?" Dale walked into Rav Zimmerman's home the next day, and the first thing he did was put a stone on the *rav's* table. "Last month, I visited one of the concentration camps where your people died. When I left, I took the liberty of taking this stone out of a wall of one of the crematoriums. Now I have second thoughts about having taken it, so I'm going to leave it with you." Before the *rav* could respond, Dale got up and walked out the door.

Rav Zimmerman thought about the stone. His first concern was that if there was any human residue on it, it required burial. After determining that that was not an issue, he gave the matter some thought. On the one hand, if there was no *halachic* issue, then he could simply toss the stone in the river. As sentimental as it was, it was still only a stone. On the other hand, it *did* come out of the crematoriums. So what to do? He decided to consult his *rebbe*, Harav Dovid Soloveitchik *shlit"a*.

Reb Dovid closed his eyes and thought about it for ten minutes. "The *pasuk* says, '*Even mikir titzak*, The stone cries out from the wall.' That stone has a *tachlis*, which is to cry out over what it had witnessed in that crematorium. That stone should be put back in the wall it came out of." On his next trip to Poland one month later, Rav Zimmerman replaced the stone.

COMMENT: *That stone had a task. So, too, every single person has a job to do in this world. No one in history was ever or will ever be given your task. Do the job right.*

"HIS WIFE" (Naso 5:12)

THE families got ready for the Shabbos *sheva berachos seuda*. Mr. Hertz passed the *becher* over to Hershel, his new son-in-law, to make *kiddush* for everyone. "I don't want him to make *kiddush*," his daughter Henna, the *kallah*, said.

"Why not?"

"I just don't."

"Henna," Mr. Hertz said in one of those irritated whispers while keeping a false smile on his face, "please don't make an issue now. *Chasanim* always make *kiddush*."

"I don't want him to."

"Are you worried about his voice?"

"No, he has a nice voice."

"Are you worried he'll mispronounce the words?"

"No, not at all."

"So what *is* it?"

"I don't want him to do it." The baffled Mr. Hertz had someone else make *kiddush*, but he couldn't figure out what Henna's problem was and it bothered him all night. Finally, after the *seuda* ended and just about everyone had left, he asked her again. "I want that the first *kiddush* he makes with us married should be for me alone."

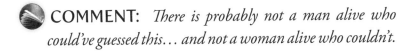 **COMMENT:** *There is probably not a man alive who could've guessed this… and not a woman alive who couldn't.*

"HIS WIFE" (Naso 5:12)

IT had been a great morning *seder*. Ariel and his *chavrusa* hadn't wasted a second, and then Ariel asked two questions in *shiur* that the *rosh kollel* said were truly of a high caliber. Ariel decided to treat himself to a deli sandwich for lunch instead of having the fish being served in the *yeshiva*.

He went down the block to "Gary's Garlic Galaxy" and came out with two thick monstrosities containing slices of meat from just about every kosher beast known to man. He sat down at the table with the *bochurim* in the *yeshiva* and spread out his repast – pickles, ketchup, chips – everything. Ariel, now salivating heavily, was about to get up to wash, as the boys eating the *yeshiva* lunch looked on in envy.

Just then, Ariel's cell phone rang. "Hi, Ariel." It was Ariella, his wife. "I'm in the neighborhood shopping, and I'm going to stop in at "Nice Slice" for some pizza. How about if we have lunch together?"

Groan. It was one of those moments. "Uh, are you *sure* you want pizza?" he asked weakly. The boys at the table noticed what was happening and started smirking. Ariel glared at them.

"Yeah. I've actually ordered mine already. Come quickly, okay?"

He took a deep breath. "Okay. I'm... coming... as... quickly... as... possible." The boys' evil grins got wider. "Take it all, you vultures," Ariel growled as he pushed his treasures towards their outstretched arms.

COMMENT: *Nothing like marriage to stop you from being selfish. And becoming* fleishig.

"AND DISSOLVE THEM INTO THE WATER"
(Naso 5:23)

Chazal *say we see from here how important* shalom bayis *is, because Hashem allows His Name to be erased for the sake of making* shalom *between a husband and wife.*

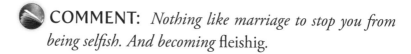

"**N**OW *this* is uncomfortable," Ari thought to himself. He was sitting at the Shabbos table with the Leavits, who had been married for barely a year. The couple was having an argument in front of him. It had started over some trivial remark that the husband, Levi, had made about the gefilte fish being on a salt-free diet. His wife Leora snapped back that only sweet people can taste salt. From there things got progressively worse. They actually started yelling at each other, right there in front of Ari.

After the shouting match, they lapsed into silence, a *very* uncomfortable silence for Ari. It dragged on for what seemed an eternity, with no end in sight. Suddenly, Ari jumped up and, imitating a karate motion, sliced through the air, ending with a long "ahhhh" sound.

"What are you doing?" the fighters asked simultaneously.

"I'm just… cutting the tension," he said with a grin.

COMMENT: *Good grief! Hey, you two, the idea behind inviting guests is that they should be comfortable in your home, remember? Levi and Leora, you should remove any further thoughts of inviting guests until you are sure – and I mean absolutely sure – you've got your act together. And you shouldn't have to be reminded by your guest putting on an act. Good grief!*

"SPEAK TO AHARON AND HIS SONS AND TELL THEM, 'SO SHALL YOU BLESS *BNEI YISRAEL*'" (Naso 6:23)

AS I approached the *shul* for the second *minyan*, I saw a man standing just outside the *shul* door. Knowing that he was a *kohein* and being a *kohein* myself, I realized immediately that the first *minyan* must be doing *bircas kohanim* and that for some reason he couldn't *duchen*. He must have left the *shul* as *halacha* requires.

I asked him what happened. Normally, if a *kohein* leaves for *duchening* it's because he didn't start heading for the front on time because he himself may have finished his *shmoneh esrei* late. In such a case he is required to exit the *shul* until the other *kohanim* finish. Or it could be that he was hoarse, and since he was unable to project his voice he needed to step out.

I was a bit taken aback by his response. "There's someone in there that I hate," he said matter-of-factly. He was referring, of course, to the *halacha* that a *kohein* may not *duchen* if there is anyone in the *shul* whom he hates.

This is not something very common. As a matter of fact, this was the first and only time that I'd ever seen a *kohein* step out for this reason. "Oh." It was the best I could do as an initial response, pretending this was just something one sees every day. "What is it that's causing you to hate him?" I asked, trying to sound casual.

"He owes me money for a job I did for him. I've asked him several times to pay me but he hasn't. So I hate him."

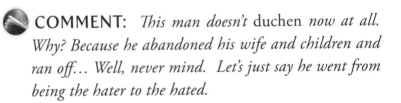 COMMENT: *This man doesn't* duchen *now at all. Why? Because he abandoned his wife and children and ran off… Well, never mind. Let's just say he went from being the hater to the hated.*

BEHA'ALOSCHA

"WE REMEMBER THE FISH THAT WE ATE FOR FREE... AND THE MELONS"
(Beha'aloscha 11:5)

L EV L'Achim is one of the best known outreach organizations. One of their activists was once sitting with a group of fresh-out-of-the-oven *baalei teshuva* in a restaurant. At the end of the meal, watermelon was brought to the table as dessert. One of the *baalei teshuva* reached for a piece, made a loud *shehakol* and started to indulge.

The activist gently corrected him and told him that the correct *beracha* on watermelon is *ha'adama*.

"Well, *I* make *shehakol*."

When the man again told him it was a mistake, he said, "Look, that may technically be so, but I want to tell you something. During the war, my tank division was in the Golan Heights and we were surrounded by Syrian tanks. Alarmed, the commander asked if any of us knew a *tefilla* to say. I mean, we were goners and we knew it. The only religious thing I knew how to say was the *beracha* of *shehakol*. I don't even know why I knew it, but I did. So I started saying it and our gunner knocked out a Syrian tank. The entire division started saying it and we kept knocking out tanks. All you heard was '*shehakol nihiye bidvaro…* BOOM!!!' Over and over. It was *unbelievable!* So my attitude is, if it works for Syrian tanks, it works for watermelon."

COMMENT: *He's wrong, of course. But you gotta admit it is hard to argue with his logic. I wonder if the Syrians answered* amen.

"TO PLACE THE HEAVY BURDEN OF THIS NATION UPON ME" (Beha'aloscha 11:11)

Moshe Rabbeinu was expressing the challenge involved in being the leader and shouldering the responsibility of Klal Yisrael.

THERE was a sudden loud knock at the door. "Who could that be at this hour of the night?" Irene asked. It was ten thirty and Max and Irene Nadel had just started getting ready to go to sleep for the night. "I don't know," Max said, even though he was pretty sure he did. "Who's there?" he asked.

"Open up, Nadel," came a rough voice. "Mr. Carmizzo sent us to, uh, have a word wit' ya'." Max felt his heart in his mouth, but he knew he'd better cooperate and let them in. Two big burly ruffians entered and sat themselves down at the dining room table. "Look, you got twenty four hours to pay up or we're gonna break your legs. No more delays. Da boss is impatient and he wants the money. Got it?"

Max got it, all right. He was in over his head with gamblers and he was in trouble. Real big trouble.

Irene, ever the good wife, decided to see if a little Jewish hospitality might not soften their visitors up a little. "Why don't you fellows have something to eat?" she asked, as if being gracious to thugs in the middle of the night was the most natural thing in the world. So saying, she set down some honey cake and drinks on the table in front of them. She then brought out a plate of herring. "I made it myself," she said with a touch of pride.

"I love herring!" one of the ruffians half-shouted, and he went to work on the goods.

Irene decided to distract them from the unpleasant business at hand by striking up a conversation. Max thought she was out of her mind. "So where are you from?" she asked.

"I'm from New Yawk."

"Me too," said the other, while swallowing his third piece of honey cake.

"And what's your name?" she then asked.

"Tony."

"And I'm Ira," said the herring fiend.

Irene wanted to keep the conversation going as long as possible, but she really didn't know what to talk about to two knee-breakers. "Uh, Ira, what's the hardest job you ever had?"

"The hardest job? Ha! That's easy! The hardest job I ever had was being *president* of my *shul*."

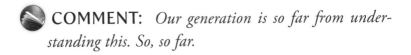

COMMENT: *Taking on communal responsibility is never easy. Yehoshua even suggested that Moshe Rabbeinu saddle Eldad and Meidad with that sort of occupation in order to put a stop to them prophesizing. I guess this gangster found it a bit too much. Or perhaps they didn't have enough herring at the* shul kiddushim.

"THE ATTENDANT OF MOSHE SINCE HIS YOUTH" (Beha'aloscha 11:28)

It was as a result of being Moshe Rabbeinu's disciple that Yehoshua merited becoming the leader after Moshe was niftar.

A BOCHUR once asked a very prominent *rosh yeshiva* for guidance in a certain complex matter. "You have to ask your *rebbe*," he responded.

"But you are my *rebbe*. I've been in your *shiur* for two years."

"Two years!?" he asked incredulously. "Two years!? Two years isn't a *rebbe*. I was in Rav Elya Meir Bloch's *shiur* for *ten* years – do your hear? – *ten years*. That's a *rebbe*!"

COMMENT: *Our generation is so far from understanding this. So, so far.*

"AND THE MAN MOSHE WAS EXCEEDINGLY HUMBLE" (Beha'aloscha 12:3)

THE meeting of the *Moetzes Gedolei HaTorah* had gone on for some time. The issue being dealt with was a tricky one and there were different opinions as to what the proper course of action should be. At a certain point one of the *rabbanim* gave a *klap* on the table, calling for everyone's attention. It was Harav Moshe Feinstein *zt"l*, and giving a *klap* was out of character for him. "Before Rav Aharon [Kotler] *zt"l* was *niftar*, he said that *I'm* to be the *manhig*, and I say this is what we should do. Therefore, that is what we are going to do. The meeting is adjourned."

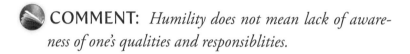 **COMMENT:** *Humility does not mean lack of awareness of one's qualities and responsiblities.*

"AND MOSHE CRIED OUT TO HASHEM"
(Beha'aloscha 12:13)

LIKE many families who have children of marriageable age, the Newmans were totally consumed with the subject of *shidduchim*. From morning till night, the subject was being discussed, phone calls were being made, and tears were being shed. In general, that's what their world revolved around. After a few days of this, six year old Miri came in from playing jump rope and announced that her friend Penini also had a brother in *shidduchim*. "Do you even know what *shidduchim* are?" her mother asked with a laugh.

"Yeah, of course I know. *Shidduchim* is when you *daven* to Hashem that someone should get married."

COMMENT: We're *the ones who don't know what* shidduchim *are. But it's never too late to learn – even from a six year old.*

SHLACH

"THE PEOPLE ARE STRONG" (Shlach 13:28)

This was the beginning of the lashon hara *spoken by the* meraglim.

CONSTANT *divrei Torah* were heard at the Shprechers' table. The *parsha*, interesting *halachic* questions, *vertlach* – the works. And none of it was forced. They were a *Toradik* family with an interest in all Torah topics. They had little interest in mundane topics and conscientiously avoided *lashon hara*. One *leil Shabbos*, at some point, the conversation drifted into the recent community *mazel tovs*. Then, in an almost unheard of occurrence in their home, someone started saying something slightly deprecating about one of those people. Suddenly, there was a loud crash – a picture fell off the wall and the glass shattered. No big deal. It's just that it happened to be a picture of... the Chofetz Chaim.

The conversation went back to Torah.

COMMENT: Siyata d'Shmaya *can come crashing down on us in surprising ways.*

"HOW LONG FOR THIS EVIL CONGREGATION" (Shlach 14:27)

The congregation here is the meraglim, *the spies. From the fact that there were ten of them and they're called an* eida, *a congregation, we learn that a* minyan *is made up of ten men.*

MOSHE Aaron prided himself on the fact that no matter how busy he was and no matter what was going on, he did not miss *minyan.* He was thirty years old and had missed *minyan* only once since the day he became *bar mitzva.* He had only missed a *mincha* on the day of his grandfather's *levaya,* when he hadn't left the cemetery until after *shkia.* Other than that, he had a perfect track record.

Now, he was in an office in central Tel Aviv and there wasn't a *shul* anywhere near. The business meeting had gone on longer than he'd expected, and there was only about a half hour until *shkia.* There were three other men in the office who wanted to *daven,* but no one else around who they could realistically approach to help make a *minyan.*

Moshe Aaron suddenly came up with a sparkling idea. He called six cabs and told the drivers to keep their meters running. "I'll pay you every shekel," he promised them, "just please come and help us make a *minyan.*" They came and *davened* with him, and his streak was left intact.

🔖 **COMMENT:** *We may not all be on the level to do* that, *but there probably* is *room for improvement in getting to* minyan *on time. At least to say some of* pesukei d'zimra.

"IT'S A LAND THAT CONSUMES ITS INHABITANTS" (Shlach 14:32)

"I T might be an aneurism. You'd better get to a hospital quickly." Phil Frank was in a small town in America's heartland on business and hadn't been feeling well. He thought it was just overall fatigue, but the doctor's suspicion sent him into a panic. After two days in the hospital, he only felt worse. He was so weak he could barely move.

At some point, the door of his room opened and a bare-headed man entered. "I'm the Reform rabbi in this town," he began in a reassuring voice. "I know you're Orthodox, but you have nothing to worry about. I know how to say the *viduy*." Phil was *not* reassured.

Two days later the doctors found it was only a nasty virus, and three days later he left the hospital.

🔖 **COMMENT:** *And four days later, he went looking for that rabbi...*

"THEY SHALL MAKE *TZITZIS*" (Shlach 15:38)
The Torah tells us that wearing tzitzis *will serve as a*

reminder that will protect us from the yetzer hara.

AT five feet ten inches tall and five feet ten inches wide, Tommy Rosen looked every bit the special squad helicopter cop that he was. With his head shaven and wearing a pull-over shirt, it was easy to confuse him with a big-time wrestler or a small truck. A slightly bulldoggish look on his face made him… well, let's just say I was more comfortable around him when he was smiling. When the police were on a stakeout, he was one of the guys up in the air tracking the suspect and providing instructions for the cops on the ground.

The reason I knew him was because his brother Sean, now Simcha, had become *frum* and was doing his best to be *mekarev* Tommy. Problem was – and still is – that Tommy's wife Janet is not Jewish and has no interest in Judaism. Tommy wears a *yarmulke, davens* sometimes, learns on the phone with Simcha once in a while and is really interested in *Yiddishkeit.* But not at the expense of his wife and two children. Hopefully, *Hakadosh Baruch Hu* will provide a solution.

Anyway, the local day school in his city somehow found out there was a Jewish helicopter cop on the force, so they invited him in to speak to the kids, figuring it would be a real thrill for them. He walked in dressed in full police gear, helmet and everything, and the kids just stared in awe. He showed them his weapons and then spoke for a few minutes about his bullet-proof vest. Then he slowly unbuttoned his shirt… and pulled out the big woolen *tzitzis* he was wearing. "This is my real protection," he said with a chuckle to the astonished, wide-eyed kids.

COMMENT: *Now there's protection and there's protection. In Tommy's case, we're still waiting for the type of protection that will resolve his intermarriage problem. Hopefully by the time the next book comes out...*

"AND YOU SHALL REMEMBER ALL THE MITZVOS OF HASHEM AND DO THEM"
(Shlach 15:39)

S HALE Zeldon and Brad Rogow, friends since kindergarten, both arrived at Ohr Somayach together. Both were in their third year at Princeton and both were smart. Very smart. They made it clear from the outset that they were there for one semester and then would be heading back to finish their degrees, Shale in engineering and Brad in pre-med. They also made it clear that their interest was an intellectual curiosity. They wished to find out more about their cultural background. They weren't in it for the religious stuff.

Shale maintained a certain aloofness and distanced himself from anything inspirational. He simply wouldn't allow the *ruchniyus* end of *Yiddishkeit* to penetrate. He'd make cynical comments in classes, and he'd roll his eyes whenever Torah values were presented.

Brad, on the other hand, responded differently. Although his mission statement was to remain above any sort of *neshama* stimulation, he really got into things. Whereas Shale related to *davening* as something polite to do in order not to insult his hosts, Brad was enchanted by it. He studied the meanings of the *tefillos* in an English *siddur* and asked many questions about how *tefilla* works. He was also very impressed by the idea of character development through Torah. But more than anything, he was taken by the truth of *gemara* study, unlike Shale who saw it as just another intellectual challenge.

With two weeks left to their trip, Brad decided to stay on for another semester. Shale, convinced Brad had a screw loose, told him repeatedly that he was out of his mind, but to no avail. Shale ended up leaving and Brad stayed.

One of the *rebbeim* in the *yeshiva*, who had seen the two come in and had worked with both, was curious. How was it that two boys, so similar, could have such different attitudes towards *Yiddishkeit*? He called Brad over and asked him frankly if he had an explanation.

"It's funny you should ask," Brad began. "See, I've been wondering about it myself, and there's only one thing I came up with. Look, both of us have parents who are totally secular. Neither of us observed anything at home, except Shale's family lit Shabbos candles and we had a Pesach *seder*. But other than that, nothing. However, my mother's father was *frum,* whereas all of Shale's grandparents were totally secular. When I was little, I'd go to spend the weekend with my grandparents once in a while. My grandfather would take me to *shul* on Shabbos morning, and being little, I enjoyed going under his *tallis* with him. He let me stay there for as long as I wanted. When I arrived at the *yeshiva* and I smelled the *talleisim*, it reminded me of the warm moments in *shul* with a man who I really loved. My grandfather died when I was nine, but somehow doing all this stuff keeps me connected to him. I don't think Shale had the chance to feel that sort of connection. That's the only explanation I have."

 COMMENT: *If only more little boys would end up under their* zaidys' *talleisim.*

"I AM HASHEM YOUR G-D" (Shlach 15:41)

T HE following story appears in my book *The Kiruv Files,* but there is an interesting addition to it which doesn't. The addition took place after publication of the book. Long after.

"What is your goal in life?" That was the question I asked the young man who had come to Ohr Somayach.

"I am a member of the Ohio State marching band," Pierce Polstein told me. "I am the senior tuba player. At halftime of the biggest game of the year, the band stands in formation and spells out the words 'Ohio State.' The senior tuba player is given the singular honor of being the one to dot the 'i' in the word Ohio. My goal is to dot the 'i.'"

Pierce eventually developed more significant goals. Today he goes by the name Pesach, and is "f & f " – *frum* with family.

His original goal, though, left me with an interesting insight. A dot in Hebrew is called a *dagesh,* which literally means "emphasis." Pierce was really speaking for society at large when he said his goal is to dot the "i." The main focus of all unfocused people is to put emphasis on the "I" – i.e., to live for themselves.

One *leil Hoshana Rabbah* I told this story during a talk given to *talmidim* at Ohr Somayach. When I finished and opened the door of the *shiur* room to leave, who do you think was waiting for me to say hello, having come to Israel for Succos? That's right, it was Pesach himself, whom I hadn't seen in… *seventeen years!*

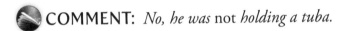 **COMMENT:** *No, he was not holding a tuba.*

KORACH

"AND WHY DO YOU PROMOTE YOURSELVES" (Korach 16:3)

Korach's complaint and subsequent rebellion was brought on by his intense desire for kavod.

THE Lev Simcha of Ger opened the envelope. A quick look disclosed it contained twenty thousand dollars, a nice donation by anyone's standard. He looked up at the wealthy donor and said softly, "*Ah dank,*" his customary declaration of thanks for a donation of any size. The man left.

A few minutes later, the *Rebbe's gabbai* came in. "*Rabbeinu*, the man who gave the large donation a few minutes ago left quite unhappy. He said something to me about not being appreciated. I mean, he was really upset."

As always, the *Rebbe* showed little emotion. "Tell him to come back. Tell him I didn't realize he wanted *kavod*. Tell him to come back, and I'll give him *kavod*." The man declined the *Rebbe's* offer.

COMMENT: *What one man calls appreciation, another calls* kavod *– and the line between the two can be quite subtle. And the latter is usually what it is.*

"YOU'VE TAKEN TOO MUCH FOR YOURSELVES" (Korach 16:3)

Korach was a chacham, *yet his jealousy drove him to take such foolish action.*

E LDAD Eichorn was the prize of the *yeshiva*. Eldad was extremely smart, a big *masmid*, very nice looking and, on top of all that, he had sparkling *middos*. It drove Merori Miller mad with envy. Merori was excellent himself, but it seemed he was always a step behind Eldad. If he asked a good question in *shiur*, Eldad asked a great one. When he did a *chesed* with one of the other *bochurim* he would inevitably hear that Eldad had done something more remarkable. And on and on.

The *yeshiva* announced its annual *chabura* contest, with the winning submission to be printed first in the pamphlet that all the *chaburas* were to be compiled in. The winner would also receive a new *Shas* and *Shulchan Aruch*.

Merori worked hard on his *chabura*, discussing his topic with his *rebbeim* and activating all of his creative energy. When he finished, he knocked on the *rosh yeshiva's* door to submit it. Hearing no answer, he took the liberty of walking in to put it on the desk… and then he saw it. Right in front of his eyes, top one on the pile… was Eldad's *chabura*.

"I know I don't have a chance against *that,*" he realized. Merori didn't even hesitate. He took Eldad's *chabura* from the pile, quickly left the office and deposited it in *geniza.*

Weeks later the *yeshiva* called an assembly and announced the winning entry. Sure enough, it was Merori's. The first one who came over to give him a warm *yasher koach* and *beracha* for continued success was, of course, Eldad.

Every *erev Rosh Hashana* Merori cried. He knew he had wronged Eldad – badly. Perhaps he had even hurt his chances for an excellent *shidduch* as well. Still, he just could not bring himself to apologize.

Some seven years later, after both had married and gone their separate ways, Merori happened to see Eldad on a bus. His heartrate suddenly increased. Eldad came over and gave him a warm handshake. "It's amazing that we should meet today," Eldad began excitedly. "Just yesterday I was reminiscing with Tuvia Teller about our *yeshiva* days, and the topic of you winning the *chabura* contest came up." Merori's heart started pounding. "You know, I had written a *chabura* and put it on the *rosh yeshiva's* desk, but it seems he misplaced it, because it disappeared." Heartbeat like a sledgehammer. "Someone probably inadvertently put it in *geniza.*" Heartbeat up to Indian war dance. "You can't believe what *mazel* that was," Eldad continued. "See, I recently learned that *sugya* again, and I realized that I made a basic mistake in Tosfos when I wrote that *chabura.* If it would've gotten published I would've made a total fool of myself, and then who knows how much it would've hurt me in *shidduchim.* I will be eternally grateful to whoever took that *chabura.*"

No heartbeat at all.

COMMENT: *Merori had tried to advance himself at Eldad's expense and instead caused himself seven years of suffering. A person consumed with envy must strengthen his* bitachon. *It works much better than hiding things in* geniza.

"MOSHE SENT TO CALL DASAN AND AVIRAM" (Korach 16:12)

Rashi points out that Moshe Rabbeinu was trying to avoid the machlokes *by making peace with them.*

SOMEHOW, word got back to the *rosh yeshiva* that two boys in the *yeshiva*, Lazer and Luzer, had had some sort of dispute and were not speaking to each other. Two days later, on the fast of the seventeenth of Tamuz, the *rosh yeshiva* called Lazer over right before *mincha* and went with him down to the lunchroom. He brought over a bowl with a bottle of milk and a box of cereal and told Lazer to start eating. Lazer didn't know what was going on, and he gave the *rosh yeshiva* a quizzical look. "Well, go ahead," the *rosh yeshiva* repeated.

"But, *rebbe*, it's… it's… *shiva asar b'Tamuz*."

"You're right. But you don't care about the cause of the destruction of the *Bais Hamikdash*, so you can eat." Lazer got the message.

The *rosh yeshiva* then repeated the same thing with Luzer. "The entire *yeshiva* is going to wait and not *daven mincha* until the two of you make *shalom*," he said sternly. "And I mean *real shalom*."

They did.

COMMENT: *Aharon Hakohein made* shalom *using all sorts of tricks, and the* mishna *in* Pirkei Avos *says one should strive to be a* talmid *of Aharon. The* rosh yeshiva *was a very good* talmid.

"AND IT SWALLOWED THEM"
(Korach 16:32)

"**O**H, no, I don't have my car here!" Ami had just gotten a Hatzalah call, but he had walked the two blocks to *shul* that morning. He ran over to Ron Reifman. "Ron, quick, I need your car – a Hatzalah call."

"Sorry, I just bought a new Jaguar and I don't want it being sped around town. I'm sure other Hatzalah guys will get there." Ami ran over to two or three other guys but they also hadn't driven to *shul* that morning. By this time, Ron, realizing there were more important things in life than his car, called out to Ami and threw him his keys. Ami raced over to the address, and it turned out he was the only responder. A little girl had swallowed an olive and was choking. She had already started turning blue by the time he arrived, but he managed to dislodge it and save her life. Her name was… Rina Reifman, Ron Reifman's six year old daughter.

COMMENT: *On a recent trip to England I was picked up at the airport by someone driving a Jaguar. It really is a nice car. But it doesn't compare with the obligation to* *save lives. To Ron's credit, he realized his folly and quickly recovered from his fit of temporary insanity. And then later, I'm sure he realized just how insane he was.*

"GIVEN AS A GIFT" (Korach 18:6)

"I'LL put up nine hundred thousand dollars for the first three years of the project." This was the commitment made by Laurence Laufer, otherwise known as "Loud Larry," to Rav Turtzin, a prominent builder of Torah who wanted to start a *kollel* near a large college campus. Rav Turtzin spent close to six months traveling around and making arrangements to get the project going.

He was in the final stages when he got a call from Mr. Laufer to meet him in his office. "I changed my mind about the project," he said. "I'll give you a one time donation of twenty five thousand." So saying, he wrote out a check and slid it across the desk.

"Have you run on hard times?" Rav Turtzin asked.

"No. I've actually had a great few months. I just don't feel like putting money into this *kollel*." He chuckled. "A guy is allowed to change his mind, isn't he?"

Rav Turtzin was not happy. At all. A lot of time and energy had been invested in the project, and now, for no good reason, the backer was pulling out. "I want to tell you something," he said, barely able to contain his anger and frustration. "I was once in Pittsburgh and a man stopped me on the street. 'My son learns in your *yeshiva*,' he began. 'I want to give you this.' He wrote me a check for five dollars. I took it because I'm not allowed to turn down money, no matter what the amount." He fixed Loud Larry with a stern gaze. "I'm taking your money only because I'm not allowed to turn it down. But I want you to know, my time is worth a lot more than what you've given me."

COMMENT: *Hashem works* midda k'neged midda. *When a person changes his mind about giving* tzedaka, *they run the risk of Hashem changing His "mind" about how much money He'll give* him. *On the other hand, if one has decided at first not to give and then does an about face, the same thing could happen in* Shamayim.

"YOU AND YOUR CHILDREN"
(Korach 18:7)

HARAV Shlomo Heiman *zt"l* once came to give a *shiur* and only three *talmidim* showed up. He proceeded to give the *shiur* with the same energy as if there would have been two hundred people there. The young men asked him how he was able to muster up that kind of enthusiasm for just the three of them.

"There weren't just three people there," he explained. "The room was actually packed full. You see, I was giving the *shiur* to you, your children, your grandchildren and your *talmidim*."

COMMENT: *A* melamed *should never underestimate the impact of his efforts. He is teaching — and reaching — future generations in ways he can't imagine.*

CHUKAS

"AND HE SHALL BE *TAMEI*"
(Chukas 19:8)

"**D**ADDY, I'm becoming *tamei* in school." That was *not* what Yonasan wanted to hear. Due to financial pressure, he and his wife Yonina had moved their family to a small town in Canada where they would be involved in *kiruv* work. One of their main concerns was that the local day school was way below par religiously for their sons, who had been in an excellent *cheder* in the large Jewish community they'd come from. So when twelve year old Yisrael said that, Yonasan realized something drastic had to be done – and he did it.

He took his boys out of the school and started teaching them himself, four hours a day. The first session was from ten to twelve in the morning and the second was from three to five in the afternoon. He prepared as if he'd be teaching a regular class of kids. It wasn't easy, because he had a full time job in outreach.

But there was a payoff. His sons told him they never enjoyed learning as much as they did now with him, and that they remember the material much better than ever. And the *kesher* they have with each other is indescribable.

When Yonasan told me about all this, my reaction was, "I would *never* be able to do that."

"I said the same thing," he answered me with a smile, "but it's amazing what a person can do when he absolutely has to."

COMMENT: *"Ein davar omeid bifnei haratzon, Nothing stands in the way of true desire." The trick is to activate the ratzon, and that happens when one realizes the urgency of the situation. Yonasan is a former talmid of mine. In this area, I am a talmid of his.*

"THIS IS THE TORAH – WHEN A MAN DIES IN A TENT" (Chukas 19:14)

Chazal tell us from this pasuk that Torah only takes root in a person who "kills" himself over it.

IT had been a couple of weeks already. Rav Weberman was feeling worn down and tired. He had always been a tremendous *masmid* who pushed himself to the absolute physical limits and he never felt any ill effects, so he didn't think it had anything to do with his exerting himself in his Torah studies. He figured it was a virus which would pass, but when it persisted his wife insisted he go to a doctor.

After doing a thorough examination, the doctor couldn't find a medical cause for the fatigue, so he decided to ask about Rav Weberman's personal habits. "How many hours of sleep do you get?"

"Uh, probably about eight."

"Well, if you're getting eight hours of sleep a night, lack of sleep can be eliminated as the cause of the trouble."

Rav Weberman grinned sheepishly. "I, uh, didn't mean eight hours of sleep a night. I meant about eight hours of sleep a week."

COMMENT: *It's probably a slight exaggeration, as no one could survive on one hour a night. But it is an indication of the importance Rav Weberman attaches to Torah study.*

"THIS IS THE TORAH" (Chukas 19:14)

HARAV Michel Feinstein *zt"l* was a tremendous *gaon* in Torah. His greatness was already apparent when he was a young man, as evidenced by the fact that the Brisker Rav *zt"l* chose him as a son-in-law. With this background information, we can really appreciate the following story.

Shortly after their marriage, Reb Michel's wife came into the room where he was learning to discuss something with him. After hearing what it was about, Reb Michel said, "Can it wait until I'm finished learning?"

"What do you mean by 'finished?'" she asked.

COMMENT: *As the daughter of the Brisker Rav, there are two plausible explanations for her response. The first is that she was genuinely puzzled, because in her father's home there was no such thing as being "finished learning." Perhaps one had an interruption, and maybe even a long one at that. But* finished? What did *that mean? The other possibility is that she was administering a gentle and friendly little dose of* mussar. What I really *suspect is that as the daughter of the Brisker Rav, she was doing both.*

"THIS IS THE TORAH" (Chukas 19:14)

HODGKIN'S lymphoma. When the test results came back confirming their fears, Shmuel and Nechami Muller were devastated. With two children under the age of four and Nechami in her fifth month, they realized their world had just been turned upside down. The doctor told them that the recovery rate was excellent and, as far as he was concerned, it wasn't life threatening and they should be optimistic. But illness is illness. Making matters worse was that Nechami would have to go to the U.S. for treatment, meaning she and her husband would be away from their kids for at least six months. Added to that was the fact that neither of them knew any English, plus the astronomical costs... in short, total chaos.

Before leaving the country, they were brought in to Harav Elyashiv *zt"l* to receive a *beracha*. After telling over the story, but before he could offer the *beracha*, Nechami told Rav Elyashiv's attendant that she wanted him to convey something else to the *rav*. The attendant turned to Rav Elyashiv. "She said it's not the medical matter she wants a *beracha* for. She wants a *beracha* that all this upheaval shouldn't cause her husband *bitul Torah*."

COMMENT: *Nechami responded well to the treatment and gave birth to a healthy baby girl. I have no doubt that Rav Elyashiv's* beracha *helped. And I also have no doubt that Nechami's attitude helped as well.*

As of this writing, they have settled in the U.S., where her husband has become a very successful marbitz *Torah. We have no way of knowing why Hashem does what He does. Still, it is interesting that one of the results of their upheaval is that Shmuel got a position that he would not have gotten at this stage of his life had the couple been in Eretz Yisrael.*

BALAK

"HIS HOUSEFUL OF SILVER AND GOLD"
(Balak 22:18)
Rashi points out that Bilaam desired other people's money.

"WHERE did my wallet go?" Zevvy Zala-znick asked himself in a semi-panic. He was at his daughter Zelda's *chasuna*. He had thousands of dollars in cash in his wallet in order to pay the caterer and the photographer and the band. And now it was gone. Needless to say, he did not enjoy the *simcha* as he should've with this burden on his mind.

A couple of days later at one of the *sheva berachos*, the feature attraction was watching the video of the *chasuna* together. There was one segment that really grabbed everyone's attention. Right before the *chuppa*, a hand could be seen reaching into Zevvy's pocket and lifting out his wallet without him noticing. The man doing it had his face in full view of the camera.

305

Everyone in the room was shocked. It was Zerach Zobel, a well known and upstanding member of the community. He was also… Zevvy's *mechutan*, the father of the *chasan*, Zelig.

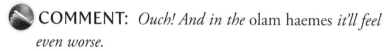 COMMENT: *Ouch! And in the* olam haemes *it'll feel even worse.*

Note: Please ask your rav about whether or not it is permissible to have a video at a chasuna.

"IF BALAK WOULD GIVE ME HIS HOUSEFUL OF SILVER AND GOLD" (Balak 22:18)

MACHLUF Ovadia, a Moroccan entrepreneur, was on a trip to France. While there, an extremely wealthy non-Jewish business acquaintance of his invited him to lunch. "I'll have kosher food for you," he promised. "I'm sure you'll want to be there – *the king of Morocco* is visiting the country *and he'll be dining with me.*"

While sitting at the table, it somehow came up that Machluf's son was having his *bar mitzvah* soon. "What is that exactly?" the king asked. Machluf explained it as best as he could. When he was finished, the king took out his checkbook and wrote out a check for *forty thousand* euros.

"That's… that's very generous, Your Excellency," Machluf stammered. "But… why so much?"

The king smiled a cocky, confident smile. "I'm the *king*," he explained. "To give any less is simply *unacceptable.*"

COMMENT: *On* Rosh Hashana, *we proclaim Hashem is the king. The degree to which we* really *believe it is the degree to which He responds to us. And He can give us much more than forty thousand euros. But it is probably a good idea to put the king of Morocco on your* bar mitzvah *invitation list.*

"HOW CAN I CURSE" (Balak 23:8)

Bilaam knew that without Hashem's approval, his efforts would be an exercise in futility.

THE Klausenberger Rebbe, Harav Yekusiel Yehuda Halberstam *zt"l,* once asked one of his *chassidim* to take care of a certain communal matter. "I'll do my best," the man answered.

"Don't say, 'I'll do my best,'" the *Rebbe* told him. "I'll explain to you why. When I was in the concentration camp, a Nazi once ordered me to pick up a boulder. It was so heavy, it would've taken four men to lift it. I said I couldn't do it. He barked at me to do it immediately. I told him I couldn't. He pulled out a pistol and pointed it at my head." The *Rebbe* paused. "I lifted the boulder. Young man, you don't *know* what your best is. Say 'I *hope* to try my best.'"

 COMMENT: *I hope you hope to try your best to absorb the message of this story.*

"I SAID I WOULD HONOR YOU, BUT HASHEM HAS WITHHELD HONOR FROM YOU" (Balak 24:11)

ABOUT twenty years ago I was driving in Columbus, Ohio and the car radio was on. The interviewer was speaking with Lorenzo Lopez, a nineteen year old local gang member. He somehow managed to convince Lorenzo to share the gang mentality with the listening public. What *was* it that made them tick?

"Ya wanna know why we beat people up? Okay, I'll tell ya. We don' wan' that people should be 'fraid of us an' look at us like we be bad. All we wan' is some respect. So tha's why we do it."

COMMENT: *I get it. They rob people so they shouldn't have to steal. And they take cars so they shouldn't have to sneak onto public transportation vehicles without paying. And they sell drugs so as not to go on welfare. It gives* "shelo sam chelkeinu kahem" *a whole new meaning.*

"IN THE LATER DAYS" (Balak 24:14)

FOR some reason, seventeen year old Shoshana did not like her name. It's an accepted, standard, beautiful name, yet she wanted it changed. Go argue with a teenage girl. Anyhow, the name she wanted was Aviva. Her mother insisted that since she once had a neighbor named Aviva whom she resented, she would not agree to her choice. Her mother suggested Chava. Shoshana, though, had once had a tough teacher named Chava, so for her that name was out.

There was only one way to settle the dispute. They had someone go and ask the Steipler *zt"l* what to do. The Steipler said not to take either name – she should just stick with the one she had. About twenty five years later, the long-married Shoshana's first son got engaged to a girl named… Aviva. And a year later, her second son also got engaged to a girl named… Chava.

COMMENT: *Whether or not you hold by the* tzava'ah *of Rav Yehuda Hachasid saying a boy shouldn't marry someone with his mother's name, this story should give you goosebumps.*

"INDEED THE NATION RISES LIKE A LIONESS" (Balak 24:24)

The Shulchan Aruch *tells us we should rise like a lion in the morning, i.e., one must muster up the strength of a lion to fight the temptation to remain comfortably in bed.*

AT age ninety eight, the leading *posek* of *Klal Yisrael*, Harav Elyashiv *zt"l*, had to undergo a serious surgery. An expert was flown in and *baruch Hashem* the surgery was successful. When Harav Elyashiv returned home after the hospital stay, he decided he must do something to "repay" the *Ribbono shel Olam* for getting him through the surgery successfully.

It's well known that for years the *rav's* schedule had been to go to sleep at ten thirty and then wake up early to learn until *shacharis*. Usually, when someone says he's going to learn before *davening*, he means something like a half hour of *Mishna Berura* or some *mussar*. In Rav Elyashiv's case, however, it meant something completely different. Rav Elyashiv would arise at two thirty (!) and then learn undisturbed until *shacharis*. He decided the best way to show his gratitude would be to devote himself even more intensely to his Torah studies... so he started getting up to learn a half hour earlier!

COMMENT: *Someone once asked Rav Elyashiv* zt"l *how he was able to learn virtually around the clock. "What can I do?" he answered. "There's a commandment of* 'v'hagisa bo yomam valayla.'" *And that was it.*

PINCHOS

"OUR FATHER DIED" (Pinchos 27:3)

ROM Shlevin, a thirty eight year old Israeli mountain climber, lost his grip and took a bad fall. He landed in a six meter deep pit with a badly injured leg. He knew there was no way he could get out and that he'd just have to wait until help arrived. Then he saw something which filled him with terror and doom and the realization that his life was over.

A huge boulder was perched on the edge of a ledge above him and would fall and crush him to death within moments. Rom tore off the back of his matchbox, scribbled on it "I'm under the rock," and managed to throw it up and out of the pit just before the rock killed him. The search party found the note and his body, resulting in his wife being spared the agony of being an *agunah*.

 COMMENT: *The* mussar haskel *is that one should do*

311

as much as one can under all circumstances. Instead of being terrified into inactivity, Rom chose to take action, a small physical *action with huge repercussions.*

"MATZOS SHALL BE EATEN"
(Pinchos 28:17)

THERE is just no place like Israel. So many things happen that make you stop and say, "only in Israel." Anyone who's been here for even a short time has a story. Well, I've been here a long time and the stories keep happening. Here's something you just won't see anywhere else.

The boys from Ohr Somayach were outside burning their *chometz* on *erev Pesach*. Just across the road from the *yeshiva* are the tracks where the Jerusalem light rail train runs. While the boys were busy with their *mitzvah*, a train suddenly stopped and the conductor opened the door and came running over. "Great," he said as he tossed a package into the fire, "I was *looking* for somewhere to burn my *chometz*." And with that, he turned and ran back so that he could resume driving his train.

COMMENT: *The joke of it all is that no one sitting on the stopped train thought there was anything out of the ordinary in this sort of thing.* Ashreinu… *I think.*

"AND IN THE SEVENTH MONTH ON THE FIRST OF THE MONTH" (Pinchos 29:1)

This, of course, is the day we know as Rosh Hashana.

THE time for *maariv* on the second day of Rosh Hashana drew near and I was lying in bed. I had flown to America for a Gateways program, and the combination of jet lag, headache and exhaustion had gotten the better of me. I knew I had to go down to the hotel *shul*, but I was having trouble pulling myself out of my horizontal position. "How am I going to do this?" I asked myself. I had zero energy – or so I thought. Suddenly I heard a frightening noise, one of the most frightening I have ever heard in my life. It was the hotel fire alarm, and I was up on the sixth floor. I can't explain how terrifying it was. No one should ever know. I was up and out of that bed *sooo* fast. I tried not to panic as I flew down the stairs, all the while thinking, "I can't believe this is *really* happening." I arrived in the *shul* fully awake and raring to *daven*. Thankfully, it was a false alarm.

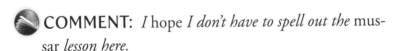 COMMENT: *I hope I don't have to spell out the* mussar *lesson here.*

"IT SHALL BE A DAY OF *TERUAH*"
(Pinchos 29:1)

ONE Rosh Hashana Shmuel noticed his friend Shaul *davening* in his *shul*. After *davening*, he greeted him and asked him what brought him to *daven* there. Shmuel figured it was something to do with where he was eating the *seuda* or something like that. Wrong. Shaul told him he wanted to hear the *baal tokaiah* who blew *shofar* in that *shul*. Now the blower was good, perhaps even excellent, but he certainly wasn't something out of the ordinary. So Shmuel asked him about it.

"It has nothing to do with the quality of the sounds," he explained. "You see, a few weeks ago I happened to see him in *beis din* at a *din Torah* he was having with someone. I don't know if you've ever been in *beis din*, but people's behavior there sometimes leaves something to be desired. Yet this man behaved with unbelievable respect towards the *dayanim* and with total self-control. That's the type of person I want to hear *shofar* from."

COMMENT: *The true test of* middos *is how a person behaves in a stressful situation, and there is very little as stressful as being in* beis din. *I'm impressed by what Shaul used as a criterion to measure the quality of the person.* Teki-ya-ah-ah!

"AND YOU SHALL CELEBRATE A *CHAG*"
(Pinchos 29:12)

The Torah here is referring to the chag *of Succos, known as* zman simchaseinu.

"HASHEM expects us to be on such a high level," Harav Chaim Shmuelevitz *zt"l* said through his tears to those gathered in his *succah*. It was Succos of 1973 – the height of the Yom Kippur war. "On the one hand, there is a Torah command to rejoice. On the other hand, Jewish boys are falling in battle. It's not easy. We have an obligation to fulfill, and we will. But you must understand the control over our emotions that's expected of us."

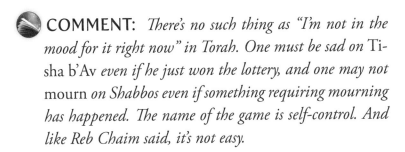 COMMENT: *There's no such thing as "I'm not in the mood for it right now" in Torah. One must be sad on Tisha b'Av even if he just won the lottery, and one may not mourn on Shabbos even if something requiring mourning has happened. The name of the game is self-control. And like Reb Chaim said, it's not easy.*

"ON THE EIGHTH DAY SHALL BE *ATZERES*" (Pinchos 29:35)

THERE was no sign of religion on Kibbutz Ein Chaim. Quite the contrary, they were virulently opposed to anything even remotely Jewish. Pork on Yom Kippur, a barbeque on Tisha b'Av, soft rolls on Pesach… it was all fine.

It was a mystery to the younger members why a handful of the old-timers would sneak off to some unknown location for some unknown reason one day a year. Maybe it was some sort of gambling night which they didn't want anyone else to know about, or perhaps they got together to reminisce about something or other. Any time one of the participants was asked about it he'd say, "It's nothing too important and it's certainly nothing that would interest you. It's just something for a bunch of old guys." For some reason, no one ever made any further attempts to find out what it was all about.

Well, one year, Yigal ben Efess could contain his curiosity no longer, so he decided to follow the group and see what they were up to. He watched from a distance as they headed all the way out to the farthest corner of the kibbutz where all the old rusty equipment lay in disuse and then entered an old abandoned shed. He waited a few minutes and then followed them in. There was a decrepit stone staircase that led downwards and ended in front of a heavily reinforced metal door. He pushed the door open a crack… and saw something that froze him in place and sent shivers up his spine. It was a sight he knew he'd never, ever forget. The men were in a well-lit cellar which they'd equipped with bright lights. But it wasn't the light that he was focused on. The men were holding a *sefer Torah* and dancing round and round with undisguised emotion, most of them with tears rolling down their cheeks. You see, it was Shmini Atzeres night. These men had all been in Europe before the war and had all learned in *cheder*. The *simcha* they had experienced as small children on that special day had never left them, and they relived it once a year in a clandestine cellar on an anti-religious kibbutz.

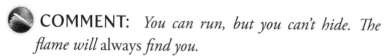 **COMMENT:** *You can run, but you can't hide. The flame will always find you.*

MATOS

"LIKE ALL THAT COMES OUT OF HIS MOUTH HE SHALL DO"
(Matos 30:3)

HOARSE for weeks, black-hatted Rav Nachshon Naiman decided to go to voice therapy. The knitted-*kippa* clad therapist gave him some exercises to do and told him to come back a week later. When he returned, the therapist asked if there was any improvement. "Not really," Nachshon answered.

"Well, have you been doing the exercises religiously?" asked the therapist.

"Uh, Modern Orthodox," Nachshon said with a grin.

COMMENT: *Nachshon was the one who was hoarse, but it was the therapist who suddenly didn't have what to say.*

"AND BILAAM BEN BE'OR THEY KILLED"
(Matos 31:8)

DURING a conversation with one of the boys at Ohr Somayach, the subject of Chicago, my hometown, came up. Hal Haller happened to overhear us. "I had a horrible experience in Chicago and almost killed someone," Hal interjected. Now, you must know something about Hal. Hal was the two-time U.S. judo champion, built like a slim rhinoceros and just as strong.

Of course, being a rabbi I had to show indifference, but I was bursting to hear his story. "What happened?" said I in my most disinterested voice.

"I was visiting a friend of mine. In the middle of the night, a member of a certain ethnic group broke into the apartment. He was high on methadone, and he had a screwdriver with him. I confronted him, and he stabbed me a number of times. There was lots of blood. I was able to disarm him and render him unconscious." Hal gave me a very grave look. "Rabbi, I want to tell you – I had a serious *nisayon*. I wanted to kill the guy! My adrenaline was pumped and this guy had just tried to kill *me*. It was really a test. I stood over him for a few moments struggling with the decision. My rational mind took over, and I passed the test. We called the cops and they hauled him away. Great city, Chicago."

 COMMENT: *No one can imagine the tests* baalei teshuva *have been through. Personally, I still like Chicago.*

You just have to avoid the wrong people, that's all. By the way, what's methadone?

"THEY TOOK AS SPOILS" (Matos 31:9)

WOLF Wolitzky is the owner of a kosher grocery store. One of the popular attractions is the huge selection of candy sold by weight in open displays. There was one man who would come in regularly. As he filled his bag, he'd make a *shehakol* and pop sweets into his mouth. When his generosity with himself became excessive, Wolf approached him and asked him to stop. One or two to sample was standard, but to treat oneself without limit was not.

The next time he was in the shop, the man did it again. Again, Wolf told him to please *not* help himself. Still, the man continued in his ways. Wolf didn't want to make an issue out of it, so he just looked the other way.

A few months later, Wolf was sitting in his office and glanced at the camera that gave him a view of the store. A young girl was taking candy and putting it into her pockets, glancing around furtively to make sure no one saw. Wolf raced upstairs and confronted the girl. He told her to come into his office and he called her father, who drove down to the shop. As soon as he heard what happened, he approached his daughter with clear intent to slap her.

Wolf grabbed him before he did so and pulled him into the next room. "If you slap her, I'll slap you!" he barked at the father. Sure enough, her father was the man who had been helping himself, against the express wishes of the exasperated Wolf. His daughter was simply following his example.

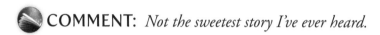 **COMMENT:** *Not the sweetest story I've ever heard.*

"AND YOU WILL RUIN ALL THESE PEOPLE"
(Matos 32:15)

A FRUSTRATED young man blamed his father's rigidness for his disinterest in *Yiddishkeit*. He met with a well known *rav* who was an expert in these matters. After hearing out the son, the *rav* arranged for a meeting with the father. It didn't take him long to see that the son was right in his various complaints. The father was indeed a rigid and somewhat irrational person.

One of the things that came out in the conversation gives us all some food for thought. The father lamented that his son almost never did as he was told. He therefore adopted a policy of *commanding* his son, thereby activating the obligation of the Torah command of obeying one's father. The *rav* realized that any effort on his part to reason with the father would be an exercise in futility, so he arranged a meeting with the Steipler *zt"l*, whom he was close with.

When the Steipler heard the story, his face assumed a horrified look. The frightened father asked the great man what was wrong. "When your son disobeys you," the Steipler said, "you can wipe out all his *aveiros* by simply saying that you forgive him. But when you give your son a command…" the Steipler paused. "When you give your son a command, you are transgressing the Torah command of not putting a stumbling block in front of a blind person, because you know he won't obey you." He paused again, and then in a voice choked with emotion said, "That's an *aveira* which you transgressed *dozens* of times. *No one* can forgive you for that."

 COMMENT: *It takes a lot of strength not to act in a strong manner.*

"OUR CHILDREN" (Matos 32:17)

SOMEONE once asked Rebbetzin Kopshitz, the mother-in-law of Harav Nissim Karelitz, how she was *zocheh* to have sons and sons-in-law who are all such big *talmidei chachamim*. "I wanted it," was her simple answer.

"But a lot of people want it," the asker persisted.

"True. But that's *all* I wanted," said the *rebbetzin* softly.

 COMMENT: *Do we want, or are we wanting?*

"OUR CHILDREN" (Matos 32:17)

HERE'S another one. Someone, maybe the same person as in the previous story, asked Rav Nissim Karelitz's wife how her parents were *zocheh* to such sons and sons-in-law. "Any time one of my brothers was unable to attend *cheder*," she answered, "my father fasted the entire day."

 **COMMENT:** *Not too complicated.*

MASEI

"AND THEY CAMPED" (Masei 33:5)

AT the end of his routine, a famous comedian would thank his audience and then finish by saying, "Good night, Mrs. Calabash, wherever you are." No one knew who this Mrs. Calabash was and why he always mentioned her. He was asked repeatedly to reveal the secret but never did. He would offer various explanations, but everyone knew he was joking around.

After he died as a very old man, someone investigated in order to find out who this mysterious Mrs. Calabash was. What he discovered is a powerful lesson for all of us. When this comedian was first breaking into show business, he was broke. There was an older lady named Mrs. Calabash who was his landlord, and she let him stay in his apartment even when he couldn't afford to pay the rent. It was out of a feeling of gratitude, even after so many years had passed, that he mentioned her at the end of each performance.

COMMENT: *There is no statute of limitations on hakaras hatov. We must show our gratitude for the good we receive from others, and we must do so for a long time. Although we know that from the Torah, thanks for the reminder, Mister Comedian.*

"YOU SHALL DRIVE OUT ALL THE INHABITANTS OF THE LAND" (Masei 33:52)

One of the ideas behind this command is that Bnei Yisrael *should not be influenced by their corrupt and evil ways.*

THERE are over seven billion people on the planet, so some of them are bound to be a little, uh, different. With that introduction, you should have no problem believing the following. There is a kid in Brazil who is known as the "magnet kid." For some reason, which even doctors are baffled by, his body has a magnetic field which allows metal to stick to him. His father has capitalized on this amazing talent by taking him around the world and using him as an attraction. He is put on public display, and all the onlookers may then – after paying, of course – put various metal objects against his body and gasp in wonder when they don't fall off. Pots, hammers, and anything else metallic that is placed against him stays attached due to the magnetic force in his body. Now isn't that worth paying to see?

COMMENT: *Although circus geeks are out of our realm of interest, we can gain an important insight from this kid. The reality of life is that stuff "sticks" to us. Whatever we're exposed to leaves an impression. A Torah Jew must do all in his power to avoid exposure to these influences, because at the end of the day we all have a "magnetic field" inside us – even if we don't speak Portuguese.*

"ACCORDING TO ITS BORDERS"
(Masei 34:2)

THE train was doing its ride around the zoo on an elevated track that allowed the visitors to see down into the cages of the various animals. As they circled past the creatures in their enclosures, twenty eight year old Hector Jamalo suddenly stood up in his seat and jumped out of the moving train over the sixteen foot reinforced fence surrounding Terry, the Bengal tiger.

Terry was not happy about having his space invaded and spent the next ten minutes doing things to Hector that took up almost a paragraph of newspaper print to describe. Just about every part of Hector's body suffered serious injury. The zoo people managed to get him out of there alive somehow, remarkably enough.

When he was able to speak, the authorities asked him *what* he was thinking. "I wanted to experience the essence of tiger," was his rational explanation.

COMMENT: *If a human being is capable of getting to a stage where he wants to jump a wall to get to a tiger – which most would agree is not that tempting – we can* *gain an insight into why* Chazal *felt we need barriers and fences to keep us away from various temptations, all of which* are *more enjoyable than "essence of tiger."*

"WHEN YOU COME TO THE LAND CANAAN" (Masei 34:2)

HERE'S one that has to be an entry for the top-ten list of "only in Israel" stories. A woman in Tel Aviv parked her car and went shopping. When she came back, she found her car was gone. In the place where her car had been, there was now a handicapped parking marking. Turned out city workers had painted the designation around her car and then had her car towed away. She was also informed that she was being fined 1350 shekels for her violation. Livid, the woman spoke to one of the security people in the area who mentioned to her that the area was teeming with security cameras. Sure enough, the entire fiasco was on film. At last report, the woman was consulting an attorney.

COMMENT: *You're probably thinking that this reminds you of some of those* midrashim *regarding* Sedom. *Well, not quite. That would apply if the city sues her for causing the city workers unnecessary labor.*

"THE MANSLAYER SHALL FLEE THERE" (Masei 35:11)

The mishna *states that one who has gone to the cities of refuge does not leave for the sake of giving testimony.*

THE *chuppa* was about to begin. The *chasan* and *kallah* were in place, the parents were standing alongside them, and the most important person of all – the photographer – finally had the angle he wanted. The *rav* who was *mesader kiddushin* turned to the *aidim*, the witnesses, and said, "Let me see your cell phones, please." Each one of the two took an i-phone out of his pocket. The *rav* shook his head and said, "I'm sorry, all the *gedolei Yisrael* have *assured* those things. You're *possul* to be *aidim*." And he wouldn't begin the ceremony until two kosher *aidim* were chosen as replacements.

COMMENT: *I heard this story took place in two different locations. One has been fully confirmed.*

"TO GIVE THE PORTION OF TZELOFCHOD OUR BROTHER TO HIS DAUGHTERS" (Masei 36:2)

Chazal *tell us Tzelofchod's sin was Shabbos desecration.*

AIRLINE pilot Mickey Michaelson and his family became *baalei teshuva*. Due to his new Shabbos observance, the company changed his regular route. It was such an insignificant thing to Mickey that he never bothered telling his wife about it. What *was* significant was that his original flight was… number 193, one of those that crashed on 9/11. His former co-pilot and crew were all killed. His wife thought he had perished as well, until she received the call from him that he was alive and well.

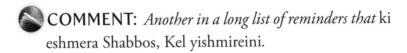 **COMMENT:** *Another in a long list of reminders that* ki eshmera Shabbos, Kel yishmireini.

DEVARIM

DEVARIM

"AND YOU SHALL
JUDGE RIGHTEOUSLY"
(Devarim 1:16)

"**S**O I told Tamar I couldn't come over," Tali was saying to Tobi when she was interrupted by the girl sitting behind them on the bus.

"Why couldn't you go over there?" the stranger asked. Tali had no idea what this girl wanted.

"Well, I had to help my mother that day," she said with annoyance, and then turned back to continue speaking to Tobi. "Last Wednesday we went to the zoo…"

Again the girl interrupted. "I love the zoo, especially the birds. I think the eagles are really something, don't you?"

"I'm actually a fan of the llamas," Tobi responded in an irritated tone.

This repeated itself several times. The girls would talk, and then every couple of minutes this girl would cut in.

After about fifteen minutes, she spoke once again. "I'm sorry about what I did. You see, the guy in the seat behind me kept trying to start a conversation with me, which is obviously inappropriate. So I interrupted you to make it look like we were speaking together. I hope you're *moichel* me."

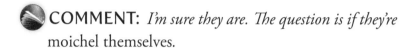 COMMENT: *I'm sure they are. The question is if they're* moichel *themselves.*

"FOOD" (Devarim 2:6)

THERE was a very impressive spread laid out for the guests by the three day Rosh Hashana program hosted by the Gateways organization. There was a sign by the pizza table that said, "YOU DON'T HAVE TO WASH." One of the African-American workers, new to the job, asked one of the African-American veterans what it means that they don't have to wash. "When they eat bray'id they hafta wash, but this isn't bray'id so they put up that sign. But the joke is," she added with a chuckle, "if they eat enough of this they have to wash *anyhow*. Um, hum."

COMMENT: *Ever stayed in a hotel? We certainly do eat enough of it. Um, hum.*

"AND WE TOOK" (Devarim 3:8)

MONEY in a Baptist church in Arkansas kept disappearing. The plate was passed around on a regular basis, but it seemed that some of the attendees were taking rather than giving. The heads of the church spoke to a consultant in Baltimore. He suggested putting large screen videos all over the walls. They immediately implemented his suggestion. The next month there was a surplus of $5000.

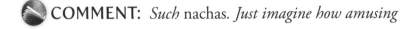 **COMMENT:** *None of our* shuls *ever need these cameras because we know we're being watched. The trick is not to need them in our homes.*

"YOU MUST GUARD YOUR HEALTH VIGILANTLY" (Devarim 4:15)

EVERYONE knows that cigarette smoking is not good for one's health. That did not deter Maygar Punzeej of Indonesia, who was in the habit of smoking two packs a day, a total of forty cigarettes. Now, there are millions of others in the world who do the same, so what's the big deal, right? What made Maygar unique was that he was... two years old! That's right – two years old. And the joke of it all was that his parents didn't see anything wrong with it. "He used to scream a lot until we found that cigarettes calmed him down," explained his father matter of factly. "Now he screams when he *doesn't* get them," he added with a chuckle.

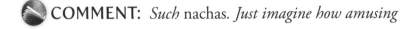 **COMMENT:** *Such* nachas. *Just imagine how amusing*

it would be if Maygar screamed because he wasn't allowed to play with a Kalashnikov assault rifle. On a more serious note, there are things we shouldn't be allowing our children, and they are far more dangerous to their ruchniyus *than cigarettes.*

VAESCHANAN

"I AM HASHEM YOUR G-D"
(Vaeschanan 5:6)

Included in this command is that we believe Hashem can do anything at any time. He has absolutely no limitations of any kind.

THERE is an elderly Jew, a survivor of the concentration camps, who says *kaddish* to this day. His niece once asked him who it is that he's saying *kaddish* for. "When I was in the camps," he explained, "I used to walk around saying *kaddish*. The words declaring that 'Hashem created the world as He saw fit' filled me with the hope that He could get us out of the camps, too. There were other prisoners in my barracks who kept laughing at me. 'If He's so powerful, why doesn't He help us?' they chided me.

"One day there was a round-up and the prisoners were led off to the gas chambers. As the line inched closer, the men ahead of me kept turning around and saying, 'So where's your G-d *now*, huh?' They entered the chambers, and I was to follow next. A Nazi guard dropped something and I bent down to pick it up for him. Just as I did, the gas chambers door closed. As it closed, the men inside shouted from the depths of their *neshamos*, 'SAY *KADDISH* FOR US!! SAY *KADDISH* FOR US!!' I managed to survive the war and since then I've been saying *kaddish* for those *kedoshim*."

🏔️ **COMMENT:** Bitachon *does not mean that things will turn out the way we want. On the other hand, we must always remember that no matter how bleak the situation, things* can *turn out the way we want.*

"AND YOU SHALL LOVE HASHEM YOUR G-D" (Vaeschanan 6:5)

The gemara *(Yuma 86a) says that this* pasuk *teaches that one should behave in a way which causes Hashem's Name to become beloved among people. People should see his actions and react by saying, "How fortunate is one who has studied Torah."*

EVERY morning, dozens of buses leave the various neighborhoods of Yerushalayim, packed with *kollel* men on their way to study at the illustrious Mir *yeshiva*. The same thing is repeated in the afternoon and evening, both on the way to the *yeshiva* and on the way home. One day, one of the buses was pulled over by a cop. Apparently, the driver had inadvertently crossed a white line which he shouldn't have, something very minor. The cop gave him a ticket anyway. The officer was really nitpicking.

The driver got back on the bus and was not in a very good mood. "Two hundred and fifty shekels for *what*?" he asked no one in particular. "*That* guy was in a bad mood so *I* have to lose money for something so silly!? *He* had a fight with his wife so *I* have to suffer!?" He carried on grumbling to himself for a couple of minutes.

Little did he know that Mutty Shafer, one of the *avreichim* on the bus, would grab the opportunity to make Hashem's Name beloved to this secular bus driver. Mutty left his seat and went up and down the aisle of the bus, asking the other *avreichim* for five shekels each so that they could pay the driver's ticket. Every single one of them participated. There were about fifty *avreichim* on the bus so it worked out nicely. When Mutty presented the money to the bus driver, he was stunned speechless… but the tears in his eyes showed clearly what he was thinking.

 COMMENT: *One doesn't have to wait for an unreasonable cop to come along in order to do something like this. There are countless opportunities every day.*

"AND YOU SHALL TEACH THEM WELL TO YOUR CHILDREN" (Vaeschanan 6:7)

This pasuk *is the source of the* mitzvah *for a father to teach his sons Torah.*

IT is well known that Harav Chaim Kanievsky is fluent in *Shas* and that he makes a *siyum* on all of it each year. I recently heard that Rav Chaim has also learned the entire *Shas* with each one of his sons. That in and of itself is enough to impress us big time (or *depress* us big time). What stopped me in my tracks was the fact that this was done before each one's *bar mitzvah*! And the *seder* when they learned it was in the morning before *shacharis*!!

COMMENT: *To teach it, you have to know it. And you also have to have sons who are willing to sit for the amount of time needed to do all that learning. And they have to be willing to get up before* shacharis. *And the person doing the teaching has to be willing to get up before* shacharis. *We all know all the excuses and reasons why we are excused. But maybe we should take steps to make it a little more relevant. At least a little.*

"ON THE DOORPOSTS OF YOUR HOME"
(Vaeschanan 6:9)

ALTHOUGH "anti" in almost every way imaginable, there was one religious "superstition" that Avital had absorbed from her grandparents. That was that there should be a *mezuzah* on the front door, and that if things are going wrong in the home you have to check it.

Her husband had fallen off the ladder in their Tel Aviv home and broken an elbow two weeks earlier, and her daughter had lost her job at the accounting firm that week.

Avital herself was involved in a collision and ended up with slight whiplash two days previously, and then today she got a bad cut when making salad for the family's dinner. As much as it went against everything she stood for, she called her friend Chagit to find out who does *mezuzah* checking.

Avital took their *mezuzah* and went to the little *safrus* shop at the address that Chagit had given her. The *sofer* opened up the case, took one look at the parchment and shook his head. "Uh uh," he said. "It's pointless to even begin checking or fixing this. This is totally *possul* all the way and has been so for some time."

Avital groaned. Then she was quiet for a few moments, clearly making some sort of calculation. "Do you know how long it's been *possul* for?" she asked.

"Oh, I don't know. Probably about four or five years."

"Well, that explains it then," she said in an exasperated tone of voice. "That explains what happened to us. See, about five years ago, our son – against our strongest protests – went ahead and became a *baal teshuva*. We couldn't understand what we did to deserve that. Now I know. We didn't have any protection, because our *mezuzah* was *possul*."

 COMMENT: *It could also be that if the* mezuzah *was* kosher *they'd* all *have become* baalei teshuva. *But I wouldn't tell that to Avital.*

"DO NOT INTERMARRY WITH THEM" (Vaeschanan 7:3)
This pasuk *is talking about the prohibition for Jews to marry non-Jews.*

"CAN I ask you a question about *amira le'akum* (instructing a non-Jew to do *melacha* on Shabbos)?" Tzvi asked me one day in the middle of the afternoon *seder*. Tzvi was a very studious young man. All I really knew about him was that he had attended a very fine *yeshiva* before.

"Is it important right now?" I asked him.

"Well, uh, yeah, it actually is. You see, I'm going to be going home soon for the summer break, and I need to know these laws well."

"Why?" I asked. I figured he was going to be getting a job at a hotel or something like that and he'd be working with non-Jews. Being that Tzvi was a day school kid, I wasn't ready for his next line.

"My dad is not Jewish and I'm going to be spending a lot of time at home, so I have to know what I can ask him to do for me on Shabbos."

After getting over my initial shock, which was magnified by the fact that Tzvi was such a well adjusted kid, I asked him what it was like growing up in that kind of situation and how his mother handles living such a contradiction. He said he never noticed anything different about his life than any of his friends. He then went on to describe how his mother and father have a great marriage, and how his mother was sure to send him and his brothers to day school. They keep kosher, have regular Shabbos meals together, and other than the fact that his father is not one of the tribe, everything is just hunky-dory.

 **COMMENT:** *No, it isn't.*

EIKEV

"THAT YOU HEAR"
(Eikev 7:12)

I ONCE spoke to a group of *rebbeim* in a prominent *cheder* about educational techniques. One of the things I mentioned was the benefit of adding stories to drive home the impact of a lesson. After the talk, one of the *rebbeim* told me that on the last day of the previous school year, he had asked the boys to repeat to him the stories he had told them over the course of the entire year. "They went on for *quite* a while," he told me excitedly. "I mean, I doubt if they'd have gone on that long had I asked them to repeat the *lessons* they learned during the year."

COMMENT: *I don't doubt it. Stories can be very powerful and have always been used to transmit Torah values from one generation to the next. What I'm trying to say is… please buy a copy of this book for a friend.*

"FORTY DAYS AND FORTY NIGHTS" (Eikev 9:11)

During those forty days and nights, Moshe Rabbeinu learned the entire Torah, both written and oral.

I HEARD the following from a *rosh yeshiva*, a giant *talmid chacham*, who told it over publicly in the name of another giant *talmid chacham*.

Reb Chaim Brisker is known to have been an otherworldly genius whose approach to learning has become the standard used in the *yeshiva* world. Reb Chaim is reported to have said, "The great Rebbe Akiva Eiger *zt"l* had thirteen different ways to learn *Shas*. I was *zocheh* to *one* of them."

 COMMENT: *This should help broaden our perspective on how big the Torah really is.*

"THE TRIBE OF LEVI" (Eikev 10:8)

One of the primary tasks of shevet Levi was to teach Torah to the rest of Klal Yisrael.

HARAV Aharon Kotler *zt"l* was in the hospital during his final illness. The head doctor, a non-Jew, asked Reb Aharon's son Reb Shneur *zt"l* why his father was receiving so many phone calls inquiring about his well-being. Reb Shneur explained that his father was the head of a *yeshiva*. "What is that?" asked the doctor.

"It's a place where young men study to become rabbis," answered Reb Shneur, figuring that was the extent of the doctor's capability of understanding what a *yeshiva* is.

Reb Aharon mustered up the little energy he had and called to his son, "Tell him it's for Torah *lishma*! Tell him it's for Torah *lishma*!"

COMMENT: *The most difficult concept for people outside the Torah world to grasp is study with no targeted goal in mind – that the study is a goal in and of itself. Reb Aharon zt"l is recognized as the one who planted the idea in the American Jewish mindset, an idea that has now spread to thousands. It was so much a part of him that it had to be explained, even to a* goy.

"THE WATERS" (Eikev 11:4)

AN eccentric multi-millionaire was an avid collector of exotic creatures. Snakes and other reptiles made up a significant part of his collection, with squids, sharks and other aquatic creatures also strongly represented. He once made a party on his ostentatious estate, attended by many of his fancy friends. After having a few drinks too many, he announced in a boisterous tone that anyone who would successfully swim across the shark pool could ask for whatever he wants. There was a loud splash, and one of the guests swam through to the other side, receiving a loud and enthusiastic round of applause from the thrilled onlookers.

"So what would you like?" the host asked in a generous voice.

"I'd like to know... *who pushed me in!*" thundered the survivor.

COMMENT: *Torah is compared to water. The* yetzer hara *makes it difficult to jump in, making it seem as if the water is infested with sharks. When we take the plunge, we find it isn't so.* Daf yomi, *anyone?*

"AND IT WILL BE IF YOU OBEY THESE COMMANDS" (Eikev 11:13)

All the rewards of the Torah come when we carry out the instructions given to us by the Ribbono shel Olam.

THE masked man entered the bank, pointed his gun at the teller and told him to fill his bag with cash. The reaction was much more powerful than the robber expected. Jud Reagan immediately sprang over the counter and tried to apprehend the shocked would-be robber. The robber, Cedric Wilkins, turned and ran. Jud, a former high school line-backer, chased him for a couple of blocks and finally tackled Cedric from behind. The incident made the evening news and Jud got his "fifteen minutes of fame."

The next day he was summoned into the bank president's office. Jud didn't know if he was going to receive a cash reward or words of appreciation.

"Mr. Reagan," the president began in a stern voice, "there are clear instructions for what to do in the event of a hold-up. Every employee of the bank knows them. The teller is meant to immediately comply with the demands of the robber and hand over as much cash as he asks for. We do not want any type of heroics because such behavior can bring about injury or death to customers or employees The bank would suffer from it. You did not follow instructions, and I therefore regretfully must inform you that you are no longer employed at our bank."

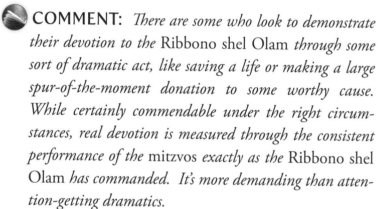 COMMENT: *There are some who look to demonstrate their devotion to the* Ribbono shel Olam *through some sort of dramatic act, like saving a life or making a large spur-of-the-moment donation to some worthy cause. While certainly commendable under the right circumstances, real devotion is measured through the consistent performance of the* mitzvos *exactly as the* Ribbono shel Olam *has commanded. It's more demanding than attention-getting dramatics.*

RE'EIH

"DO NOT DO AS ALL THAT WE DO HERE TODAY" (Re'eih 12:8)

The Torah here is putting a limitation on the usage of bamos, *private altars used for sacrifices. Once the* Bais Hamikdash *was built they would no longer be acceptable. All sacrifices had to be brought only in the B*ais Hamikdash.

HARAV Shimshon Pincus *zt"l* was once asked an intriguing, though not uncommon, question. "What would you do," began a rabbi friend of his, "if you found out that your mother's mother wasn't Jewish and that therefore neither are you?" The asker was anticipating any one of the standard answers normally given to this question: "I'd have a cheeseburger to find out what it's like." "I'd go out and have a good time for a week." "I'd attend a Saturday afternoon concert while eating a pepperoni pizza." The usual.

Yet Rav Pincus's answer was nothing like any of the

above. "What would I do? I'll tell you *exactly* what I'd do. I'd build a *bama* and offer a sacrifice, something which is only permitted nowadays for non-Jews. After serving Hashem in the best way possible as a non-Jew, I'd convert back to Judaism."

COMMENT: *Rav Pincus's attitude should push us to do a little introspection. How much do we appreciate the privilege of being chosen to serve the* Ribbono shel Olam *at the highest level?*

"AND KEEP HIS COMMANDMENTS"
(Re'eih 13:5)

WHILE attending a Catholic nursing school, Gail Greenberg made the acquaintance of a few of the nuns who taught there. They asked her questions about Judaism and various Jewish rituals. Gail decided to answer them through a live demonstration, so she invited three of them to her home for a Shabbos meal.

They were impressed by the *mezuzah* they noticed on the front doorpost as they walked in and then immediately caught sight of the candelabra with the Shabbos candles burning. They looked on with awe when her husband Gordon made *kiddush* with a shiny silver *becher*, and they listened with interest as he explained what the various *sefarim* on the shelves were about. Of course, they couldn't help but ask about the knitted *kippas* the boys were wearing, and the *shofar* on the shelf was a topic of conversation for a while, too.

As they got up to leave after the eye-opening evening, Sister Angela said in a voice full of respect, "This is truly a holy home."

COMMENT: *We really do have "holy homes." Let's try to keep them that way, a mission which is becoming progressively more difficult as technology advances and makes more and more impurity available.*

Note: One should speak with a halachic *authority before extending such an invitation. I am only reporting the reaction, as it was told to me, for the sake of the lesson learned.*

"AND THE *CHAZIR*" (Re'eih 14:8)

"YOU are a very lucky young lady," Dr. Musgrave said. Shelly Feivelson, a secular young lady, was sitting across the desk from her surgeon. Just a week earlier, her life had been in danger and she had undergone very delicate brain surgery to alleviate a problem brought on by parasites in the brain. All had gone well, and she had just finished the follow up examination. "There is one thing I'm curious about, though," the surgeon continued. "Please forgive me for asking, but you're Jewish, aren't you?"

"Yes, I am," Shelly said proudly, a little surprised and very curious about the doctor's intrusion into her private life. "Why do you ask?"

"Well, you see, the type of parasites that attacked your brain are usually brought on by consumption of pork. Not always, but in most cases. Now, I know that Jews are forbidden to eat pork, so I was wondering how it was that you ended up in this situation."

Pork was indeed something Shelly ate on a regular basis. Not anymore, though. Today, inspired by the surgeon's unintended *mussar schmooze*, she is fully *shomer Torah u'mitzvos*.

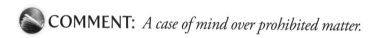 **COMMENT:** *A case of mind over prohibited matter.*

"DO NOT HARDEN YOUR HEART AND DO NOT CLOSE YOUR HAND TO YOUR BROTHER THE PAUPER" (Re'eih 15:7)

SUCH a beautiful *kiddush*! The Rosens had a new granddaughter and the entire *shul* had gathered in their spacious backyard to celebrate with them after *davening*. Cholent, roast beef, *kugels*, cake – how anyone could go home and have room for a *seuda* was a mystery.

Rav Drobkin, the rabbi of the *shul*, cared very much about his *kehilla* and never hesitated to correct mistakes the people might be making. His manner was very honest and direct and he never beat around the bush, one of the reasons most of his congregants loved him. It's also the reason a few resented him. Someone who talked in *shul* during *davening* would get a call after Shabbos informing him that his behavior was unacceptable. If the *rebbetzin* noticed a woman whose mode of dress was not up to par, she would tell her husband and the guilty party would also be informed in no uncertain terms that better was expected of them. Even habitual latecomers would receive a reminder about what time *davening* starts.

Rav Drobkin gave Mel Rosen a warm *mazel tov*, but then quickly moved on to what he felt was a more important topic. "Mel, I saw a sign on your front door that says 'NO SOLICITORS.' Tell me, did you buy that sign in Sedom?"

Mel was momentarily taken aback by the rabbi's bluntness. "Uh, you know, I just don't like being disrupted so often. I can't get anything done at home without a knock at the door every few minutes. It's not the money. I have plenty. It's just the constant bother."

"So why don't you just take the *mezuzos* off your door? That'll stop *frum* collectors from bothering you."

"Rabbi, you know I can't do that. Having *mezuzos* up is a *mitzvah d'Oraisa*."

"So is responding to requests at your door, Mel. Please remove the sign."

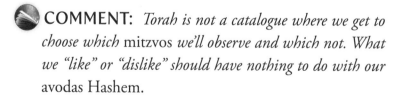 COMMENT: *Torah is not a catalogue where we get to choose which* mitzvos *we'll observe and which not. What we "like" or "dislike" should have nothing to do with our* avodas Hashem.

"YOU MUST OPEN YOUR HAND TO HIM" (Re'eih 15:8)

Chazal *say that the* tzedaka *one gives throughout the*

course of a lifetime adds up, one coin and then another. It's comparable to a suit of armor made up of metal scales which protects the one who wears it.

YEARS ago, the board of directors of the New York Times had a meeting to decide on the font they were going to use for the paper. After much deliberation they settled on a style which does not require dotting the "i." Why? Because they realized that due to the volume of sales, some eight million papers daily, the ink saved by not dotting the "i"s would add up. To how much, you ask? I hope you're sitting. Over the course of ten years, the paper would save *millions* of dollars' worth of ink! Just by not putting dots on the "i"s!

COMMENT: *Now* that's *news worthy to print – and a reminder that we should keep on giving.*

SHOFTIM

"AND THEY SHALL JUDGE THE PEOPLE WITH PROPER JUDGMENT" (Shoftim 16:18)

A SUSPENDED license, several previous arrests for drunken driving and a generally reckless approach to life made Arthur Carver a disaster waiting to happen. When he lost control of his car while speeding and crashed into a flea market tent, it was no real surprise. It was clear, though, that he needed to be put in jail for a good long time. Yet the judge at his trial, Weston Clement III, decided to go easy on him. Why? For one thing, Arthur had belonged to the same fraternity that Judge Clement had been in back in his college days. The fact that Arthur was a University of Colorado football fan and despised Colorado State, sentiments shared quite strongly by Judge Clement, also played a major role. He was sentenced to a ridiculously lenient six months of community service.

Six years later, a very drunk Arthur ran a stop sign and

crashed into a fancy Lincoln Continental, seriously injuring both occupants of the car. Oh, I can't believe I forgot to mention it. The occupants of the Lincoln were Judge Clement and his wife.

COMMENT: *I'm sure the judge enjoyed watching his favorite college football team on T.V. during his months in traction – about the only thing he could do at the time. Far better would have been to pass judgment properly in court, including locking up reckless and drunk drivers so that they cease being menaces to society.*

"AND YOU SHALL NOT TAKE BRIBES"
(Shoftim 16:19)

WE had just gotten off the flight from Israel to New York and were on the sidewalk outside Kennedy airport's international terminal. We needed to get to the domestics terminal to catch our flight to Columbus. There was a long line of cabs parked at the curb and I went to the first one and told the driver we needed to get over to Domestics.

"I ain't taken' ya," he said matter of factly. "Because then I gotta go to da back uh da line and wait for anothu' fare." I tried the next guy and got the same response. From the third guy, too. None of them wanted to take a short fare from International to Domestics and then have to wait again.

Now, I *knew* the law required a cabby to take the customer

wherever he wants to go, no matter how close the destination, so I hurried over to a big burly cop standing on the sidewalk. The man in blue would certainly rescue the victim in distress. "Officer," I said in my best "I-respect-policemen-and-I'm-a-model-citizen" tone of voice, "none of the drivers are willing to take us to Domestics."

"Well, did ya tawk the intuhnational language?!" he bellowed at me with a thicker-than-putty Brooklyn accent, clearly shocked at my naiveté. "Ya gotta tawk the intuhnational language or you gonna be standin' here all day." And he walked off to help other citizens in distress.

 COMMENT: *I should've realized the cop probably spoke the international language too. Fluently.*

"TO NOT OBEY" (Shoftim 17:12)

RENEE Ringle was the typical anti-*baal teshuva* mother. She and her husband never came to terms with their son Chuck's decision to embrace a Torah lifestyle. Even after he married and had eight children of his own, she was still militantly opposed. So it was a pretty big surprise when, on one of her visits, she asked to go to *shul* Shabbos morning. Her son took her to the *ezras nashim* entrance, and she made her way to a seat right in front of the *mechitza*.

Chuck, now Chizkiyahu, met her after *davening* and could tell right away that his hope of her attitude having undergone some sort of positive change was for naught.

"There were two men sitting by the *mechitza* talking about the Super Bowl," she hissed. "And I could hear every word they said. This is how the Orthodox behave? Your people are *no* better than ours."

COMMENT: *First of all, yes we are. Perfect – no. Better – much. Second of all, Mrs. Ringle was not in shul to daven. She was there to find a flaw in order to justify her own non-observance. If it wouldn't have been talking, she would've found something else, not that that justifies anything. But it is notable to hear that there's a woman who's interested in football.*

"AND HE SHALL READ IT ALL THE DAYS OF HIS LIFE" (Shoftim 17:19)

One should be involved as much as possible in Torah study, and as much of one's conversation as possible should be in Torah matters.

KIPPA-CLAD Avner the cab driver asked his *rosh yeshiva* passenger what the topic of study was in the *yeshiva*. Happy for the opportunity to share a little Torah with this simple Jew, the *rosh yeshiva* began explaining the *sugya* in Bava Metzia that they were in the middle of. The *rosh yeshiva* was pleasantly surprised at how well Avner was able to follow the logic of the *gemara*, even asking a pertinent question. He continued his impromptu discourse for twenty minutes, and Avner was still into it.

Suddenly, the driver's cell phone started making music.

With an annoyed look on his face, Avner answered the phone and snapped, "Not now! I'm in the middle of learning!" and quickly hung up.

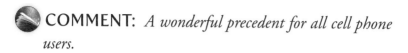 **COMMENT:** *A wonderful precedent for all cell phone users.*

"IN FIRE" (Shoftim 18:9)

SEVENTEEN year old Misha Yugoyev, a Gruzini lad, was a lazy good-for-nothing. He sat around all day eating and sleeping, periodically taking a break to *dray* around with his good-for-nothing friends. Finally, having had enough, his father Mikhail told him he wouldn't give him any more spending money. "Go out there and work like the rest of us," he barked. His mother Natasha had a soft heart, so she gave him a ruble without her husband knowing. Misha then spent the day goofing around and drinking vodka.

When Misha came home at night he said, "Look, Dad, I worked and earned a ruble." Mikhail grabbed the ruble and threw it into the fire. Misha just shrugged and walked away. This same thing repeated itself each evening for a week. At the end of the week, Natasha told her son she had no more rubles to give him.

The next day, Misha went out and worked, loading boxes on a truck. At the end of a day of this backbreaking labor, he was paid a ruble. He came home and showed it to his father. Again Mikhail grabbed it and was going to throw it into the fire, but this time Misha started shouting in protest. *"Now,* I know you *worked* for it," Mikhail said with a wise, fatherly smirk.

COMMENT: *We were put into this world to earn our eternal reward, because if we'd get it for free we wouldn't experience the same eternal delight.*

KI SAITZAI

"WHEN A MAN HAS A REBELLIOUS SON"
(Ki Saitzai 21:18)

"THANK you very much for your efforts, but I'm not really interested in a second meeting."

"Was there a specific problem, Kaila?" the *shadchanit* asked.

"Well, actually there was. You see, every time I said something, Avishai responded by saying, 'What's the difference?' or 'It doesn't matter,' or 'Big deal.' It really didn't make me feel important or interesting."

Leah the *shadchanit* was puzzled. The reports about Avishai had been outstanding. Although his father was sour on *yeshivas* and objected to long-term learning, Avishai had earned a reputation as a *masmid*. He had plans to stay in learning and was said to possess sterling *middos*. "Why did you talk like that?" Leah asked him.

"Well, when I was about to go out, I asked my *rebbe*

for advice. After all, I've never had social interactions with girls. He said it's not a big deal. I should just talk to her like my father talks to my mother. So I did."

COMMENT: *The single most powerful influence on children is their parents. Children are the greatest imitators in the world. Better give them something worth imitating.*

"DON'T TAKE THE MOTHER WITH THE CHILDREN" (Ki Saitzai 22:6)

One of the explanations given for this mitzvah *is that it's the mother bird's compromised position of being within arm's reach, due to her hovering over her children, that makes it possible for someone to take her. The Torah will not allow us to take advantage of the vulnerability which comes about through her* mesirus nefesh.

IT was tough having a mother who only had one eye. Jeff Weinstein was embarrassed when his friends would come over, and he was embarrassed to be seen with his mom in public. True, she had a glass eye where her original one had been, but after a few minutes of looking at her, one could tell the eye wasn't real. Even after Jeff got married he still cringed whenever anyone new met his mother. Eventually, his mother died at the ripe old age of eighty eight.

During the *shiva,* the family was reading some of the letters and notes she had left behind. One of them was addressed directly to Jeff. "To my loving son, Jeff. I know I was a source of embarrassment to you and I always felt bad. Had I lost my eye in an accident, I wouldn't have felt guilty, as it wouldn't have been my fault. But you see, my not having an eye was entirely my fault. When you were born, you were missing an eye. The only way you'd be able to have a functioning eye was if a human eye would be transplanted into you immediately, which would then give it a chance to grow as an actual part of your body. I gladly allowed the doctor to remove one of my eyes so that you wouldn't have to suffer. I'm so sorry for causing you all that embarrassment. With all my love, Mom."

COMMENT: *Children have no idea how much parents sacrifice for them. Jeff finally got it. And I think he was far more embarrassed* after *she died than while she was alive.*

"WHEN A MAN TAKES A WIFE"
(Ki Saitzai 22:13)

THERE is a story told about President Bush. I don't know if it's true, but I love it. The presidential motorcade made a stop in a service station so that one of the vehicles could fill up with gas. The First Lady, Mrs. Laura Bush, got out of the car and started speaking with one of the gas station attendants. When she got back in the car, her husband asked her what it was all about.

"Oh, when I saw him, I recognized him as someone I dated way back in high school. We just reminisced a little about old times." The president started laughing. "What's so funny?" she asked.

"Just think," he answered, "you could've married him, and instead you ended up marrying the president of the United States."

"It's not quite like that," she responded. "You see, if I would have married him, *he* would have become the president of the United States."

COMMENT: *I once told this in* shiur *and one of the guys said it's a true story. I don't know, but the message certainly rings true. As* Chazal *say, "Hakol mai'haisha," what a man becomes is due to his wife.*

"THE EXCHANGE OF A DOG"
(Ki Saitzai 23:19)

A S I approached the coffee machine in the *yeshiva*, I reached into my pocket and found only a five shekel coin. I needed change, because I really needed this cup of coffee. Ah, I was in luck. There was a young guy standing by the machine. "Do you have change for five shekels?" I asked. He did. After taking his money and giving him my coin, I said thank you.

"No problem, dog," he said. Just like that. He really said that. He referred to me as "dog." And you know what? I wasn't in the least bit insulted. As a matter of fact, I felt complimented. He considered me a "dog," one of the highest epithets possible in today's world. I had made it. I was a dog. I was one of *them*. Coffee… and being a dog. What could be better? The boy turned and walked away, never even remotely considering the possibility that "dog," inner city slang, is not really a term one should use when speaking to one of the *rebbeim* in the *yeshiva*. But I *did* feel accepted. Wanna hear me bark?

 COMMENT: *It's rough work trying to block out the influence of the insane world around us. Really rough. Rough rough! Rough rough!*

"AND YOU WERE TIRED AND WEARY"
(Ki Saitzai 25:18)

ANSHEL Spiegleman was driving everyone around him nuts, especially his good wife Braindel. He was always grouchy and irritable, and was generally unpleasant to be around. Almost nothing was good, and whatever was good could have been better. Braindel was at her wits' end. Anshel was constantly involved in confrontations in *shul*, and his co-workers at the glassmaking factory were losing patience with him. He also fell asleep during just about any *shiur* he attended or with any *chavrusa* who tried to learn with him. This added more non-admirers to his growing list.

What was the problem? Anshel had decided to become a *tzaddik*, so the first thing he did was cut back drastically on sleep. He only allowed himself two hours in bed. Anshel figured he'd put all this new-found time to good use and become a world class *talmid chacham.*

Problem was, he forgot one thing. To become a *talmid chacham,* one must learn. Due to his tiredness, the learning he did was low-quality, as his heavy head made it difficult for him to comprehend and to retain the little he did absorb.

Finally, his wife gave him an ultimatum. "Either you start sleeping more or you're going to be very lonely," she threatened.

"Why? Are you planning on leaving?" he retorted.

"Sort of. I plan on leaving *you* in the middle of the forest locked in a crate. Now, instead of being so obstinate, I want you to go to the Divrei Chaim of Tsanz and tell him what you're doing. You'll see he'll tell you to get more sleep."

"Two hours of sleep a night is too much for you," the great Divrei Chaim said after hearing Anshel's story. Anshel was gloating. He couldn't wait to come home and wag a victorious finger in Braindel's face. But the Divrei Chaim wasn't finished. "You know why two hours is too much? Because on two hours, you're tired all day, and you make everyone *meshuga* and get very little accomplished. So you may as well sleep for half an hour a night and *then* get very little accomplished the next day." Anshel's rude awakening (oohh) motivated him to head home and get more sleep. And he did no finger wagging.

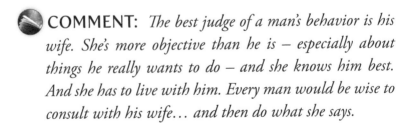 COMMENT: *The best judge of a man's behavior is his wife. She's more objective than he is – especially about things he really wants to do – and she knows him best. And she has to live with him. Every man would be wise to consult with his wife… and then do what she says.*

KI SAVO

"AND HONEY"
(Ki Savo 26:15)

HARAV Eliyahu Mishkovski *zt"l*, the *rav* and *rosh yeshiva* of Kfar Chassidim, suffered from constant pain in his feet. He related what it was that caused this chronic problem. "When I learned under Harav Shimon Shkop *zt"l* in Grodno, he told us *bochurim* that whenever he gives a *shiur* outside the *yeshiva,* we should not attend. He said it would weaken the *sedarim* in *yeshiva* if *bochurim* are missing. Well, I once left the *yeshiva* to hear him even though I wasn't supposed to. After the *shiur*, Rav Shimon said to me, 'I understand how your *heart* could want to do such a thing, but I don't understand how your *feet* could take you.' As soon as I got back to the *yeshiva* my feet started hurting, and they've been hurting ever since. But," Rav Eliyahu added with a huge smile, "the *shiur* was *so* sweet... it was *worth* the pain!"

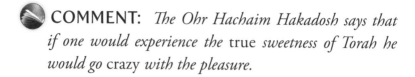 **COMMENT:** *The Ohr Hachaim Hakadosh says that if one would experience the* true *sweetness of Torah he would go* crazy *with the pleasure.*

"AND THE NATIONS WILL SEE HASHEM'S NAME CALLED UPON YOU" (Ki Savo 28:10)

HAT could be better than venturing out to the jungles of Africa? In the mind of Yotam Dayan, nothing. So the young Israeli, fresh out of the army, packed his stuff and set off on his own in an effort to "get away from it all."

At one point, he rented a jeep and started driving through the villages in the surrounding area. The locals were unbelievably poor, so it was only natural that when he saw a little kid on the side of the road pointing to his mouth in a gesture meaning "I'm hungry," he stopped the jeep. He started looking through his backpack to find a candy bar for him. When he looked up again, he saw to his very unpleasant surprise that his jeep was surrounded by about twenty five unfriendly looking natives. *Very* unfriendly. *Extremely* unfriendly.

This was a standard trick employed by the locals. They would send out a pathetic looking kid, the vehicle would stop, and then they would rob the driver of all his money – or worse. Usually worse. Yotam had served in one of the elite Israeli army units and was normally fearless. Right now he was scared. *Very* scared. *Extremely* scared.

One of the men asked him in broken English where he

was from. "Israel," Yotam answered hesitatingly. And then something totally unexpected happened. The men all slowly backed away from the jeep in what was unmistakably a state of awe, bowed slightly, and started chanting, "You the chosen piple. You the chosen piple." They apologized for inconveniencing him and sent him off on his much relieved way.

Upon his return to Israel, Yotam decided to investigate why it is that we're referred to as the "chosen piple." Predictably, he became a complete *baal teshuva*. Today he learns full time and runs a night *kollel*.

COMMENT: *Better late than never. And in this case, it could've really been never. Very never. Extremely never.*

"HASHEM WILL STRIKE YOU WITH MADNESS" (Ki Savo 28:28)

IT'S not clear what was bothering him, but sixty two year old Terry Thomas of Zanesville, Ohio was truly disturbed. He pulled a stunt that left all the schools in the area closed, with warnings broadcasted that none of the residents should leave the safety of their homes. What exactly did he do? He released over sixty dangerous pets that he had been raising – lions, tigers, leopards and other hazardous creatures – into the public. He then took his own life. Police had to hunt down the animals on the streets and highways before giving the all clear that life could be resumed normally.

COMMENT: *I had a rebbe who once told us that insanity is contagious. What could be expected from someone who lives in a state where there's no law against raising dangerous animals and where animal rights people protest – as they did – against the police killing the animals that were roaming free? The man was obviously insane. But the danger hasn't passed. Please keep in mind that there are i-pods and laptops and other dangerous creatures still on the loose.*

"AND YOU WILL GO CRAZY" (Ki Savo 28:34)

HARAV Koppleman *zt"l*, the legendary *rosh yeshiva* of the Lucerne *yeshiva*, was *niftar* at the age of 106. The stories about this great man abound. He was once walking down the hall of the *yeshiva* and passed by just as one of the boys slapped another boy. The *rav* immediately launched into a harsh rebuke about how one who strikes his fellow is considered a *rasha* and that Jewish boys don't hit. As he turned to walk away, one of the other boys said to him softly, "*Rebbe*, it's not his fault – he's a bit of a *meshuganer*."

"A *meshuganer*?" challenged Rav Koppleman. "If he's a *meshuganer* then he should've hit *himself*. He didn't. He hit someone else. That's no *meshuganer* – that's a *rasha*!"

COMMENT: *Sometimes a person makes a mistake and then says, "I could just hit myself." According to Rav Koppleman zt"l, that would be an even bigger mistake.*

"AND ON YOUR DESCENDANTS"
(Ki Savo 28:46)

THERE'S an old Russian legend that goes like this: Little Ivan had a favorite hobby of killing bugs and insects. The more pain he could inflict, the better. His parents would just look on and laugh, and then go back to drinking their vodka. As Ivan got older he felt more of a need to express the Eisav streak within him, so he got into hunting. Nothing gave him more of a thrill than shooting an animal and watching it die. "Ahhhh, *blood*," he would whisper with a deep sense of satisfaction.

As his blood lust increased, he found the only real fulfillment he could find was in killing *people*. Of course, he was careful to choose his victims carefully so as not to get caught by the police, so his opportunities were limited.

Well, one day, after a particularly long dry streak of not being able to murder anyone safely, Ivan and his son went on a manhunt trip together. He figured that out in the country, they'd be bound to find someone alone who would serve their purpose perfectly. Alas, no luck.

After a full day of not finding any hapless victims, Ivan could wait no longer... so he killed his son. Upset at what he'd done, he then took his own life. The two of them were buried next to each other.

Before he died, Ivan somehow managed to leave instructions for the inscription on his tombstone, which read, "It was my parents' fault."

COMMENT: *We don't have to look to Russian legends for guidance. The* Navi *says that Dovid Hamelech* *never rebuked Adoniyahu and that resulted in his rebellion. Parents must be on the watch from day one and never falter, because complacency can be disastrous.*

NITZAVIM

"IN THIS BOOK" (Nitzavim 29:19)

AVRAHAM Randolf is a *ger tzedek* from Canada. Being black allows him to travel in places which Jews would usually avoid, such as Muslim countries of any sort. Avraham simply puts a cap over his yarmulke and tucks in his *tzitzis*. That makes places like Indonesia, Saudi Arabia and Iran, which are heavily populated by Muslims, open turf for him on his business travels.

He was once sitting in the airport in Indonesia looking at a *sefer* when a Muslim came over to him. "If I didn't know better, I'd say you were Jewish," he began.

"Why?" Avraham asked cautiously.

"Because Jews are the only ones who sit off to the side in airports and look in books," the man explained.

 COMMENT: *It's nice to be noticed. Usually.*

"AND YOU SHALL RETURN
TO HASHEM YOUR G-D"
(Nitzavim 30:2)

The pasuk *is discussing the concept of* teshuva.

W E'VE always heard how every character trait can be used for something positive. However, quite frankly, we do sometimes wonder how blatantly negative forms of behavior can be good. One such example is the profitable profession of pickpocketing. Honestly, how can this form of crooked behavior *possibly* be something positive?

Well, a group of pickpockets in London, wishing to atone for their past misdeeds, actually came up with a novel way of putting their skills to good use. First, they presented their plan to the authorities and received approval, making sure to coordinate the entire thing with the police. Then the deft-fingered individuals went around slipping money *into* the pockets of unsuspecting tourists in the busy metropolis. Ten and twenty pound notes would be found by the surprised and delighted "victims." Over one hundred thousand pounds was distributed in this rather creative manner.

"I've stolen so much over the years, it feels good to give back," pocket-putter Trevor McFarlane said with satisfaction.

COMMENT: *Dickens's Artful Dodger would be disappointed.*

"WHEN YOU RETURN TO HASHEM YOUR G-D WITH ALL OF YOUR HEART"
(Nitzavim 30:10)

SNUG as a bug in a rug. Stanley Hanks was as comfortable as can be, just waking up from his inebriation-induced slumber. He was *so* comfortable, he didn't really feel like moving. He probably wouldn't have moved for some time, but there was a terrible odor. The more awake he became, the worse it got. Stanley propped his head up and noticed he was lying in the back of a city garbage truck. How he'd gotten there and how long he'd been there he didn't know. He actually chuckled to himself. After all, he'd woken up in some pretty strange places before. There was the time he awoke in a tub full of motor oil and another time that he ended up in the back of a bakery covered with whipped cream.

As he slowly sat up, he heard a terrifying roar. It was the sound of the huge garbage compressor being turned on. In a matter of moments he'd be crushed to death. Stanley screamed at the top of his lungs... and startled sanitation worker Hal Corker managed to hear him and shut off the compressor in time. "Weirdest piece of garbage I've ever seen – and I've seen some doozies," Hal said later to his disbelieving friends.

COMMENT: *When stuck in the "garbage truck" of sinful behavior, one must remember that it's never too late to "get out." Sincere* teshuva *is accepted, but it must be done before the eternal compressor is activated.*

"WHO SHALL GO UP FOR US"
(Nitzavim 30:12)

A S he walked towards *shul* for *maariv*, Berel suddenly stopped in his tracks. Could it really be? He moved a few steps closer to get a better look. Sure enough, there was the great Rav Avraham Genechovski *zt"l*, the *rosh yeshiva* of the Chebin *yeshiva*, standing on a ladder and making faces into a second story window. Berel tried to get himself to move so that the *rosh yeshiva* wouldn't know he'd been seen in this rather awkward position, but the *rosh yeshiva* had already noticed him and clearly gestured for him to wait until he came down.

"I'll bet you're wondering what I was doing up there," Rav Genechovski began. Berel tried to brush off any need for an explanation, but Rav Genechovski wouldn't allow it. "You see, I was on my way to the *yeshiva* when I heard hysterical crying coming from up in that apartment. I ran up to the front door and knocked, but there was no answer. The crying persisted and I could tell it was children who were crying. So I took a ladder and started making funny faces at the two little children in the room until they started laughing. Their parents had obviously stepped out for a few moments. They just walked back in, so I came down from the ladder."

COMMENT: *It's a big chesed to alleviate people's fears. And there are plenty of opportunities with both feet on the ground.*

"LOOK, I PRESENT YOU TODAY
THE OPTION OF LIFE... OR DEATH"
(Nitzavim 30:15)
The Torah tells us we can choose life or choose death.

EASYGOING, fun-loving, popular and charming was how you'd describe Adam Zeldman. It seemed he had everything going for him from A to Z. Apparently, though, he didn't think so, because he started searching for *something.* Like countless others before him, he ended up at Ohr Somayach.

One day in *shiur* we did a Tosfos, one of the first Adam had ever done in his life. He really got a *geshmak* out of the way everything fit together so perfectly and how the *gemara* could now be understood in a different way. At first he just started laughing, a laugh of complete satisfaction from the depths of his sweet *neshama.* Not loud, just the sound of pure joy. "Rabbi," he exclaimed, smiling from ear to ear, "I feel like I've been asleep for the first twenty years of my life and that I've just woken up."

COMMENT: *There's no greater form of truly living than being involved in vibrant Torah learning. Today Adam is wide awake – and getting wider every day. I'd be very surprised if in a few years he isn't involved in waking others up.*

VAYEILECH

"ONE HUNDRED AND TWENTY YEARS"
(Vayeilech 31:2)

RUDY Rosensweig's wife Rosie did not like Reuvain, Rudy's son from his first marriage. She wanted their entire inheritance to go to the three children the two of them shared. When Rudy became bedridden with his final illness and needed a full time nurse, Rosie gave her instructions not to let Reuvain in for a visit. Each time he came, the nurse would make an excuse why he couldn't come in to see his father.

After about three months, Rudy realized the end was near, so he drew up his will. Rosie convinced him to cut Reuvain out, as he didn't even have the decency to come and visit. Rudy wrote that after he dies, his son Reuvain gets nothing.

After the *shiva*, Reuvain went to Rav Henkin *zt"l* to complain about the way he'd been cheated out of his inheritance. Rav Henkin told him he'd have to take the issue to court, but that someone should translate the will into Hebrew.

When they met in court, the judge, who obviously couldn't read Hebrew, asked Rosie to translate what was written. She said, "It says clearly that after *meah v'esrim*, which means one hundred and twenty years, his estate is to be divided among Rosie's three sons only, and Reuvain gets nothing."

"Well, that sounds pretty clear to me," snapped the judge. "That means that in a hundred and twenty years he'll have to give up what he gets right now. And what he gets right *now* is a full share! Case dismissed."

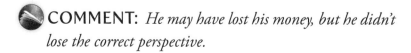 COMMENT: *Wanna laugh? Just picture the baffled look on Rosie's face when she asked herself, "What went wrong?"*

"TO GIVE TO THEM" (Vayeilech 31:7)

T was the annual Lakewood Yeshiva fundraising dinner. One of the regular wealthy donors stood up to speak. "I lost most of my money in the financial crash," he began, to a suddenly very quiet ballroom full of people. "But what I lost was *my* share. I still have Hashem's 'share.' And I'm giving it to the Lakewood Yeshiva." He then wrote out a check for seven hundred and fifty thousand dollars. The *yeshiva* had their most successful dinner *ever*.

COMMENT: *He may have lost his money, but he didn't lose the correct perspective.*

"PLACE IT IN THEIR MOUTHS"
(Vayeilech 31:19)

THE long-anticipated pogrom began. The ghetto dwellers ran and hid wherever possible to stay out of sight of the bloodthirsty mob. One group of people was hiding in a *beis medrash*. Eizik Perkovski saw two *yeshiva bochurim* hiding under a bench and whispering to each other. He figured they were encouraging each other not to be afraid and to have *bitachon*. He edged closer to hear what they were saying, and what he heard made him realize that our enemies will never defeat us.

"That can't be *pshat* in the Tosfos," one was saying, "because the Rashba clearly says not like that." The other responded by reminding him of the Tosfos in Bava Kama. And they continued on with their learning, despite the fear and panic surrounding them.

COMMENT: *We have the opportunity to do the same* without *hiding under benches. Why wait?*

"AND NOW WRITE FOR YOURSELVES THIS
SONG" (Vayeilech 31:19)

THREE hundred and fifty bucks an hour isn't bad by *anyone's* standards. That's what B. Franklin Groffman, senior partner in the firm of Groffman, Reelback, Sloan and Flint was billing his clients. He had whatever he wanted and was pretty satisfied in life. To assuage his Jewish conscience, he was active in his Conservative synagogue's youth group. There wasn't too much religious stuff going on, of course, but he went up with the kids on the annual fishing trip to Canada and accompanied them as one of the adult escorts when they went to amusement parks or museums. He was proud of himself for his selflessness.

One day, for some strange reason, the school arranged a trip to the local *cheder*. From their point of view, this was no different than a trip to any other museum containing relics of a long forgotten past. Expecting a sterile environment and a detached manner, the group was somewhat rattled by the warm and friendly welcome they received from the *frum* principal. The group was then given a tour of the various classrooms. B. Franklin Groffman was moved by what he saw. Really and truly moved. The kids in every classroom were singing the *davening* or happily chanting *pesukim* from *Chumash*.

"Boy, those cute little buggers really seem happy," he thought to himself. "*We* were never that happy in public school. *We* never sang or chanted anything with such joy."

Yes, today Binyamin Pesach Groffman is totally *frum* with a totally *frum* family. And he is a *big* supporter of the local *cheder*, along with many other important Torah causes.

 COMMENT: *And he's one happy* big *bugger.*

"AND HE TAUGHT IT" (Vayeilech 31:22)

HARAV Yisrael Yaakov Fisher *zt"l* and his three brothers all became huge *talmidei chachamim.* The four were once sitting and having a Torah discussion with different opinions being put up for analysis. Rav Yisrael Yaakov offered a complex explanation on the topic, but his brothers would not accept it. He tried again, and again it was rejected. When a third attempt also failed, he started crying.

His brothers were shocked at the sight of his tears and asked him why he was so upset. After all, it's standard procedure to disagree when engaged in the battle of Torah ideas. Why the tears?

"You don't accept what I'm saying because you don't understand what I'm getting at," he explained. "And if you don't understand, then it's *my* fault. It means *I'm* not explaining it properly, because if I did then you *would* accept my premise. It's *my* fault." And he cried some more.

COMMENT: *The Brisker Rav* zt"l *said that very complex matters can be understood even by children if explained properly.* Rebbes *and* morahs *often get frustrated when students fail to understand. A clearer explanation may very well solve the problem. This applies in other areas, too. It's quite common that our point of view isn't understood by others because* we've *been unclear. Husbands and wives should keep this in mind when discussing the myriad issues that come up in life. They must try to calmly explain their positions… and then the husband should give in – even if he doesn't understand.*

HA'AZINU

"ASK YOUR FATHER AND HE SHALL TELL YOU" (Ha'azinu 32:7)

ACH night, Effie Englander would put his daughter Elke to sleep by having her give *tzedaka*. He would give the one and a half year old a few coins, and she would put them in a *pushka* by her crib, announcing "*tzedaka, tzedaka*" as she dropped each coin in. One night after putting her to sleep, Effie heard her voice coming from the room. He went to check on her and found that somehow some coins had fallen into her crib. Instead of putting them in her mouth, as just about any kid her age would, she was dropping them into the *pushka...* and chanting "*tzedaka, tzedaka*."

COMMENT: *A coin in the mouth of a baby is life threatening. Yet another example of* tzedaka tatzil mi'maves. *I mean* really – *it can't get much more obvious than* this.

"THEY WOULD COMPREHEND THEIR END" (Ha'azinu 32:29)

ZEVULUN Zupnick was a very rich man, but much to the consternation of his future heirs, he gave away a lot of money to *tzedaka*. "Why do you have to give *so much?*" they asked him at a family meeting. Zevulun smiled broadly. "I'm just smuggling money into *Olam Haba.*" His explanation put an end to the discussion.

COMMENT: *What a smart man. A* really *smart man. And when he gets to* Olam Haba *he sure won't be treated like a smuggler.*

"YOU WILL PROLONG YOUR DAYS" (Ha'azinu 32:47)

"WHO here knows English?" barked the commandant at a line-up in Auschwitz at four in the morning. "Anyone who knows English will be rewarded with extra rations and a job working indoors." Seventeen year old Herman Pearlman felt himself raise his hand, even though he didn't know a word of English.

The Nazi approached him. "I have to know how to say something in English to send to a friend," said the Nazi. "If you fail me I will shoot you on the spot." Herman started muttering the *Shema* under his breath. "How do you say '*Ah gute glukeshe yar*' in English?" the subhuman asked.

"A happy new year," Herman responded without a moment's hesitation. And how *did* he know? Herman's father had been a wealthy man before the war and he would send generous donations to various Torah institutions in America. These institutions would send him Rosh Hashana greeting cards, all of which had "A happy new year" printed on them. "A happy new year" were the *only* English words he knew. Herman got the rations and the indoor job, which helped him survive the war and be able to tell over the story.

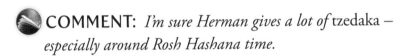 COMMENT: *I'm sure Herman gives a lot of* tzedaka – *especially around Rosh Hashana time.*

"AND DIE ON THE MOUNTAIN WHICH YOU WILL ASCEND" (Ha'azinu 32:50)

A SECULAR Jew once entered Rav Shlomo Freifeld *zt"l's succah* and immediately noticed the pictures of the *gedolim* on the walls, hung as decorations. "Who are those people?" he asked.

"Those are people who are now an extinct species," Rav Freifeld answered. "They're called 'human beings.'"

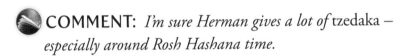 COMMENT: *There is so much wisdom in what Reb Shlomo said. "If the earlier generations were humans then we are like donkeys," is how the* gemara *puts it.*

"YOU SHALL SEE" (Ha'azinu 32:52)

POOR eyesight caused Harav Michel Yehuda Lefkowitz *zt"l* to consult with an eye doctor, who recommended new glasses. He bought the new glasses but didn't start wearing them until a few months later, in Nissan. Knowing everything Rav Michel Yehuda did had a reason, someone asked him what it was. "If I would have walked into the *beis medrash* with new glasses, the *bochurim* would've noticed and would've started talking about it, which would've been *bitul Torah*. So I waited until *bein hazmanim*. By the beginning of next *zman*, people will have gotten used to them, so there will be no harm done."

COMMENT: Bitul Torah *is often thought of as an "inyan" or "chumra." It's neither. It is a full fledged aveira, and must be avoided like all other aveiros.*

V'ZOS HABERACHA

"REJOICE ZEVULUN IN YOUR TRAVELS AND YISSACHAR IN YOUR TENTS"
(V'zos Haberacha 33:18)

Zevulun and Yissachar had the most famous Torah partnership in history. The tribe of Zevulun engaged in commerce and supported the tribe of Yissachar, who sat and leaned.

ONE of the most successful Torah programs nowadays is called "Partners in Torah." A partnership is made between those who are observant and those who are not as yet observant. They engage in one-on-one Torah study, the most potent *kiruv* tool known to man. The uninitiated are exposed to the beauty of Torah, which in many cases is followed by a full commitment to a Torah lifestyle.

Betzalel Weisbraun had been studying with his secular partner Jack Fogelman for over two years. Each day they sat and learned for an hour. Jack was a lawyer, so he really enjoyed the logic and the challenge of *gemara*. However, there was no perceptible movement in his religious commitment.

Somewhat frustrated, Betzalel approached Harav Pam *zt"l* about the matter. "Is it worth it for me to continue with him?" he asked.

"No," Rav Pam answered, "it's not worth it. If you don't understand what an hour a day of Torah learning does for someone, then it's really not worth it for you to continue learning with him." Betzalel continued.

COMMENT: *We don't see any immediate tangible effects from breathing air or drinking water either, but no one questions the value. Torah study is our air and water.*

"AND YISSACHAR IN YOUR TENTS"
(V'zos Haberacha 33:18)

The tribe of Yissachar was involved in constant Torah study, the highest level mitzvah *that exists.*

YOUNG, newly married Fruma Hoffman was excited to meet her husband's *rav* and to have a chance to chat with the *rebbetzin*. Besides being a serious *talmid chacham*, Rav Plessner was known as an incredible *baal chesed*. His home was open to a virtual non-stop flow of people who needed help. As Fruma sat *schmoozing* with the *rebbetzin*, she saw how the *rav* distributed money to the needy, advised parents, referred people to doctors and even lent people equipment for home repairs.

Fruma could barely contain her excitement – actually, she couldn't contain it at all. With an effervescent personality, Fruma kept gushing about how impressed she was and what a *tzaddik* the *rav* is. The *rebbetzin* smiled and thanked her for her compliments.

When Fruma and her husband got up to leave, the *rebbetzin* told Fruma she'd like to tell her something. "It's all great and wonderful. My husband is doing really big *mitzvos*. But just remember... all of it together does not compare to one *blatt* of *gemara*."

COMMENT: *We shouldn't be shocked or surprised. After all, every one of us says v'talmud Torah k'negged* kulam *each and every morning.*

"FULLY SATISFIED" (V'zos Haberacha 33:23)

THERE is a wealthy man who arranged for cartons of chickens to become available to poor people. Each week, some seven hundred families benefit from his benevolence. But the beauty of it is that they do not get the chickens as a handout. The chickens are sold to the poor families at a ridiculously low price, having been told that it's a special purchase deal. This way they can buy the chickens and enjoy them, their dignity having been maintained by being able to pay. And even *more* beautiful is that they fill out a form indicating which of three *hechsherim* they prefer, giving it even more of a feeling of not being ordinary *tzedaka*. And even *more* beautiful still is that there is a "customer service" call made from a secretary, asking if there was full satisfaction with the product and the delivery service to their home.

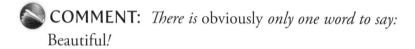 **COMMENT:** *There is* obviously *only one word to say:* Beautiful!

"AND HE BURIED HIM " (V'zos Haberacha 34:6)

Chazal say the Torah is chesed from beginning to end. It begins with the chesed of Hashem providing clothing for Adam and Chava, and it culminates with the chesed of Hashem burying Moshe Rabbeinu.

"HI, Shmuli, do you happen to know of anyone who could use some *succah* wood?" Shmuli Ganz was on the way out of *shul* when Yishai Kliers threw this question at him.

"You're not gonna believe this, Yishai. Just yesterday, I got a call from my brother who's a rabbi in Queens asking me if I know of any available *succah* wood for a new family that moved in."

After this initial incident, Shmuli realized that if there was one person who needed *succah* boards, there were bound to be others. One thing led to the next, and Shmuli became known as the *succah shadchan,* matching up people all over the place with *succos*. At last count, he'd made four hundred and fifty three "*shidduchim*."

The best one of all was when he got a call from an out-of-towner (town being New York) asking for help in locating a *succah*. Shmuli actually had the name of someone from that area who wanted to unload his *succah* wood. It turned out the two were... next door neighbors.

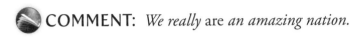 COMMENT: *We really* are *an amazing nation.*

"ALL OF YISRAEL"
(V'zos Haberacha 34:12)

I CAN think of no better story with which to end the book. At one of the *hespedim* for Harav Nosson Tzvi Finkel *zt"l*, the Mirrer *rosh yeshiva*, one of the eulogizers said the following: Rav Leizer Yudel Finkel *zt"l* was a Jew who kissed every *Shas*. Rav Nosson Tzvi *zt"l* was a *Shas* ... *who kissed every Jew.*

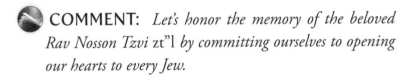 COMMENT: *Let's honor the memory of the beloved Rav Nosson Tzvi* zt"l *by committing ourselves to opening our hearts to every Jew.*

HOW TO RUN A SHABBOS TABLE

A PARENT'S GUIDE TO CREATING A MOST ENJOYABLE SHABBOS TABLE

INTRODUCTION

A FEW years back, a very fine *avreich* called me to ask about what to do at his Shabbos table. "My wife finds Shabbos boring," he lamented. It was not the first time I'd heard about people being challenged by the Shabbos table and it was not the last time. Sometimes the kids are restless, and sometimes it's the parents who are exhausted. Sometimes it's a lack of knowing what to talk about, and sometimes it's simply a feeling of inadequacy in dealing with apathetic teens.

I know that many families are missing out on something that could be both fulfilling and productive, and it's a shame. Here we present ideas and techniques that can, with just a little preparation and effort, turn the Shabbos table into something the entire family will look forward to week after week. Remember, perfection is rarely achieved in any realm. Any improvement is a major accomplishment.

The benefits of the ideas presented here will be best achieved if the parents, especially the father, give these concise ideas a quick review every few weeks.

The ideas presented here do not all apply to all families under all circumstances. All people are different and the chemistry and structure of each family is different. Some of the ideas may actually seem to contradict each other. It is up to the parents to choose which ideas are most suitable for their specific family. It would be very surprising if there isn't something here that every set of parents will find useful.

We will be discussing how to conduct a Shabbos table with children and/or teens. This is not a guide for conducting a table where the guests are secular and the goal of the evening is *kiruv rechokim*.

You will find that the most important points are repeated in different sections, due to how crucial they are.

Wishing you many wonderful *Shabbosim*!

GOALS AND EXPECTATIONS

The goals which should be first and foremost in your mind are:

Your kids should have an **enjoyable** experience at your Shabbos table.

They should **look forward** to the Shabbos table each week.

This is achieved by creating an atmosphere which is warm, relaxed, fun and productive.

DON'T EXPECT TO RELAX

W HEN the kids are young, don't expect the Shabbos table to be relaxing. It's very normal to feel that "I've worked hard all week and I'd like to have a nice relaxed meal." The reality is that Shabbos and the Shabbos *seudos* may actually be the most challenging time of the week. This is especially true for fathers, as they are often not around the kids as much during the week and not as accustomed to the constant tumult. Just reducing your expectations can actually help you have a more relaxed table.

One way to avoid frustration over not being able to unwind is to divide the *seuda*. Eat the appetizer. Then, when you are no longer famished, you can spend time with the kids and have a nice productive and enjoyable Shabbos table. After that, when they've gone to sleep or are winding down, the father and mother can sit and eat the main course in a more comfortable setting.

TO HAVE GUESTS OR NOT TO HAVE

T HERE are different stages and phases in life, and none of them are forever. At the stage **when the family is young, the unchallenged priority at the table is your children.** Since they are your priority, the question of whether or not to have guests is one which must be considered carefully. It's a good idea to consult with a competent rav.

Even if you do have guests, it should be made clear to them that you will be focusing your attention on your children. Of course, in an exceptional situation, you might put your energy into the guests. But, as a rule, at this stage of life it's all about the kids. When your children are older, you will be able to give more of yourself to guests.

Of course, it's a good idea to have guests once in a while so that the kids are taught the importance of *hachnasas orchim*. One *rav* I know has one *seuda* with guests and one *seuda* without, so that his kids absorb the importance of the *mitzvah*. However, since no two families and situations are identical, it's advisable to ask for guidance in this important area.

HOW LONG SHOULD CHILDREN BE EXPECTED TO SIT AT THE TABLE?

W HEN children are young, make sure your expectations of how long they should sit at the table and how disciplined they should be are realistic. Little children have trouble sitting. In many

cases, a good ten minutes with some semblance of coopera-
tion and participation should be seen as a major accomplishment. It's good to keep in mind that if one *seuda* went
well, even if the other two didn't, it should still be seen as a
successful Shabbos.

A Shabbos table that involves threats, punishments
and tension, because the father wants to increase the
ruchniyus at the table or because the parents want a for-
mal environment, is dangerous. It can easily result in
kids who despise the Shabbos table, *chas v'shalom*, and
can even be the first step in their eventually going off the
derech, chas v'shalom.

DON'T COMPARE

Please do not make the common mistake of thinking
about what other people's Shabbos tables are like. For one
thing, some level of chaos is perfectly normal for families
with young children. What's going on at your table is
probably going on at other people's tables as well.

Also, you may have been somewhere where you've seen
a beautiful Shabbos table and you would like to emulate
it in your own home. Not being able to do so causes you
frustration. However, you may very well be forgetting that
you saw that family at a time when their children were
somewhat older than yours are right now. They were,
therefore, more capable of sitting attentively and partici-
pating maturely, so any comparisons are not valid.

Furthermore, please keep in mind that you, the parents, are different than those parents, and your children are

different than those children. The father in that home may be a very lively personality capable of keeping his family entertained for hours, whereas the father in your home is less animated. That father may be an energetic singer with a melodious voice, whereas the father in your home may not be.

The mother in that home may have been a strict disciplinarian who demanded that her family sit, whereas your home has a mother with a softer approach, with its advantages and disadvantages. The mother in that other home may have a natural hunger to hear *divrei Torah* and has transmitted that feeling to her children, whereas the mother in your home may just have a natural hunger and wants to eat.

So again, comparisons are not productive. Rather, focus on the strengths that you do have and use them at your Shabbos table. Of course, if there is some specific activity or idea which you've seen by others that you appreciate and which can be implemented at your table, then by all means do so.

PREPARATIONS

A NAP IS A MUST

FOR many men, Shabbos meals are the only time they have for any meaningful interaction with their children. It is vital, therefore, that the father comes to the Shabbos table refreshed and energetic. If at all possible, the father needs to make it a priority to take a nap on

Friday, even if it means trading some Friday hours at work for more hours during the week.

The mother should also try to get some rest on *erev Shabbos*. She certainly deserves it. Emphasis was placed on the men because, in most homes, it's the father who conducts the table. Therefore, he must be in top form. This is one of the most overlooked areas of achieving a successful Shabbos table. Even if the father's nap means the absence of some of his help on *erev* Shabbos, which means the home will not be as tidy as the mother would like, it's worth the tradeoff.

Many men doze during *kabbalas Shabbos* and rely on that to get them through the meal. However, for quite a few men that simply isn't enough and they're still tired at the table. Of course, if the husband can be at his best without a nap, he should be up and helping his wife as much as she feels is necessary. If there isn't enough time during the day to get a proper nap, a *shaila* should be asked of a qualified *rav* whether the husband should forgo *kabbalas Shabbos* in *shul* in favor of a nap so that he'll be able to fulfill the *mitzvah* of being *mechanech* his children.

PREPARE SEATING BEFOREHAND

BE sure you know where everyone is going to be seated. This is especially important if you're having guests and the logistics have to be worked out. Having kids fighting over seats gets the *seuda* off to the wrong start. Little place cards add a touch of *kavod* and boost the kids' feeling that Shabbos is special.

OF *ZEMIROS* BOOKS AND *CHUMASHIM*

THE *zemiros* booklets should be on the table before the *seuda* starts. Having to get up and bring them can cause a delay which will break up the spontaneity of the moment, resulting in little or no singing.

There should be *Chumashim* on or near the table. There should be one for each person and ideally they should be uniform. That way, if the father wants to call attention to something inside the *Chumash*, everyone will be able to find the place quickly. A one-time investment in ten or twelve small uniform *Chumashim* really doesn't cost that much, especially if you realize their importance.

FOCUS ON THE CHILDREN

AS we mentioned before, if you have a young family and somehow have ended up with guests, they should be told in advance that most – if not all – of the *seuda* will be focused on your children. One prominent *rav* I know had a lot of requests from *bochurim* for Shabbos meals. When his children were young he would tell them that they were welcome to come, but he was going to ignore them. He used such strong language to make sure there would be no misunderstandings. The only time he had to spend with his children was Shabbos, and that was his priority at that stage of his family's development.

In most homes, the mother spends hours preparing for Shabbos. Sometimes it's the better part of two or three days. The father must follow her example and spend time preparing for the Shabbos table. A quick peek at a *vort* from a *sefer* during *kabbalas Shabbos* is simply not good enough. You can make time for preparation on *erev Shabbos* or you can make time during the week. It really doesn't matter when. You can prepare *divrei Torah* on the *parsha*, stories, songs or activities. The bottom line is that you should come to the table with some sort of idea of what you'd like to accomplish and how you will do it.

Please keep in mind that even if you aren't a very exuberant or colorful personality, the act of preparing will inject you with enthusiasm and what you give over will have some zip. One word of caution: You may come to the Shabbos table and find that the time is not ripe or the general atmosphere is not receptive to what you prepared. If that happens, don't force it. Whatever you do, don't force it. You'll be rewarded for your preparation, and next week there will be another Shabbos when you'll be able to try again.

GETTING STARTED

BEGIN PROMPTLY

I T'S important to get off to a good start. As soon as the father comes home from *shul*, the *seuda* should begin. If there are guests, pleasant introductions should be made and then the singing should begin. Don't start with "Where are you from?" and "What do you do?" types of conversations. People are hungry and there will be time for chitchat later. If it turns out there wasn't time later because the *seuda* was entirely focused on your children, that's most probably perfectly okay.

IF YOU BEGIN *SHALOM ALEICHEM*, THEY WILL COME

I F all the children are at the table except for one or two, don't wait for them to arrive in order to start *Shalom Aleichem*. If you do wait, it often happens that by the time the missing one comes in, a different one has left. That leaves everyone standing around waiting for longer and the mood quickly sours. Additionally, if everyone is present in the dining room, don't wait for them to assemble around the table. The fact that one is on the couch and another is on the floor doesn't matter. Just begin singing. That's usually enough to get everyone to start moving towards their seats at the table.

KEEP THINGS MOVING

I F one of the kids is still not around by the time you're ready to make *kiddush*, don't wait too long for him to show up. You have to consider that those present are hungry and eager to start. Waiting for one child can put people into a bad mood and torpedo the success of the entire *seuda*. That child should be given a cup of grape juice when he or she arrives to make their own *kiddush*. During the week, the parents should talk to the child about the importance of being present for *kiddush*. Even if it happens again, follow the same plan. Eventually the child will fall into line.

POURING THE WINE

P OURING the wine or grape juice after *kiddush* often leads to bickering among the children about who got more and who got first. One idea to help avoid this frustration is to pour some grape juice into each child's cup at their place before *kiddush*. Then, after *kiddush*, simply pour a drop into each of their cups. This one little idea can make the difference between an enjoyable *seuda* and a frustrating one. I've been told it really makes a difference.

RECOGNIZE MOMMY

A TALMID *chacham* that I know has a beautiful *minhag*. Before *kiddush*, the children all take turns saying what their mother did for them that week.

If you can implement that idea, it's wonderful. However, if you see that people are hungry or that the kids are restless, it might be a better idea to leave it until after *hamotzi*. It can also be done once in a while, instead of every week. If there are guests present and the kids are self-conscious, don't pressure them or force them to participate.

WHAT TO DO AT THE TABLE

K EEPING everyone's interest at the table is extremely challenging, especially when there are children and teens of different ages. The goal is to have some sort of Torah-based interaction, although that's not always so easy to achieve. Discussing the *parsha* may interest some and bore the others. Sometimes the people at the table, including the father, do not know enough about the *parsha* to get any kind of energized conversation going. Telling stories is good, but you may not always have a story, or at least not one that no one has heard before. Also, stories don't necessarily lead to conversations which everyone can be involved in.

So, what to do? What I have found to be the best of all worlds is to **present an interesting and provocative** *halachic shaila* which grabs people's attention and then leads effortlessly into an enthusiastic discussion. The father should throw out a question and then allow everyone to respond, stimulating a lively discussion.

Here are two examples of the types of *shailos* I'm talking about:

 A cab driver in Israel was given a Coke by a passenger. It turned out to be drugged. The cabby slept for twenty minutes and awoke to find that he had been robbed. He called a *posek* to find out if he had to make a *borei nefashos* on the drink. His dilemma stemmed from the fact that had he known the drink was drugged he would not have drunk it in the first place. (The answer was that he did have to make a *borei nefashos*.)

A man wanted to take a bus from Bnei Brak to Yerushalayim. When he opened the baggage compartment to insert his suitcase, he found it was full. In order to make room, he climbed into the compartment to move the baggage around. The driver, unaware that the man was in the baggage hold, closed the door and drove to Yerushalayim. The man endured a very uncomfortable ride but emerged unhurt. The *shaila* was whether or not he had to pay for the trip. (The answer was no.)

These types of *shailos* generate interest in people of all ages. Even youngsters and people with limited Torah knowledge will offer opinions and feel part of the conversation. This usually turns into a lively discussion, often leading to other Torah ideas. This is a particularly efficient method of getting normally apathetic teens involved, as well as showing them that the Torah can actually be quite exciting.

These types of *shailos* can be found by the hundreds. I will list a few good sources to help you get started.

The "Aleinu Leshabayach" and "Borchi Nafshi" series contain hundreds of contemporary *shailos* that have been presented to Harav Yitzchok Zilberstein *shlit"a*.

There is a series called "Veha'arev Na" which also presents dozens of *shailos* that have been dealt with by contemporary *poskim*.

"Mishpitei HaTorah" by Harav Zvi Shpitz *shlit"a*

presents many fascinating questions in monetary law.

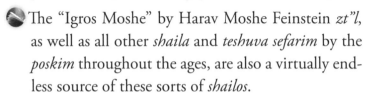 The "Igros Moshe" by Harav Moshe Feinstein *zt"l,* as well as all other *shaila* and *teshuva sefarim* by the *poskim* throughout the ages, are also a virtually end-less source of these sorts of *shailos.*

Be sure to point out that there may be differing opin-ions among *poskim.* This won't affect the discussion. Re-member, the main goal is not to teach the *halacha* – it's to engage your family in a productive *Torahdik* discussion. The side benefit is that a lot of *halacha* gets learned along the way.

The father will have to invest some time looking for the types of *shailos* that will stimulate your family. It's wise to keep some sort of notebook or file and accumulate a collec-tion. Remember, *shailos* can be brought up for discussion more than once. People at the table sometimes enjoy the fact that they remember the answers to questions that were presented and discussed in the past.

Similarly, if you discuss the *parsha,* the ideal way to do so is by throwing out a question, as opposed to saying a *vort* or sharing a thought. This doesn't mean there isn't room for that as well, it's just that for the sake of what you're trying to accomplish, the question approach is much more effective.

BE CREATIVE

TRY to be as creative as possible when coming up with ideas about what to do at the table. For exam-ple, kids love rhymes, even bad ones. So if you can tell a story in rhyme, or at least have a few lines of rhyme in it, your kids will be more attentive. They love to guess what the rhyme will be, so you can pause before the last word in each line and let them shout out what they think the ending is. And again, anything you come up with should be recorded in a notebook so that it will be available for future reference and use.

TELL STORIES

STORIES should certainly be told over at the table. It's a good idea to record stories in a notebook so that you have them handy. That way, when the kids say, "Tell us a story," you won't have to rack your brains trying to come up with one. The impetus for the "Impact" series was situations such as the Shabbos table. The feedback I've gotten from people is that it has been very helpful. There are other excellent storybooks available as well. Take some time to look up a few before Shabbos and write them down.

IMPROMPTU RELAXING

THE following is an idea I stumbled across quite unintentionally, but I've found that it fosters family unity and warmth in a remarkable way. Once in a while, the father can leave the table, perhaps after the first course or before dessert is served, and stretch out on the couch to sing or tell a story.

What is likely to happen – and indeed happened in our

home when I took a stretch after the first course one *leil Shabbos* – is that the children gather around you to sing along or hear the story, which then turns into a miniature *kumzitz*. For some reason, the informal setting draws the kids in a way that sitting at the table may not, even the older kids. (The side benefit is that the mother can sit alone at the table while the kids are distracted and eat in peace for a little while.) You may want to do this weekly or only occasionally. Either way, I highly recommend it.

CONVERSATION AND COMMUNICATION

COMMUNICATION – NOT EDUCATION

PLEASE keep in mind that children of all ages, especially teens, are looking for *communication*, not *education*. They would like to be heard and involved in discussions or hear stories and points of interest. They don't want to be in a classroom, and they don't want to hear a *drasha*.

If the father is a *rebbe* or teacher of some sort, he must be particularly careful not to dominate the conversation. A teacher is accustomed to doing most, if not all, of the talking. It is very easy for him to expect the same sort of attentiveness from his children that he demands from his students. Be very careful here and constantly check with your wife to find out if you've slipped into lecture mode. If it's the wife who leads the Shabbos table or is very talkative, she should ask her husband if she's dominating.

DIVREI TORAH NEED NO INTRODUCTION

IT'S not a good idea to introduce a *dvar Torah* by giving a *klap* on the table and announcing, "Now there's going to be a *dvar Torah*." There are a couple of reasons for this. First of all, just hearing those words causes some people to tune out. The instant they hear the words "*dvar Torah*" they think of a classroom or a long-winded sermon and inwardly groan. This is particularly true if the orator – whether the father, an older boy or even one of the younger children – has a track record of being long-winded or boring.

Also, announcing that there's going to be a *dvar Torah* makes it sound as though Torah is a novelty which is only spoken about under certain circumstances. This is not a good message to communicate to the family. Torah should be interspersed throughout the conversation, and it should come as no surprise that someone offers a brief and interesting Torah idea. Whoever is speaking should simply start talking about his Torah concept just as he would talk about anything else. For example, the father might say, "Oh, you gotta hear this," and then mention an interesting *vort* or present an interesting *halachic* dilemma or tell over an interesting *midrash*.

DO NOT DISCUSS JEWISH SOCIAL ISSUES

DO not discuss Jewish social issues at the Shabbos table. This includes topics such as the so-called *shidduch* crisis, the housing shortage, difficulties of getting accepted into seminaries or *yeshivos*, Israeli political policies and so on and so forth. These discussions usually lead to people expressing their opinions and not listening to anyone else's, with nothing much accomplished. These types of discussions are not considered *Torahdik* discussions, even if the word "*hashkafa*" is used repeatedly. They also tend to include a healthy dose of *lashon hara* and criticism of *gedolei Yisrael*.

These discussions are a terrible waste of the Shabbos table. The one exception to this rule is in a situation where there is a teen who is having difficulty with an issue on a personal level, and the only real opportunity to discuss it with him and be *mashpia* is at the Shabbos table. In such a case, the parents should bring up the issue. However, you must be certain that it will not lead to a shouting match or any other form of unpleasantness.

BEWARE OF *LASHON HARA*

IT'S common for the father or sons to report the various *"mazel tovs"* when they come home from *shul.* This can often lead to questions about those families, which then easily leads into discussing those families, which then easily leads into *lashon hara.* It's best to simply tell the good news, wish everyone a *mazel tov,* and then go on to a different topic of conversation.

Family reminiscing can be a lot of fun, and should not be discouraged. However, **analyzing family and parental policies is usually not a great idea**, as it often leads to tension at the table and puts teens in a bad mood. If the conversation somehow drifts in that direction, switch to something else – quickly. The Shabbos table must always be pleasant and enjoyable.

OF SPORTS, POLITICS AND OTHER TRIVIALITIES

THERE is always a question as to what the approach should be with regard to non-Torah topics that people would like to talk about, such as world events, scientific discoveries, sports, and just about anything else under the sun. Parents must exercise good judgment in this tricky area. If their kids are generally non-responsive to Torah discussions, then talking about other things should not be discouraged. Of course, every effort should be made to present a Torah outlook on the given subject and to sneak in a *Chazal* here and there. As long as the conversation is enjoyable, it should not be discouraged.

Politics are best avoided, and Israeli politics, being particularly distasteful, should never be spoken about. Obviously, if the family is capable of a more *Torahdik* discussion, the other topics should be held to a minimum. Again, parents must exercise careful judgment here.

FOOD

GOOD FOOD AND LOTS OF IT

I T'S important that the family members be excited about coming to the Shabbos table. This excitement begins with good and abundant food. Don't expect your children and husband to be such spiritual giants that all they want is to come to the table and speak Torah.

The mother must make sure to prepare the kind of food her family is crazy over and make it in large amounts. Some women have little interest in food themselves or are dieting. They must set aside their personal preferences for the sake of the cause.

Of course, a limited budget means there is a limit to what cuts of meat or how many portions of chicken can be served. But even on a limited budget, the mother can make mouthwatering side dishes, dips and salads. It may mean taking the time to learn some new cooking skills, but it's well worth the effort.

VARY THE MENU

T HE menu should be varied periodically. Even the best foods tend to lose their luster if served week after week. That doesn't mean changing everything. One or two new dishes or a different flavor of chicken can do the trick.

DESSERTS SHOULD BE EXCITING

E ATING canned peaches week after week just doesn't do it for most people. Cakes, cookies, ice creams and sherbets should be served in various sizes, shapes and colors. You know you're on the right track when the dessert is followed by exclamations like, "Wow, this pie is fantastic!" or "These cookies are awesome!" The more exciting the desserts, the better the chances of keeping children and teens at the table until the time the desserts are brought out.

IT'S ALL IN THE PRESENTATION

W ELL-PRESENTED food creates excitement and brings an element of *kavod* to the table. The food should be arranged nicely on the platters, not just dumped on. Little touch-ups, like a sprig of parsley next to the food, enhance the interest in whatever is being served. Surprisingly, even small children appreciate the subtleties of food appearance. If you are not creative in this area, please speak to someone who is.

CLEAN DISHES

T HE serving dishes should be sparkling clean and unstained, so that there is a feeling that something *mechubadik* is taking place. If the family is using disposable dishes and serving platters, they should also be as *mechubadik* as the budget allows. The more *mechubadik* the children feel, the more *mechubdik* they'll act.

DESSERT AND NOSH

IT'S a good idea to have various "munchies" to bring out with dessert, as this will keep people, especially teens, sitting at the table longer. A variety of seeds and nuts is a good start. Sunflower seeds, pumpkin seeds, peanuts, watermelon seeds, and whatever else is available is great – the more the merrier. One or two of the expensive kinds, like cashews or pistachios, might also be included. And a tray with popcorn, potato chips and some bisli is sure to keep family members at the table for longer, and even bring back those who have already left.

LIMIT THE SWEETS

WE all want to avoid too much sugar. One or two sugary candy treats for Shabbos is not unreasonable. However, it's not a good idea to put out a tray with a variety of candy on the table when little children are present. They often lose control and just start grabbing, which defeats the purpose of putting it out.

SODA

MANY families wisely avoid having soda and other sugary drinks during the week. It is advisable to provide soda on Shabbos, or at least on some Shabbosim. Obviously, parents should supervise the quantities consumed.

VARIOUS DO'S AND DON'T'S

DON'T TURN YOUR SHABBOS TABLE INTO A CLASSROOM

P LEASE don't turn your Shabbos table into a classroom. Even if the father doesn't have time to learn with his boys during the week, the Shabbos table is not the place to "*shtup*" in the learning. The kids will consider it as an unpleasant experience. Handouts from school can be used as guides for what to talk about and some questions can be asked, but the kids should not feel that this is their weekly exam.

REWARDS AND TREATS

Y OU can and should use candy and treats as a way of generating interest and participation. However, it's not a good idea to reward individual answers from individual children, because then the brighter children tend to come out with more. Rather, provide all the children with treats at various intervals during the *seuda*. Each child can be asked a few questions about what they learned that week as part of the Shabbos table routine, with no expectation of reward for the answers. (Children should be motivated through rewards for good behavior and effort in their studies, but how and when to do so is beyond the purview of our discussion.)

DON'T CRITICIZE

PLEASE do not use the Shabbos table as an opportunity to point out the various flaws you may have
noticed in your family members. And certainly
never criticize your spouse at the Shabbos table.

DON'T DISCUSS FAMILY ISSUES

AVOID bringing up unpleasant family issues or problems which have come up in the course of the previous week or which have been lingering for a while.

NEVER CORRECT YOUR WIFE IN FRONT OF OTHERS

IF the mother says something at the table, even if it is objectively incorrect, the father should do whatever he can
to help her save face. He should bend over backward and
be as creative as possible to save the situation. For example,
if she said the Vilna Gaon lived at the time of the Rashba,
the response might be, "Well, even if he didn't, he was close
in stature to those who lived in that era." This one piece of
advice carries untold benefits for the home.

THE MOTHER'S PRESENCE AT THE TABLE
DURING THE FATHER'S DVAR TORAH

SOMETIMES the mother gets up from the table as
soon as her husband begins saying something about
the *parsha* or any other Torah topic. This obviously

sends the wrong message to the rest of the family, and every effort should be made to avoid this.

If it's a subconscious reaction because she knows there's going to be an oppressive ten minute *drasha*, then she should speak to her husband about it – tactfully – during the week. They should decide together what sort of style he should use at the Shabbos table.

PRAISE YOUR CHILDREN

FIND reasons to praise the kids at the table. It could be something they've done recently or a good *midda* they possess. It doesn't really matter. The main thing is that they should hear themselves praised. With teens, this is trickier because of their unpredictable nature. They may see you as being condescending or see themselves as so "mature" that they've outgrown any need for praise. Assess their needs carefully and proceed with caution to make sure their response isn't negative.

DON'T SHOW ANGER

NEITHER parent, but especially the father, should ever show anger or any form of irritation at the table. If something happens that ticks you off and you can't overlook it (kids bickering, a spill, a comment from a teen), walk into another room and stay there until you're completely in control of yourself. Don't storm out – just walk away calmly. However, walking away from the table isn't ideal, and should only be resorted to if absolutely necessary.

IRON OUT *SHALOM BAYIS* ISSUES
BEFORE YOU COME TO THE TABLE

ANY differences between the parents which may have arisen due to *erev Shabbos* tension or anything else must be resolved before coming to the table. Nothing is more unpleasant and damaging to kids than sitting with parents who are upset with each other.

PRAISE YOUR WIFE

AT the end of the *seuda*, the father should thank the mother loudly and clearly for the meal and for all her efforts on behalf of the family. The kids should also be told to thank their mother, but the most efficient way of teaching them is for them to see the father doing it.

ZEMIROS

It's very important that:
- *Zemiros* **booklets should be on the table** at the beginning of the *seuda*.
- All of the *zemiros* **booklets should be uniform**.
- There should be more than enough to go around.

This way, everyone can easily find the page and song by your simply announcing the page number.

DON'T SING WITH YOUR MOUTH FULL

WHEN you begin singing, **make sure those whom you want to have singing along with you have finished the course** that's been served. It often happens that the father is served first and therefore begins eating first. He is then finished before anyone else and all ready to sing, while those around him are not. He also might only want one portion, while some of the others want two or more. This is particularly true of teenaged boys, who have a well-deserved reputation for consuming massive quantities of food. So before you start singing, wait for just about everyone else to finish eating so they will be able to participate.

ANNOUNCE THE *ZEMIROS*

WHEN the time is right to sing, announce, "We'll sing *zemiros* now," along with the page number, but then don't wait too long for everyone to get focused. Sometimes people are *schmoozing* or looking in *sefarim* or whatever, and they won't stop what they're doing until they actually hear something being sung. So simply start singing. That's usually enough to get everyone to join in. If what you'd like to sing is not one of the standard Shabbos *zemiros*, say, "Let's sing a little," and just start singing.

NO PRESSURE *ZEMIROS*

IF any of the children don't feel like joining in the singing, don't pressure them. You may ask them if they'd like to sing, but without pressure. (You can ask them at a different time, not at the Shabbos table, why they don't join in the singing.) And never put one of the kids on the spot by forcing him to sing a solo, even if he has a good voice.

On the other hand, those who aren't singing should not carry on conversations while the singing is going on. It is disruptive, and it interferes with creating the warm, *ruchni* atmosphere which *zemiros* can generate. Mothers and daughters must be particularly careful here, as their non-participation in the singing can easily tempt them to chat. Also, if a mother is chatting during *zemiros*, she's sending a message to her family that the *zemiros* are not that important.

INVOLVE THE KIDS

ASK your kids if they would like to pick out the *zemer* or *niggun*. They may want to pick it and have you start singing, or they may want to start singing themselves. Whatever the case, it's a way of having them feel more involved.

VARY THE TUNES THAT ARE SUNG

MANY of the *zemiros* have more than one *niggun* they can be sung to. Also, sometimes *zemiros* can be put to the tunes of well known contemporary songs. For example, "*V'li Yerushalayim*" by "*Deveykus*" fits "*Menucha v'simcha*" perfectly. And "*K'ayal ta'arog*" fits "*Ka ribbon*" flawlessly. You can also teach your kids some old songs which have gone out of style. If you are really gifted, you can make up original *niggunim* and fit the *zemiros* to them.

MAKE A LIST OF SONGS

MAKE a list of the different *niggunim* the various *zemiros* can be sung to, as well as a list of the other songs your family enjoys singing. You can divide the list into categories of slow "*neshama*" songs and faster "*leibidik*" songs. You can add to the list as time goes on and accumulate a nice selection to choose from. Keep the list handy at the Shabbos table so that you can refer to it easily. This way, you avoid a situation where the mood is right for singing but you just can't think of a song. This one piece of advice makes a very big difference at the Shabbos table.

Also, kids are likely to ask what other songs are on the list, and then you can sing them one after another, leading to a nice long family singing session.

WAIT A LITTLE WHILE BETWEEN
COURSES IN ORDER TO SING

IF the mother brings out the next course as soon as the previous one is finished, the singing will not get off the ground. And if the singing is going well and the kids are really into it, hold off on the food as long as possible. Remember, once the first course has been served, nobody is starving. Of course, if the singing isn't happening – for whatever reason – and there's no productive *schmoozing* or discussion, the food should come out right away.

I hope these tips help you achieve a fulfilling Shabbos table.

Wishing you again many beautiful and enjoyable *Shabbosim*!

REVIEW LIST

DETERMINE GOALS:
1. Be realistic (how long can kids sit, how much Torah, etc.).
2. Your main goal is that the table should be enjoyable.
3. Carefully consider if you should have guests.
4. Don't think about what's going on in other homes.
5. People want communication – not education.

PREPARATIONS:
1. The father should nap on Friday.
2. Food should be exciting (dips, desserts, presentation, etc.).
3. Provide uniform Chumashim and zemiros.
4. Inform guests you'll be focusing on family.
5. The couple should discuss logistics (seating, wine distribution, cutting challa, dealing with a disruptive child) beforehand.

THE FATHER'S SPECIFIC PREPARATIONS:
1. Halachic questions.
2. Discussion starters.
3. Stories.
4. Parsha vorts.
5. Poems.
6. No politics (especially Israeli).
7. World events acceptable, conclude with Torah outlook.

AT THE TABLE:

1. The father mustn't dominate.
2. One shouldn't announce the dvar Torah before beginning.
3. The mother shouldn't leave for the dvar Torah.
4. It's good to wait between courses.
5. Don't reward individuals.
6. Don't test kids on material.
7. Don't dwell on simcha announcements.
8. Start right away; don't wait for a missing child.
9. Leave the table to sit on the couch.
10. Don't discuss social issues (shidduch crisis, Sefardi/ Ashkenazi, protektzia in yeshivos, acceptance policy in seminaries, etc.).

ZEMIROS:

1. Announce the zemiros and start right away.
2. Vary the niggunim.
3. Have the kids choose.
4. Keep a notebook.
5. Make up your own niggunim.
6. Be sure all are ready to join.
7. Don't force people to join.

GLOSSARY

Adam gadol – A great Torah person

Agunah – Woman who is forbidden to remarry

Al chait – Prayer of confession of sins

Aliya – Being called up to say Torah reading blessing

Amos – Handbreadths

Apikores – Heretic

Aron (Kodesh) – Ark

Ashreinu – We are lucky

Assur – Forbidden

Aveira, aveiros – Sin(s)

Avinu – Our father

Avodah – Service in the *Mishkan* or *Bais Hamikdash*

Avodas Hashem – Serving Hashem

Avos U'banim – Father and son learning program

Avreich(im) – Married man (men) studying in *yeshiva*

B'ezras – With the help of

Baal – Master

Baal gaava – Arrogant person

Baal habayis – Head of the household

Baal korei – One who reads the public Torah reading

Baal simcha – Someone celebrating a happy occasion

Baal tokaiah – One who blows the *shofar* in *shul*

Baal(as) (pl. baalei) teshuva – Someone who was previously secular and chose a religious lifestyle

Bais Hamikdash – The Holy Temple

Balagan – Mess

Badecken – Marriage ceremony where groom covers bride's face

Baruch – Blessed

Becher – Goblet

Bein adam l'chaveiro – Between man and his friend

Beis din – Torah court of law

Beis medrash – Place of Torah study

Ben – Son of

Ben Torah – Someone who lives his life always striving to grow in Torah

Bentch goimel – Say prayer of thanksgiving for being saved

Bentcher – Book used for Grace after Meals

Bentching – Blessing

Beracha achrona – After-blessing

Beracha, brachos – Blessing(s)

Bitachon – Trust in Hashem

Bitul – Waste

Blatt – Page

Bnei Yisrael – The Jewish people

Bochur(im) – Unmarried young man (men)

Chabura – Torah discourse

Chag – Holiday

Chanukas habayis – Celebration of a new home

Chareidi – Ultra-Orthodox

Chasan(im), chatan – Groom(s)

Chassidim – Hassidim

Chasuna – Wedding

Chavrusa – Study partner

Chazal – Sages

Chazir – Pig

Chazer – Review

Cheder – Jewish day school for boys

Chein – Charm

Cherubim – Angels on *Aron*

Chesed – Acts of kindness

Chevra kadisha – Burial society

Chillul – Desecration

Chinuch – Education

Chiyuv – Obligation

Cholent – Shabbos stew

Chometz – Leaven forbidden on Pesach

Chumash – Bible

Chumra – Stringency

Chuppa – Wedding ceremony

Chutzpa – Insolence

Daas Torah – Torah outlook

Daf – Page (of *Gemara*)

Daf yomi – Daily page of *Gemara*

Dan l'kaf zechus – Give benefit of the doubt

Daven, davening – Pray, prayer

Dayan(im) – Judge(s)

Derech – Way

Din Torah – Jewish court case

D'Oraisa – From the Torah

Drasha – Speech

Dray – Delay, hang out

Duchen – When a *kohein* blesses the congregation

Emes – Truth

Emunah – Belief

Eretz Yisrael – Land of Israel

Erev – Eve

Eirusin – Engagement

Ezras nashim – Women's section

Fleishig – Meaty

Frock – Rabbinical coat

Frum – Religious

Frummy – Conspicuously religious person

Gaava – Arrogance

Gabbai(m) – Sexton(s)

Gadol hador, gedolei haposkim/ Yisrael, gedolim – Torah leader(s) of the generation

Galus – Exile

Gan Eden – Paradise

Gaon – Genius

Gebruchts – Wet matzah products

Gehenom – Hell

Geniza – Holy works retired from use

Geshmak – Sweet

Get – Divorce document

Gevir – Rich man

Gilui – Revelation

Giyores – Woman convert

Goy – Gentile

Hagba – Ceremony of lifting the Torah in *shul*

Hakadosh Baruch Hu – G-d

Hakaras hatov – Gratitude

Halacha, halachos, halachic – Jewish law(s), pertaining to Jewish law

Halevai – If only

Hashem (Yisbarach) – G-d (may He be blessed)

Hashgacha – Providence

Hashkafa – Outlook on life

Hasmada – Diligence

Hatzalah – Emergency services

Hatzlacha – Success

Hechsher(im) – Kosher certification(s)

Hesped(im) – Eulogy, eulogies

Hishtadlus – Effort

Hy"d – May his name be avenged

Imeinu – Our mother

Inuyim – Afflictions

Issur – Prohibition

Kabbala – Esoteric Torah studies; decision to do something

Kaddish – Prayer said in memory of the departed

Kallah – Bride

Kashrus – Kosher

Kavana – Intent

Kavod – Honor

Kehilla – Community

Keilim – Vessels

Kepaida – Grudge

Kesher – Connection

Kesubos – Marriage contracts

Kever – Grave

Ki eshmera Shabbos Kel yishmireini – When you keep the Shabbos Hashem watches over you

Kiddush – Prayer over wine sanctifying Shabbos

Kiddush Hashem – Making Hashem's Name respected

Churban – Destruction

Binyan – Building

Hadasim – Myrtle branches used on Succos with *lulav*

Shtetl – Village

Kippa – Yarmulke

Kiruv (rechokim) – Outreach

Kisei hakavod – Hashem's throne

Klal Yisrael – The Jewish people

Klap – Hit

Koach – Strength

Kochi v'otzem yadi – The strength of my hands

Kohein gadol – High priest

Kohein, kohanim – Priest(s)

Kollel – Yeshiva for married men

Korban(os) – Sacrifice(s)

Kosel, Kotel – Western Wall

Krias Yam Suf – The splitting of the Red Sea

Kugel – Pudding

Kvetch(y) – Complain(ing)

Leibidik – Lively

Levaya – Funeral

L'vatala – Unnecessary

Ulpan – Course to teach Hebrew

Levi'im – Levirate

Lishma – For its own sake

Lashon hara – Gossip

Lukshen – Noodle

Lulav – Palm branch used on Succos

Maariv – Evening prayer

Machala – Disease (cancer)

Machlokes – Fight

Machmir – Stringent

Madreiga, madreigos – Level(s)

Maggid shiur – Someone who teaches Torah

Chapping pshat – Understanding the topic

Malach hamaves – Angel of Death

Malach(im) – Angel(s)

Manhig – Leader

Marbitz Torah – Disseminator of Torah

Masechta – Tractate

Mashgiach(im) – Spiritual guide(s); supervisor(s)

Masmid(im) – Diligent student(s)

Mazel – Luck

Mazel tov – Congratulations

Me'ein Olam Haba – A taste of the World to Come

Mechalel – Desecrator

Mechanech(im) – (n.) Teacher(s); (v.) to teach or educate

Mechitza – Separation

Mechubadik – Respectable

Mechutan – Family of your child's spouse

Mechutan(im) – People whose children have married each other

Mefarshim – Commentators

Meikel – Lenient

Mekarev – Bring someone closer to religion

Melacha – (Forbidden) work

Melamed – Teacher

Meraglim –Spies

Mesader kiddushin – Person who leads marriage ceremony

Meshugane – Crazy

Mesirus nefesh – Martyrdom, devotion

Mevater – Give in

Midda k'neged midda – Measure for measure

Middos – Character traits/ development

Midrash – Oral Torah explaining the written Torah

Mincha – Afternoon prayer; (sacrifice in *Mikdash*)

Minhag – Tradition

Minyan – Quorum of ten men

Mishkan – Tabernacle

Mishmar – Learning session

Mishna, mishnayos – Body of text of Jewish law, predecessor of the Talmud

Mishpat – Judgment

Mispallelim – People praying

Mitzvah goreres mitzvah – One *mitzvah* leads to another

Mitzvah, mitzvos – Commandment(s)

Mizbei'ach – Altar

Moichel – forgive

Morah – Teacher

Moshiach – Messiah

Motzai Shabbos – Saturday night

Musaf – Shabbos and holiday prayer

Mushchas – Despicable person

Mussar (shmuessen) – Discourse on ethical growth

Mussar haskel- Lesson for life

Nachas – Satisfaction

Navi – Prophet

Neb(by) – Nerd(y)

Neshama, Neshamos, Nefesh – Soul(s)

Niftar – Died

Niggun – Tune

Nisayon – Test

Nogei'a badavar – Has personal bias

Nosh – Snack

Olah – Type of sacrifice

Olam Haba – World to Come

Olam Ha'emes – World of Truth, i.e., Heaven

Olam Hazeh – This world

Pshat – Explanation

Parnassa – Livelihood

Parsha – Weekly Torah reading

Pasuk, Pesukim – Verse(s)

Petirah – Death

Pikuach nefesh – A matter of life and death

Posek, Posek hador – (The leading) rabbi who determines Jewish law

Possul – Not fit for use

Potch – Spank

Pasken – Decide the Torah law

Pushka – *Tzedaka* box

Rav, Rabbanim, Rebbeim – Rabbi(s)

Rebbe – Teacher

Rebbetzin – Rabbi's wife

Ribbono shel Olam – Master of the World

Rikud – Dance

Rosh chodesh – First day of the month

Rosh yeshiva – Head of a yeshiva

Ruach hakodesh – Divine inspiration

Ruchni – Spiritual

Ruchniyus – Spirituality

Safrus – Writing holy scrolls

Schlepped – Dragged

Schmooze – Talk

Seder – Learning session; Pesach night meal

Sefer – Book

Seuda/seudos – Meal(s)

Shacharis – Morning prayers

Shadchan(im) – Matchmaker(s)

Shaila – Question

Shalom – Peace, hello

Shalom aleichem – Greetings

Shalom bayis – Harmony in the home

Shamayim – Heaven

Shas – Talmud

Sheketz – Disgusting thing

Shelo asani goy – That He didn't make me a non-Jew

Shelo sam chelkeinu kahem – That He didn't make our portion like theirs

Sheva berachos – Celebrations after a wedding

Shevatim – Tribes

Shidduch(im) – Match(es) made between two people looking to marry

Shira – Song of praise

Shiur(im) – Lesson(s)

Shlamim – Type of sacrifice

Shlit"a – May he live a good long life

Shloshim – Thirty day mourning period

Shmoneh esrei – Main prayer

Shteiging – Learning seriously

Shtup – Stuff

Shul – Synagogue

Simcha – Happiness; happy occasion

Siyata d'Shmaya – Heavenly assistance

Siyum – Completion of a section of the Torah

Sugya – Topic

Tachlis – Purpose

Talmid Chacham, Talmidei Chachamim – Man (men) learned in Torah

Talmid(im) – Student(s)

Techias hameisim – Revival of the dead

Tefilla, tefillos – Prayer(s)

Teshuva – Repentance

Tzaddik(im) – Righteous person (people)

Tzedaka – Charity

Yeshiva, yeshivos – School(s) for learning Torah

Yetzer hara – Evil inclination

Yid(den) – Jew(s)

Yiddishkeit – Judaism

Yiras Shamayim – Fear of Heaven

Yisrael – Israel

Yom Tov– Holiday

Zaida, zaidy – Grandfather

Zechus(im) – Merit(s)

Zemer, zemiros – Shabbos song(s)

Zt"l – May the righteous be remembered for a blessing

Shuckle – Rock back and forth

Shomer Shabbos – Shabbos observer

Shtick – Tricks

Simanim – Signs

Shteibel – *Shul*

Shver – Father-in-law

Simchadik – Happy

Sofer – Scribe

Shtar – Contract

Taiva – Ark

Talmud Torah – Religious elementary school

Tatty – Father

Tumah – Impurity

Tochacha – Rebuke

Tenaim – Contract stating intent to marry

Tallis, talleisim – Prayer shawl(s)

Tzaros – Troubles

Tzava'ah – Will

Tzibbur – Congregation

Vaad – Council

Tznius – Modesty

Vasikin – Sunrise

Yeshua, yeshuos – Salvation

Yichus – Lineage

Yasher koach – Well done!

Yishtabach Shemo – May His Name be blessed

Zman simchaseinu – Succos

V'hagisa bo yomam valayla – You shall study them day and night

Vidui – Confession

V'talmud Torah K'negged kulam – Learning Torah is equal to everything

Tzedaka tatzil mi'maves – Charity saves from death

Vertlach – Short *divrei Torah*

Divrei Torah – Torah thoughts

Tanach – Bible

Tzidkus – Piety

Tzara'as – Biblical disease

Vaadim – Learning groups

Shkia – Sunset

Zav – Spiritual impurity

Se'ais – Spiritual sore

Nega – Spiritual sore

Middos tovos – Good character traits

Issur – Prohibition

Peyos – Sidelocks

Kashrus – Laws of keeping kosher